My Story

TOMMY HUNTER

with Liane Heller

My Story

🄽 METHUEN

Toronto New York London Sydney Auckland

Canadian Cataloguing in Publication Data
Hunter, Tommy
   Tommy Hunter: my story

ISBN 0-458-99620-3

1. Hunter, Tommy. 2. Country musicians - Canada - Biography. 3. Television personalities - Canada - Biography. I. Heller, Liane. II. Title.

ML420.H85A37 1985   784.5'2'00924   C85-099410-1

Lines from "I Saw the Light" and "Mansion on the Hill" quoted by permission of Acuff-Rose Opryland Music Inc.

Printed and bound in Canada by John Deyell Company
1   2   3   4   85   89   88   87   86

CONTENTS

INTRODUCTION

It's 10 o'clock at night, and Studio 7 is just about deserted, except for me.

I thought I'd just hang around for a few minutes and kind of feel the quiet. It's a very unusual sound to hear around this place, where we spend so much of our time making music, singing, talking, trying our very best to put our television show together in such a way that you, at home, will enjoy our show as much as we enjoy creating it for you.

Our show. That's what I've always called it. I just don't think of The Tommy Hunter Show as myself alone, and I never have, because there are so many people, from the producer to the lighting crew to the cameramen to the makeup artists, who always put so much of themselves into the show that it belongs to them as much as it does to me.

Only a few moments ago, we just finished the taping of our last show of the season, and that's always a very special time for us. We're always looking forward to a bit of rest and relaxation after a pretty gruelling schedule that often stretches into 12 or 13-hour days (and nights). And yet, there's some sadness, too, when we realize it's going to be some months before we see each other again. We're all going to miss that shared feeling of working together toward a common goal: the very best country music show that television can achieve.

While we may feel that we never quite get there, still it's the shared effort that makes us all enjoy our work as much as we do.

It *is* quiet in here.

Our guests, by now, are all winging their way back to Nashville, Calgary, Halifax and Montreal (they really *did* come from coast to coast tonight!). Donna and Leroy Anderson, our resident songbirds, have flown off to a romantic late-night dinner uptown. And one of the sound men had to leave early; he got the happy call from the maternity ward up at Toronto General.

Les was the last to leave, as usual (well, second-to-last), and I could tell by that little knowing smile he gave me on the way out that he thought we'd done ourselves proud tonight, and all season, too. That's Les Pouliot I'm talking about, our producer and writer.

"See you next season," he said as he left, and then, noticing my grin, "be the good Lord willing."

So here I am, in this great big empty studio on Mutual Street, with the banks of lights dimmed for the season, the cameras all wheeled back from the stage, the sound equipment silent, the hallways quiet and dark.

The blue suit I was wearing on the show tonight is hung up and packed away until next year, and I've carefully sorted out my scripts and stored them safely at the bottom of my briefcase. But as I sit here, I can still hear the faint echoes of that beautiful three-part harmony we sang, Donna and Leroy and I. I can still see Al Cherny's wonderful smile as he warms up to a favorite fiddle tune. I can still feel the tremendous excitement of reaching out to an audience that's reaching out to you.

Some things, you never forget.

Oh, here's something I forgot . . . my guitar. I didn't put it back in the case. Still leaning up against the stool, just as it was when I did the gospel song tonight. Only there's no spotlight on it now, or on me. Just me and my guitar.

Seems like it's always been that way.

CHAPTER 1

Childhood

I'd like to tell you about another guitar of mine, which I keep right here in my office, close at hand, so that every once in awhile I can open up the case and have a peek at the smooth, shining wood and brightly polished strings.

Oh, I don't play it anymore; I guess you could say it's retired. See, it only looks new; this guitar's probably got thousands of miles on it, and a million memories of county fairs, rodeos, bars, concert halls . . . It's taken so much bruising and battering that even the cracks in the wood had cracks.

A couple of years ago, I thought I'd at least try to get it fixed up a bit, so I turned it over to some restoration experts and wished them the best of luck. Well, I don't know how those craftsmen did it, but when they finished repairing, rebuilding, sanding, polishing and restringing, that old guitar looked exactly the way it did when Mom and Dad bought it for me, just about 35 years ago.

It's now safely tucked away, wrapped in tissue paper and locked in its case, the way you might carefully mend a childhood heirloom, dust it off, and gently place it on the shelf of your favorite cabinet.

Now, to hear me go on about that guitar, you might think it's made of solid mahogany and inlaid with pure gold. Fact is, it might just as well have been mahogany, gold and the Hope Diamond that my folks were buying when they counted out forty-nine hard-earned dollars for it.

Not a whole lot of money by today's standards; that's true. But you know, that $49 was really a very considerable sum for Mom and Dad to be spending on something like a guitar, since extras figured pretty low on the list when it came time to draw up the household budget. Even so, they managed to scrimp and save and squeeze every penny out of every dollar, until, finally, there was enough.

My folks did all that because they believed in my dream, and they knew that guitar was going to be a big part of it. So you see it makes me feel proud to be able to tell them their wonderful gift looks just as good as new; and the dream, well, it's never grown old.

Sometimes, it's amazing what you'll turn up when you dip into the past.

So when I was first asked to do this book about my life, I got to thinking that my folks could probably tell me a million stories about our family history; and I figure that talking about roots makes a pretty good beginning to anyone's life story.

Well, I just barely *mentioned* to Dad one time that I'd like to know a little bit more about his side of the family, when suddenly I was regaled with visions of covered wagons crossing the plains. That's right; covered wagons, bumping and jiggling along in the dust and heat.

You see, my grandfather, William Hunter, may have been born in Eastern Canada (Brantford, Ontario, to be precise), but he must have had some of that pioneer spirit in him to leave the security of his home and follow his dream across the Western United States.

Remember now, this was still the 19th century, and homesteading was still very much a way of life for many families, who spent weeks hauling all their earthly belongings across the country in heavy, slow-moving wagons, until they finally reached their tract of land and began carving out a life for themselves: a home, a small farm, and a golden opportunity.

Nebraska was where Grandpa chose to settle, and where he met my grandmother, Emma Hunter, who was Pennsylvania Dutch. They homesteaded near Havelock, Nebraska, which is now part of Omaha. But back then, it couldn't have been much more than a tiny speck in the vast sea of prairie that stretched endlessly to the horizon.

My grandparents must have had their hands full trying to raise a family, and it certainly was a big one. Five boys. My dad, James Hunter, was the middle child, born in 1902.

Must have been plenty of room for a boy to wander around, because Dad told me he used to go on long rambles with the cutest little puppy which his father had brought home one day; the only thing was, that tiny pup turned out to be a coyote.

But it wasn't all roaming around in search of adventures, the way Dad recalls his childhood. The covered wagons were still heading west to California, sometimes rolling by so close he could see them through the clouds of dust. Life was still pretty basic; I mean, Dad even remembers going out on the prairie to collect buffalo chips for kindling.

Grandpa's rules were pretty basic, too, and they seem to have stood the test of time. I remember Dad saying to me, "You know, it's like my father always told me: you get yourself into trouble, you get yourself out of trouble." As for the third generation (mine), that little expression is a philosophy I go along with 100 per cent.

Dad was only about 10 years old when his folks decided to move back to Canada, settling down in London, Ontario, where Grandpa worked as a blacksmith at Empire Brass, a big company that's still in business today. Grandma, now, she pretty much had her work cut out for her with five boys at home.

But the boys didn't really spend a whole lot of years playing around the house; matter of fact, they didn't even spend that many years at school. Dad was about 14 when he was apprenticed as a blacksmith and went to work with Grandpa at Empire Brass, and he's pretty sure all his brothers were about the same age when they took on full-time jobs. That's just the way it was, Dad said. You know, if you don't get up early enough, you might just miss the bus.

After a few years at Empire Brass, Dad went to work for the Canadian National Railway in London; but the CNR started laying workers off, and since he'd only been there three years, he didn't have the seniority to hang onto his job. He heard that the Illinois Central Railroad in Chicago was hiring, so he spent a few years down there. Then, one day, he got the word from London that the CNR was taking back some of the laid-off workers, so home he came.

Dad never changed jobs again; he stayed with the Canadian National Railway until he retired, 47 years later. But, you know, it's always sort of bothered me that the CNR never credited him for those first three years. If they had, he could have had that 50-year pass he always wanted. As it is, his long service pass gives him pretty much unlimited travel on the CN line, but I guess that 50 years was what he'd rightfully earned.

Of course, at the time, he was probably just happy to be back in his job and home again. Besides, there were other plans to think about.

You see, the call that brought him back to London came from a certain young lady he'd been seeing for a number of years. Her name was Edith Stunden, but it seemed that name might be due for a change before too long.

As it turned out, it was only a short time after Dad returned to London that he and Mom were married.

Now, Mom and Dad have a great deal in common, which is probably why their marriage is coming up on 60 years now, with no stormclouds in sight. They both come from large families; five children in both cases, but Mom has three sisters and only one brother. Their backgrounds, too, are very similar, even though Mom's family comes from England. I mean, there wasn't any great wealth or nobility or anything; the Stundens were strictly working-class, just like the Hunters.

Mom's family immigrated to Canada from Greenwich, England; but for many years, they lived in Bermondsey, a highly industrialized suburb of London, England, where Mom was born. I visited the area with Shirley about 10 years ago, and got a very strong sense of Mom's background.

One of Mom's relatives, a very pleasant man named Alvie, came into London to help us find my mother's birth certificate, and afterwards, we all took the bus to Bermondsey, with me snapping pictures all the way and Alvie pointing out the store where Grandma shopped and the little town hall where the family went for civic meetings. At the corner where we got off was a tiny pub with a brightly painted sign hanging over the door. "Your grandmother worked in there, you know," Alvie said, and I just stared in disbelief. *My* grandmother . . . well, we just had to go inside and have a look.

Shirley, Alvie and I sat at the long, polished wooden bar of the small, crowded pub as the men joked and laughed over their dart game and the ladies, in their bright hats and felt tams, chatted over their pints and half-pints. I kept trying to picture Grandma wearing a big white apron and serving beer in this bustling English pub, and the owner very kindly allowed me to take a photograph, so I could have the memory with me always.

Even more remarkable was visiting the area where Alvie lived with his parents. The English television series called Coronation Street looks just *exactly* like Alvie's neighborhood: row upon row of long, narrow houses, each with a tiny back-garden and a little strip of grass out front.

Somehow, as we sat talking, the subject of the war came up, and they began to tell us about the day the bombs went off in their neighborhood. They ran for the shelter as the air-raid sirens screamed, got to safety just in time, heard the terrible explosions and slowly crept outside to find that all the houses, including theirs, had been reduced to a heap of rubble. But there, in the midst of all that debris, was a bottle of whisky, untouched; so they sat down, had a little drink, and walked over to a nearby house which was, miraculously, still standing.

The tremendous courage, the sheer guts of that family just rendered me speechless. I mean, I just gaped at them in awe. All I could think about was how much it reminded me of a point in the George Chuvalo-Floyd Patterson fight when Patterson had just hit Chuvalo so hard on the jaw that I thought it was going to take Chuvalo's head off. But Chuvalo just kept on coming. Don Dunphy, the sportscaster, said that if a boxer throws his best Sunday punch and hits you square on the chin, but you keep coming — that's frightening.

So if some guy throws his best bomb at you, and you keep coming, even with your home in a pile of rubble right in front of you, that's amazing. You dust yourself off, you have a little drink, and you start again, from the ground up. Absolutely amazing.

We all have to do that, in a way, although we don't all have to pick ourselves up from the blow of a war in our own backyard the way many families did, including Mom's. But if you're able to get up and keep going, even when life throws you her best Sunday punch, I think that's a tremendous accomplishment.

Not too long ago, with another question about Mom's family on my mind, I paid a visit to her brother, Albert Stunden. Uncle Albert is a man I greatly respect and admire; besides being a fine carpenter and a religious person, he is the kind of man that many individuals would do well to model themselves after.

We talked about my grandmother, Ellen Stunden, and Uncle Albert told me how she used to go out to do housecleaning in London, England, back around the turn of the century. Then, the subject shifted to my grandfather, Tom Stunden. "You were named for him, Tommy, did you know that?" asked Albert, a warm smile lighting up his finely etched features. "I always thought so," I replied, "but now I know for certain. But there's something else I'm not at all sure about, and maybe you can shed some light on it."

"What's that, Tommy?"

"You know the factory where my grandfather worked; what was it, the Thames Iron Works?"

"That's right. Thames Iron Works."

"I've always heard that Grandpa helped manufacture the propeller blades for the Titanic there. Is that true?"

Uncle Albert sat back in his armchair for a moment, and scratched his nose thoughtfully. "To tell you the truth, Tommy, I don't know for sure," he finally said. "And you know, I think it may have to remain a mystery, because, you see, just before the First World War, the Thames Iron Works closed down. That's why your grandfather and grandmother decided to leave England and emigrate to Canada."

Mom was only six when her family settled down in the east end of London, Ontario, and began getting their bearings in a strange new place. Well, not all that strange, really; if Grandma and Grandpa had searched across Canada for a place that reminded them of home, they couldn't have done better than London. I mean, even the name of the river was the same (the Thames) and the parks all had English names and even looked like English country gardens, only with more trees; it's not for nothing that London is called the Forest City.

In fact, you didn't have to go much further than the nearest street corner to see how close the resemblance was; the signposts all had names like Queen, Piccadilly, Wellington, Talbot, Richmond . . . and Hamilton Road, which was where Mom's family first lived.

A short time later, once my grandfather had gotten himself set up in a job (basically the same kind of factory work he'd been doing in England) he chose a home for the family on St. Julien Street. Funny thing was, that house where Mom was growing up couldn't have been more than a 20-minute walk from Dad's place on Dundas Street.

Mom's house was one of the very few in the neighborhood that had two storeys instead of one; Grandpa worked in a factory and Grandma added to the family income by going out to do housework and raising chickens in a coop she set up out in back of the house.

When I was about six years old (so I am told), I toddled out back to watch Grandma kill a chicken for Sunday dinner. Well, it looked pretty easy to me, so I just grabbed one and — wham! — chopped off its head. Unfortunately, I'd just killed Grandma's only rooster.

But even before I came along and put a dent in the poultry production, those chickens Grandma was raising just weren't enough to ensure that the family made ends meet. Most of the children, including Mom, had to go out to work in their early teens. As Mom recalls, in those days just after the First World War, chances were pretty slim that a youngster would even enter high school, much less graduate. Their parents, like Mom's, just couldn't afford the luxury.

Mom's first job was on a farm, looking after kids for the summer. She was barely 12 years old. The following summer, she was back on that farm again, and by the time she was 14, she had her first full-time job, at the McCormick biscuit and chocolate factory in London. Knowing Mom, the only reason she didn't take a permanent job even earlier was that 14 was the minimum working age.

You see, nobody ever had to make a case for my mother to go out to work; she *wanted* to help support her family, and help put food on the table. It would have been close to impossible to talk her *out* of working, and once she got started, it was just go, go, go, working at McCormick's, going out and doing housework, and I mean getting down and scrubbing and polishing and waxing. Take a rest? Does a whirlwind take a rest?

I'd be hard-pressed to think of any other individual with more energy than Mom. Work is what she's always poured it into, and probably always will. To this day, she finds it difficult to slow down even for the briefest moment, though Lord knows, I've tried to get her to relax a bit and enjoy life. But you see, work *is* Mom's life; she understands work the way you and I understand the pleasure of relaxing when the working day is done, and nobody, including me, is ever going to tell her different; she's far too independent ever to be budged off a point she really believes in. I guess I've inherited my fair share of that, too. I mean, there's absolutely no way that I ever have or ever would ask anybody to do my work for me; if it's going to happen, it'll be because I make it happen, whether it takes 10 days, 10 weeks, or 10 years of struggle.

16

Mom used to tell me about riding her bike to the biscuit factory, and one time, as she was passing the train station, her path was blocked by a westbound freighter. Well, no train was going to stop my mother; she simply dismounted, hauled the bike (and herself) through the couplings, and continued on her way. But you know, there was an occasion on which Mom did stop while pedalling past the station, and that was when a young railway worker came over to introduce himself.

"My name's Jim Hunter," he said. "Could I ask yours?" So they chatted for a moment or two, and finally he worked up the courage to ask her for a date.

"Well, that sounds nice," Mom said, "but you'll have to ask my mother first."

Well, no time like the present, Dad figured, and off he went that same afternoon to St. Julien Street, where Grandma readily gave her permission, smiling up at the earnest young face. Mom and Dad's first date was that very evening, and about four years later, in 1926, they were married.

My folks often tell me how important it was for them, in the early years of their marriage, to work toward getting a home of their own. That was their dream, and they worked six days a week to achieve it. At first, it was an uphill battle; after all, there was a heavyweight contender to take on: the Depression. But my parents won out in the end, and in 1936, they bought a two-bedroom bungalow on Brisbin Street, where they still live to this day.

Their little house was typical of east-end London, with its cozy, modest frame homes, very few of them two storeys high and even fewer with garages, since most families, including my folks, didn't have cars. There was the streetcar and the bus, and both my parents rode bicycles. (It was only a short time ago that Mom reluctantly turned in the old bike that had taken her to and from work so many years.)

My father still doesn't own a car. A few years ago, when he and I were out for a ride in my new car, I noticed him glancing at me as I drove. "How'd you like to take her for a spin, Dad?" and he nodded. So we switched places and off we went; and I mean, we *went*. He was so utterly terrorized that his foot went rigid on the accelerator, and his hands gripped the wheel so tightly that his knuckles went white. Well, we brought that little excursion to a halt rather quickly, and I'm afraid that marked the beginning and end of Dad's driving career.

Oh, there I go, rambling all over the place. Let's head back to Brisbin Street, some time after I was born on March 20, 1937.

Wait a second; there's nobody home, and the sun's not even up yet. What could be going on? Hey, look, there's a taxi going up the street, and that looks like Mom and Dad in the back. A *taxi* . . . must be something really important, because they never take taxis. Let's follow them, all right?

Look over there; the taxi's pulling up at Victoria Hospital. Is someone sick? No, no, Mom's smiling, and so is Dad, and they're heading down the corridor to the maternity ward . . .

Awww, you guessed it was my birthday I was talking about. Well, so much for mystery introductions!

Of course, the *real* suspense lasted a good many hours for Dad, as he paced back and forth across the waiting room enough times to leave permanent footprints on the linoleum. He probably tested many a nurse's patience, too; Dad's idea of an update was to head back to the nursing station five seconds after being told there was still no news.

Finally, after hours of waiting, came the words he'd been longing to hear. "Congratulations, Mr. Hunter; you have a son." It was 1:30 in the afternoon.

Over at the nursery, Dad peered through the glass until he found the tiny crib with a blue card bearing the name Hunter. He drew a deep breath as his son's mouth opened wide in every baby's favorite song: Waaaaaa! (Well, the lyrics aren't much, but it's a catchy tune.)

I'm glad Mom was at home when I was little; there isn't a safer, more reassuring feeling I can remember from earliest childhood. Mom in the kitchen, all the familiar sounds of her pots and pans, and her footsteps as she came to the doorway to check on me every once in awhile.

At Eastertime, she'd make hot-cross buns, and I'd watch, wide-eyed, as she worked the yeast dough in a great big bowl, covered it with a cloth, and set it down on a counter while she waited for it to rise. Then, I'd head for the warmest spot in the living room (right over the hot-air vent), curl up in a blanket, and listen to Aunt Jenny's True Life Stories on the radio. I can't remember what the stories were about, but it was a warm, friendly voice that I enjoyed hearing, maybe because one of my own aunts is named Jenny.

Sunlight streaming in all the windows, Aunt Jenny's True Life Stories, Mom working in the kitchen, the smell of dough rising . . . those are memories I treasure.

You know, to this day, the smell of home baking takes me back to my childhood, and Mom's hot-cross buns, fresh raisin bread, pies . . . I can almost taste them now.

Of course, I also had to work my way through certain foods that weren't at the top of my list of childhood favorites, too; like spinach and carrots and liver (which I actually enjoy now). I don't know how many times I had the following conversation:

Tommy: But I don't *like* it!

Dad: It's good for you, Tommy.

Tommy: But, DAD . . .

Dad: Eat it, Tommy, or you'll get scurvy!

My folks were also very careful about germs, and I remember times, at the supper table, when we'd have to stop the meal and put cloths over the food because there was a fly in the room. Or if I got up during supper and touched a doorknob that someone had handled, it'd be, "Tommy, go scrub your hands before coming back to this table!"

All this may sound strange today, but you've got to realize that this was a time when there weren't the vaccines and antibiotics we have now, and certain diseases, like pneumonia, were often fatal. Many parents, including mine, place great stock in preventive methods, like guarding against germs and eating the right foods.

Foods were purer, and there couldn't have been many preservatives in them, because Mom was always telling me to put things like bread into the refrigerator so they wouldn't spoil. Foods *looked* different, too, especially in one store in the London market; Chauncey Smith, I think it was called. There'd be all these dried fruits, raisins, currants, various kinds of peels for baking, all set out in huge bins so you could see what you were getting, Even the teas came in big tins; none of these little packages of tea-bags covered in plastic wrapping.

Home remedies were still very popular in the forties. Does anybody remember mustard plasters? I start sweating just thinking about them. If I was home with a cold, I'd have to bundle up under the covers, and then Mom would come in with one of those plasters. I couldn't understand how anything so cold and clammy going on could be so hot coming off. (Of course, being sick had its good points, too; it was the only time, other than Christmas and birthdays, when I'd get gingerale.)

I don't know if it was the food, or the mustard plasters, or watching out for germs, but something must have worked, because I never had any serious illnesses as a child. About the only times the doctor came to our house (Mom would go to our next-door neighbor's house to call, because we didn't have a phone till I was in my teens) was when I had the usual childhood trio of measles, mumps, and chickenpox. Usually, it would be Dr. Callaghan, the same doctor who delivered me.

On one of those rare occasions when I was home in bed for more than a few days, I remember my grandmother (Mom's mother) coming to visit me. She sat in a little chair beside my bed and told me stories from the Bible; her soft voice painted wondrous pictures of ancient times, and then, just as quietly, she began to describe a homeless, persecuted people whose once-strong nation would, someday, be restored.

"But, Grandma," I asked, "how do you know all that?"

"Why, because it's written in the Bible, Tommy," she answered calmly.

I recalled that prophecy a few years later, when Israel became a nation.

I liked having my grandparents only a short walk away when I was little. When I was a bit older, they moved even nearer — right onto our street. The whole family got together to build the house for them; Uncle Albert, as a carpenter, was in charge, with Dad and a few of his brothers-in-law helping out. (I tried to lend a hand, too, but I guess I wasn't destined for a big career in the building trades. It seemed my major contribution was getting underfoot.)

Come to think of it, Mom's relatives made up quite a clan in our neighborhood: Grandma and Grandpa four doors down from us; two aunts and their families only a few streets away, and a third aunt in northeast London. There wasn't a week that went by without our seeing them all at least twice or three times, not counting Christmas, birthdays, and special outings. My father's family lived out of town, and visiting them would be a special treat.

I'm an only child, and they say that a child on his own in a family can have a pretty hard time of it. I'm sure this is true in many cases, but my experience was different; I had that big family around me, and as they never made a big fuss over my being an only child, I never thought about it much.

Every Saturday I went with Dad and Grandpa to Jackson's Bakery. My grandfather would be on his bike, and my father on his, with me on the handlebars, and we'd all ride over there late in the afternoon. They'd just be unhitching the wagon when we got there, and we'd watch them back the horses into the stall, take off the harnesses, groom them and put on the feedbags. Inside, all the breads and cakes that hadn't been sold during the day would be all stacked up, and the smell was mouth-watering. "How much is the cheese bread?" Dad would ask. "Five cents," said the man behind the counter. So we'd take a pillow slip, pack it full of cheese and raisin bread, tarts, maybe some date squares or even a cake, and back we'd go on the bikes.

Another place I liked to go was Aunt Jenny and Uncle Joe's. Although it was in town, their place looked like it might have been right out in the country, with planks laid in instead of sidewalks, and there'd always be old, broken-down parts of trucks that my uncle kept out there. I'd crawl into this old shell of a truck and make "varoom-vroom" noises like I was really driving.

Then there was Aunt Venie's. Every Friday she would get a huge bag of cookies from McCormick's, where she worked. It was full of pieces of broken cookies that smashed when they fell off the assembly line, and the whole gigantic bag would cost only 25 cents. Boy, did I look forward to those days! Even the crumbs tasted good with a glass of milk.

Sometimes I'd drop by Aunt Esther's house for a glass of milk, or she'd give me a big handful of dates that I'd squish between two oatmeal cookies, like a sandwich.

When I think about it, my aunts were very much alike in a lot of ways, and they all reminded me of my mother. When they came to our house for a visit (almost every day), they all sat together at the kitchen table, drinking tea and chatting. I still picture them that way: kind, loving people who liked baking and enjoyed drinking tea and talking together after a hard day of work.

They helped each other out all the time, too. Esther would drop over to our place to give Mom a cabbage she'd bought on special, and she'd be holding two others that were going to Venie and Jenny; or when my father asked about getting potatoes from a farm just outside London, it'd be, "Well, Jim, I suppose you'd better get me two bags, and I know Venie's going to want two, and probably Jenny and Esther will want a few bags, too."

When it came to giving relatives a hand, it didn't stop with our family in London. I remember my folks putting together little packages of sugar, chocolate or cookies to send to Mom's relatives in England while the war was on. We were clipping coupons ourselves (which I'm sure some of you will remember; so many coupons for so many pounds of butter or sugar, so many times a month. But the rationing was much stricter in England, so we cut back even more in order to give them the things they wouldn't have had otherwise.

Now that I remember it, there were all kinds of foods we never seemed to get except on special occasions, like

Christmas and birthdays. Birthdays were very simple; my aunts and uncles and grandparents would come over to our house, we'd sing Happy Birthday and have a slice of cake and maybe some ice cream (a *big* treat!), and that was about it.

Presents were more for Christmas, but opening gifts was only part of why I loved (and still treasure) the whole feeling of Christmas at home. On Christmas Eve, with perhaps a gentle snow falling outside, my Uncle Ned and Aunt Ivy would be out together in the horse-drawn wagon, delivering milk. There'd be all sorts of extras because of the holiday; two quarts of homo, a quart of Jersey with all the thick, golden cream at the top of the bottle, a quart of dairy cream, butter, *and* two dozen eggs. It'd be seven or eight in the evening, and I'd watch at the window as the horse slowly pulled the cart past our house in the yellow lamplight.

Just about that time, a couple of my aunts and uncles would drop over, shaking the snow off their coats, and Grandma and Grandpa would be there, all of them laughing and talking as they came into the living room. Pretty soon, it would be my bedtime, and that was the hard part. Oh, I *knew* that the quicker I went to bed, the quicker it would be Christmas morning, but it would be difficult with all the laughing and excitement going on. I'd feel for the stocking on the side of my bed, and snuggle down under the covers . . . but then I'd hear bells jingling downstairs, and my Uncle Henry's voice booming through the house. "Yes, I think that's him coming now. That's Santa Claus," he'd say. "Santa won't come in if you're awake, you know."

Finally, I'd get to sleep, and in the morning, my stocking would be packed with an orange, some nuts, a few candies, maybe a flashlight or a little model car, and one of those great big, juicy red apples from British Columbia that we never got any time other than Christmas. Under the tree there'd be hand-knitted argyle socks from Grandma, a sweater or mitts from my other aunts. One year, there was a terrific sled with metal runners. After the big turkey dinner, I went out all by myself to the hill down the back of the street, flopped down on the sled and took off. I just seemed to fly down that hill, with the wind stinging my face and the snow billowing around me, hearing the trees cracking in the icy cold and feeling the wondrous hush of a cold winter's night all around me.

The only time I remember spending Christmas out of town was when we went to my Uncle Harry's house in St. Thomas. It seems every family has a rich uncle, and in our case, it was Dad's brother, Harry Hunter, who owned a successful hotel and a beautiful home. He was also an extremely generous man who'd give you the shirt off his back — and go back for more shirts. I always liked him a great deal and was proud of his success.

Christmas at my aunt and uncle's house would mean imported china and heavy sterling silver, with my uncle at the head of the table carving the turkey. They couldn't have been more hospitable in sharing their festivities with us, but somehow, I felt a little awkward, as if I might stick one of those big silver forks right into my cheek halfway through the meal.

I guess I just wanted to be home for Christmas, so I could open up my presents right in our living room, and play with my new toys.

The year Dad bought me a model railroad I just about brought the house down with my sheer delight. We got it all set up on the living room floor and I crouched way down on the rug so I could watch the tiny engine come wheeling around the track. I just couldn't get over how magical it all was. I guess I was seven that Christmas, and you know, to this day I still haven't gotten over the magic of trains (although I know a little more about them now).

Then there were the *real* trains, like the ones over at the railway yard, where my father worked. I loved going over there, just Dad and I, heading down to the train station after church on Sundays. We'd usually stop at a little restaurant called the White Spot and have some pancakes, and then we'd go over to the station. I'll tell you, to a kid who's train-crazy, that place is like being handed a key to the biggest toy store in the world. I couldn't take my eyes off any of it: the roundhouse, with its tracks radiating outward like spokes in

24

some giant wheel; or the engines, huffing and puffing like enormous horses. My dad knew all the engineers, so we'd be able to get real close and watch those huge steel chargers blazing in the sun as they were cleaned and oiled. Finally, it'd be time to watch them leave, one of them on the Sarnia-Port Huron-Chicago route, the other heading for Windsor and Detroit.

Dad would point out all the different cars to me, and explain how his job as a car checker was to make sure they were all on the right trains. "See that boxcar full of lumber on that track over there?" He'd point at the Sarnia-Chicago train. "Well, that car's supposed to be going to Sarnia, but if I put it on the other track, it'd maybe end up going to Detroit and the building company wouldn't have the lumber they needed."

Then, I'd suddenly hear that sound that always made me shiver: the whistle blowing as the Chicago-bound train rumbled slowly away. A few minutes later, there it'd be again: Whoooooo . . . ooo . . oo and the Detroit train would pull out. All the way home to dinner afterwards (we always had our big Sunday meal in the afternoon), I'd be thinking how lucky I would be if only I might ride one of these trains.

Well, I was fortunate indeed, because I got to ride them both. One of my dad's brothers, Fred, lived in Detroit and another one, Frank, made his home in Chicago. When Dad got a pass to ride the railway that far (the distance you could travel depended on how long you'd been with the company), Mom and I were able to go along, and those trips were fantastic. I really enjoyed the ride to Chicago, because it meant spending all night on the train, and I remember getting so excited beforehand that I'd hardly be able to eat my supper, even if we were having apple pie for dessert.

We'd go down to the station in the evening, and at 10 p.m. that train would very slowly pull out into the darkness, gradually gaining speed, faster and faster, until all I could see was the night rushing by outside the window. Then, I'd snuggle down on a pillow they rented in the day car, which is where my folks and I always travelled, and I'd listen to the steady rhythm of the wheels clacking beneath us . . . Eventually I'd fall asleep, and suddenly it would be 8 o'clock in the morning, and we'd be pulling into Chicago's Dearborn Street Station.

Now, Chicago is a city I've always liked a great deal; a big, bustling metropolis, still it has the relaxed feeling I've come to associate with the midwestern United States. On Saturday, we'd have a look in some of the big department stores, or maybe a hobby shop where I could get parts for my model railroad, and then we'd spend the rest of the weekend with my aunt and uncle before going back on the train Sunday night. Although it was a short trip, I always thought it was a great treat, and I always felt very close to Aunt Zola and Uncle Frank, who used to tell me some of his railroad experiences as a steward on the Route of the Zephyrs, from Chicago to California.

Another train trip, though a much shorter one, involved the whole family; aunts, uncles, cousins, and grandparents, all of us headed to Port Stanley for the annual picnic put on by our Christadelphian church group. We'd ride the London and Port Stanley railway — the L and PS (or the Late and Poor Starter, as it was jokingly called, although it wasn't such a bad little train. Matter of fact, it was the first electric train in Canada.).

When we got to Port Stanley, we'd climb onto an incline that would pull us straight up the side of a steep hill; two tickets for five cents, I think it cost. The ladies would have a great table set up there, overlooking the lake, and they'd be brewing coffee on a propane stove and laying out sandwiches, homemade potato salad, cakes, and pies. You could also get Mackie's hot dogs and orangeade, the best you'd ever find anywhere, as anyone who grew up in the London area will certainly attest.

Just about the only train trip I *didn't* enjoy was coming back from Toronto one time after my folks and I had been to see Uncle Albert. There was a terrible thunderstorm, and all I could think about all the way back was my little dog, Buster, out in our backyard all alone, getting ready to have puppies. Now, Buster had dug herself a hole back there, and Dad said she'd be fine, but of course we didn't expect that awful storm.

That was the longest train ride of my young life. I kept picturing Buster the way she looked when my uncle arrived at our door with this little bundle of fur, part bulldog, part Labrador Retriever, and part everything else; just the cutest and most lovable pup you could imagine, and now she was having puppies herself. I guess Buster and I had been pretty much inseparable ever since I got her, and I was terrified of anything happening to her or the family she was expecting.

The train crawled into London at long last, and then there was the bus ride, and finally, we reached our street. Well, I took off out of that bus so fast the driver hardly had time to open the door, and I ran full tilt down the street toward our house. Suddenly, I heard Mr. Lee, our next-door neighbor, shouting: "Tommy, Tommy, your dog's in your backyard having her puppies!"

I didn't wait to hear any more. I raced to the backyard . . . and there was Buster, lifting her tiny puppies up onto the edges of a blanket she'd somehow managed to stuff down into the hole. If one of the pups fell back down, she'd patiently haul it up to safety again.

Mr. Lee had brought that blanket out back when it started raining. Buster wouldn't let him come very close (dogs are like that when they're having puppies), but she grabbed one corner of the blanket and shoved it into the hole to protect her pups. I didn't know if she'd let me come near, but her tail started wagging the instant she saw me, and I lifted up every one of those pups, brought them and their proud mother down to the basement, and got them all cozy near the furnace in a box lined with a clean, dry blanket. Later on, we found homes for all seven puppies, and it was just Buster and me again.

One day, I was visiting a kid down the street, and as I was walking back, thinking that I didn't really like his company that much, I heard the horrible squealing of brakes.

I didn't even want to turn around, because I had this sickening feeling . . .

But I finally forced myself to look, and there lay Buster. We put her out in the backyard and I just sat there, sobbing, stroking her soft fur, praying it was all just a nightmare and she'd suddenly be alive again. If only I hadn't gone to visit that kid, I told myself; but I guess even at that young age I knew, deep down, that Buster could have been killed even if I'd stayed at home that day.

A few days later, a friend of the family came to visit and saw how upset I was about Buster. "Oh, don't fret, Tommy," he said. "It's only a dog, you know." Well, Buster wasn't just a dumb dog, not to me, and you know, I never liked that man again afterwards.

I never had another dog again as a child; I suppose I felt no other dog could ever replace Buster.

But, there *were* other animals . . . of a sort. The typical wildlife that boys are forever bringing home, like frogs, or grass snakes, which I'd keep in a box that I'd punch holes in so they could breathe. I'd always set them free within a few days, because I liked animals and I always figured they'd be better off back where they came from.

One time, I even brought home a catfish, which I kept alive for almost a week in a bucket of water in the basement. I didn't know what else to do with the thing; a few of us kids had been fishing down at the Thames, and I hooked this nine-inch catfish. Ugliest thing I ever saw, and flopping all over the place. I couldn't get the hook out of its mouth, so I decided to take it home, and even though it had been out of water a good 20 minutes, it revived once I got it into the bucket. I guess, thinking back, I should have thrown it back in the river, but I didn't know that much about fishing at the time (I've improved considerably since then).

Unfortunately, one of my one-boy animal rescue missions backfired miserably; I saw a mouse in the middle of the street and decided to save it from getting run over. Well, instead of being grateful, the little so-and-so chomped right down on my finger, hard. That wasn't the worst of it, either; I had to go to the hospital to get the wound cleaned, and, even more horrible, get a needle stuck in my arm.

28

I had an absolute horror of needles (still do, in fact). To this day, I remember the school nurse coming to the door of our classroom, consulting her little list while I sat there, quaking at the thought that it might be my turn to get a medical checkup, which might just include getting a needle. Then I'd hear, "Tommy Hunter, please," and down I'd go with the nurse, wondering whether it was going to be my unlucky day.

Well, the nurse and doctor would look down my throat, and get out the stethoscope to check my breathing and take my heartbeat (which must have been going a mile a minute by then). They'd check my ears and eyes, mark it all down, and all the while I'd be thinking, Oh, here comes the needle, oh no . . .

"That's fine, Tommy," the nurse would say, and I'd feel so relieved that I'd ask for a bottle of cod-liver oil just out of sheer gratitude to them for leaving out the injection.

"Oh, isn't that nice, Tommy," the nurse would say approvingly, and hand me the bottle. Of course, all the relief I'd felt in avoiding the awful needle would evaporate as soon as I got home with the cod-liver oil, which Mom would pour into some orange juice I'd have to swallow. That stuff was almost as bad as getting a needle.

Let's see, now: loves trains, dogs and snakes; hates needles and cod-liver oil. Sounds pretty typical, right?

Well, I was a fairly typical kid. School, for example (not counting things like pasting cotton balls on cut-out paper Santa Clauses in kindergarten; I seem to remember excelling at that). No, I'm thinking more about subjects like reading. It's not that I had any trouble working through the Dick and Jane and Spot and Puff business with the other kids; I just wasn't one of those students who constantly had his nose stuck in a book. In most courses, I was what you'd call an average student.

I did work hard, though; there was an hour or two of homework every night, and I never thought of avoiding it. I knew what the consequences would be; back then, it was quite straightforward. If you did well, you were rewarded, and if you did something wrong, the teacher took you out in the hall, strapped your hand a couple of times, and that was that.

However, lessons in simple justice didn't stop outside the classroom, nor was it the child who was always singled out for punishment. When I was about seven years old, I was getting ready to come home from my swimming lesson at the downtown YMCA late one chilly afternoon. I was shivering by the time the bus arrived and climbed aboard thankfully, putting my ticket in the fare box.

"Now, wait just a second," the driver snapped. "You're not going to get away with that!"

"What did I do?" I asked, looking at him in bewilderment.

"Now, none of that," he said. "That was half a ticket you put in. Now you'll just have to get off the bus, and maybe that'll teach you a lesson for next time."

I tried to protest, knowing I'd put a full ticket in the box, but he just ignored me, opened the door, and pointed down the stairs. Fighting tears of frustration, I got off the bus and started the long walk home; and I mean *long*. It took me more than three hours to get to my house, and when I arrived, it was pitch-black outside and I was cold, scared and miserable. I saw my mother peering anxiously through the window, and when she saw me coming, she ran outside and threw her arms around me.

"What happened, Tommy?" she cried. "I've been so worried . . ."

Well, when I told her, the expression on her face changed from concern to sheer fury. She quickly bundled me up in some warmer clothes and out we went to the corner and waited at the bus stop. Soon, a bus pulled up and she pointed at the driver: "Is that him?"

"No, Mom," I said, confused.

Another bus came by, but that wasn't the right one, either, and finally, a third. "Is that him, Tommy?" It was.

Mom was up those stairs and towering over the driver before I even knew what had happened. I mean, my mother isn't that tall, but believe me, she could *tower*. "You threw a seven-year-old boy off the bus in the dark to walk halfway across the city?" she shouted.

He mumbled something about the fare, but he never finished the sentence. "He *told* you he put a full ticket in that box, and that's just what he did!" she continued, and the driver looked like he wished he were somewhere else.

But Mom was just getting warmed up. "If anything had happened to him," and her finger was waving right under his nose, "you'd have had me to answer to. People like you ought to be locked up, treating a little boy like that!"

With that, she turned on her heel and marched down the steps. I glanced nervously at the driver, but he was just sitting there, absolutely stunned. I think it's a good bet that he thought twice the next time he considered ordering a child off his bus.

I must have been a pretty independent kid for my age, taking buses back and forth when I was seven; and I guess part of it was my height — I could almost pass for a teenager. I couldn't have been more than eight when I got my first after-school job as a delivery boy for a grocery.

Now, Grandpa had a real old bicycle; I don't know if many people remember the kind that had those great big wooden wheel rims, but that was it; a real antique. Anyway, I asked to borrow it because it had a good big carrying basket up front and I figured it was perfect for my new job.

At the store, I guess they decided a tall kid like me could handle a pretty good load, so they heaped that basket high with groceries. They probably didn't notice that for all my height, I was skinny as a rail (despite Mom's delicious baking) and when I sat down on the bike, it felt to me like there was a lot more weight in the basket than there was on my end. But I had a job to do, so away I went.

I was managing all right, thinking to myself, "Hey, this work stuff is fun," and just pedalling along. Then I saw a hill, and put the brakes on. Nothing happened. I tried again, frantically pumping the brake, and suddenly, the wheels locked and I came to a dead stop.

Those groceries literally flew out of the basket in every

31

direction, while I sailed over the handlebars as though I'd been shot out of a cannon. I skinned myself pretty good, but I can't remember even feeling the pain; all that was on my mind was the sickening crash of bottles, and the thought of eggs leaking through the bags, potatoes and carrots scattering every which way, tin cans thudding on the pavement. What was I going to do?

When I brought his poor bicycle home, Grandpa just laughed and laughed. "Don't worry about it, Tommy," he said, kindly. "It's just an old bike." The grocery owner wasn't quite as reassuring, though. He told me it was okay, but I could tell by the look on his face that my days as a delivery boy were numbered.

I did manage more successfully as a delivery boy a few years later, when there was a little more gristle to go with all that skin and bone. I delivered paint for a hardware store, and really enjoyed working for the couple who owned the place; after a short time, they even promoted me to working inside the store. I got to know the stock so well that I could tell where just about every nut and bolt was kept, so I could help all the customers choose exactly what they wanted.

Probably just about everyone can recall a truly memorable character from their childhood; you know, someone who was, well, *different* from the norm. For me, that person had to be Colonel Drew. Nobody was quite sure where Col. Drew came from, but some people said he'd fought in the U.S. Civil War, and others even said he'd been a Confederate soldier who had been forced to seek refuge in Canada. There were all sorts of rumors about it, and we kids could believe it all when we looked at him. There was an air of mystery about him, and he had the kind of eyes that could tell a million stories.

We were a bit scared of him, but more fascinated than frightened, really. He used to take a few of us out to help him clean out a barn on this one farm he had, way out in the country. I always felt lucky to be going out there because he was the kind of man who would ask only the kids he really liked; he wouldn't even talk to the others.

We'd go out there in this rattletrap of an old truck he had, clean out all the stalls for him, and maybe he'd let us ride one of the horses afterwards. Then, once in awhile, we'd go out at nightfall.

I'll never forget one of those trips. There was no moon on that cold November night, and I couldn't see the road ahead as we bumped and jolted along the deserted side road, heading toward a hill. I swallowed hard and crossed my fingers, knowing that the CNR main line crossed at the top of that hill; couldn't see the crossing, because there were no wigwags, but I knew it was there, and I just prayed we'd make it over the tracks in that old heap.

The gears were grinding and the whole engine screamed in protest as we inched upward. Where were we? The truck slowed, and came to the stop in the utter darkness. Col. Drew led the way into the barn . . . He lit a lantern, which cast an eerie yellow glow over the barn, my two buddies, and Col. Drew's angular, weatherbeaten face, and began to tell us stories. I guess an hour passed like seconds as he talked, and you know, I can't even recall the stories he told; just the echo of his deep, mysterious voice and the rattling of the barn walls in the cold autumn wind.

Finally, we started back across the field. All of a sudden, there was a shriek; it was one of my buddies. I looked up to see this huge, hulking form come toward me. I almost dropped in my tracks. Then I saw it was a horse.

Somehow, we all got to the truck (and back home) in one piece. We probably would have gone back again if we'd had the chance, because all that mystery really appealed to us. But we never did see Col. Drew again, and you know, I never was quite sure what happened to him. I suppose he just disappeared, as mysteriously as he'd arrived.

I should tell you about some of the mischief we got into as kids. I'm not talking about serious stuff, like breaking and smashing; we never got into bad trouble. We just played the typical childhood pranks, like ring the doorbell.

You never heard of ring the doorbell? Well, what we did was get a bunch of rotten cabbages, creep real quietly up someone's old wooden steps, ring the bell, toss the cabbage at the door, and race as fast as we could to the next targeted house. I mean, real rough stuff!

Sometimes, we climbed Mr. Lee's cherry tree and helped ourselves, and one fall, we fixed our sights on a yard with an apple tree. Bob was our advance man. Bob could really climb; he had absolutely no fear of heights. So up he went, shaking ripe apples out of the tree as he climbed. Now, Bob was also supposed to be the lookout, since he had the right vantage point, but I guess he got so excited throwing the apples down that he forgot about keeping watch, and next thing we knew, there was the owner.

"Eh there, you lot, clear out of it at once," he said, in the calm tones of a British parliamentarian. That put an end to the apple raid right there. Instead of running off with the loot, we just collapsed with laughter at the sound of that very refined English accent. Our noble scout, Bob, half-fell out of the tree in his effort to climb down while shrieking with laughter. Somehow, we managed to get out of the yard, falling down and holding our sides every few steps.

Other times, there'd be hiking trips, or we'd go swimming or hiking; there was always a group of five or six of us, and we had a lot of fun together. But very often, I'd go off by myself; one kid wanted to climb up on someone's roof, which didn't interest me, or maybe another one didn't want to take a 15-mile bike ride, like I did. There never seemed to be one kid who felt the same way I did about things; someone who you'd call a best friend.

One day, I saw an ad in the newspaper for a show that was coming to the London Arena: Roy Acuff and his Smoky Mountain Boys and Girls. To this day, I don't know why I wanted to go so badly, but I remember pestering and begging and pleading with my dad until he agreed to take me.

From the moment Roy Acuff and the other performers came onto that stage, I was completely and totally mesmerized. My ears were ringing with a sound unlike anything I'd ever heard before, and a beat that filled me with such excitement that I could hardly stay in my seat. I felt an incredible sensation that was a bit like the shiver I got when the train

34

slowly pulled out of the London station, only better. (I later found out that I'd just heard the legendary "Wabash Cannonball" for the first time.)

I had no idea what to expect from a travelling Grand Ole Opry show, but from the first moment the curtain rose and I heard the sounds of those acoustic instruments — the ringing guitar, an old bass fiddle, Dobro, southern fiddle — and listened to the natural, earthy voice of Roy Acuff, I was in seventh heaven.

When Acuff sang of tragedy, you could hear the pain and tears in his voice. To me, it was an evening spent with a storyteller whose songs painted pictures of railroads that ran from the great Atlantic Ocean to the wide Pacific shore, to a terrible wreck on the highway, to a young lady with pretty blue eyes who was left crying in the rain.

It was all woven together without the aid of electrified instruments, fancy production, or tricky lighting effects. Just plain, uncluttered soul music that was as pure and gentle as a quiet running stream. The music was simple and the words were everyday language, but they touched your very soul.

Near the end of the program, all the folks onstage gathered around a single microphone, and very naturally and respectfully sang a song of inspiration that would have inspired many a nonbeliever.

I was absolutely beside myself with the music, and with the people who were making all this happen while still being so friendly and happy, like they were visiting us in our living room.

Why, there couldn't be anything better in the whole world than that music, I thought; and suddenly, out of nowhere, it felt as if a great light had come on somewhere inside me . . . I don't know how, or why, but I suddenly *knew*; I just knew that what I wanted, more than anything else, was to make music like that for the rest of my life.

After the show, Dad and I went to see if we could get Mr. Acuff's autograph, which he kindly wrote out for me, smiling at my obviously awestruck expression. All the way home, I kept picturing his cheerful smile and hearing, like a voice inside my head, that incredible music.

I was nine years old, and I'd just found my best friend: country music.

CHAPTER 2

Early Youth

That night after the Roy Acuff show, I drifted off to sleep still hearing that beautiful music singing in my ears; and in my dreams, I could see the whole performance once again, only this time I was right up there on the stage, playing and singing in front of a huge crowd.

Between spoonfuls of oatmeal at the breakfast table the next morning, I rattled on a mile a minute about the show, the musicians, and how much I'd enjoyed it, and how much fun Dad and I had, and couldn't I please, please take guitar lessons?

"What's that?" asked Mom. "Guitar lessons?"

I looked up at her, trying to make her see how important it was to me, struggling for the right words. "Mom, see, I've gotta . . ." I faltered, "I mean, I want to, you know, play the guitar and sing . . . Please, Mom?"

My mother shook her head and started clearing away the breakfast dishes. "Now, Tommy, you know those lessons are expensive."

"Mom, please; I'll help pay for them," and I winced, remembering that disastrous first job as a delivery boy for the grocery, "somehow," I finished, lamely.

"I don't want to hear anything more about it, Tommy," she said. "Now, off you go or you'll be late for school."

But that was far from the end of it. When Dad came home, I started in again, and for the next few days, the question of guitar lessons became a familiar theme in the Hunter household. I was relentless; no logical argument could sway me. Whether my folks realized just how serious I really was, or whether they just didn't want to hear any more of my wheedling, they finally relented, and enrolled me in the Edith Hill Adams Academy in downtown London. As I remember, the lessons cost about $1.00.

I really enjoyed Mrs. Adams' lessons, because she knew all the different styles and, more importantly, was able to get them across to me simply and clearly. First, the names of the six strings and the notes they represented; then, the frets and how they worked in going up and down the scale; and finally, a little grid she drew on pieces of paper, with dots showing where my fingers should go to play chords. Her lessons in the basics stayed with me; to this day, I still use the runs and sequences of chords that Mrs. Adams showed me (although there are a few others I've managed to pick up over the years).

Now that I think about it, Mrs. Adams reminded me a great deal of one of our Sunday school teachers in the Christadelphian Church, who used to use little pictures she had painted to illustrate the Bible lessons, so that we'd understand the meaning behind the rules we had to learn. I remember thinking to myself that if I ever had the chance to express myself to people (through music, I hoped), I'd follow that example and make sure to keep things clear and simple.

But before any of that could happen, I knew I had a lot to learn. I had a natural sense of rhythm (as Mrs. Adams told me, rhythm is the one aspect of music that can't be taught) and a fairly good ear, probably to some extent inherited from my mother, who taught herself to play the piano by ear, just by listening to her sister practise the piano. But any modest gifts I was lucky enough to have certainly didn't mean I could get away without working hard.

I practised on a guitar Mrs. Adams lent me, and after about six months had gone by, my folks bought me that guitar for $14. I guess by then it was more than obvious that music was no passing fancy for me. Day after day, I'd come running home from school to practise my chords and runs, not stopping until my fingers were so raw that I couldn't press down on the strings any more.

But all the practising I was doing didn't quite prepare me for my unforgettable stage debut, at the age of 10. There were about 40 of us kids from Mrs. Adams' school who were giving a recital at the Hamilton Road United Church; the hall was packed with excited relatives and friends, pointing and nudging each other. Finally it was time for my age group, the 9-to-13s, to get up and give our performance. I think it was "Drifting and Dreaming" we were supposed to be playing, but I can't be too sure, because I never played one note of it. I was so petrified with fear that I just stood there in my white pants, shirt and bow tie, clutching my guitar for dear life.

That didn't stop me from trying again, though. If you really want something badly enough, you just keep going back until, slowly, the fear begins to fade. That's what happened to me; I just kept at it until I actually began to enjoy performing in those little shows we did.

You see, I always felt a great need to express myself, even as a child. At one point, when I was about 8, I used to struggle so to get my words out that I stuttered quite badly in frustration. Dr. Callaghan, our family physician, helped me overcome that problem with a very simple method: "Just slow down, Tommy," he'd say. "Slow down and really *think* about what you're trying to say, create the picture of it in your head and then say it *very slowly*." That approach took care of the stutter, and country music, courtesy of Roy Acuff and my $14 guitar, answered the need for something to express.

Very quickly, it seemed, music was taking over my life. You know, about the only average boyhood activities I can recall were occasional outings with the other kids, but even those were happening less and less often.

I do remember getting into a few fights when I was 10 or 11; I even started boxing lessons after one kid beat me up within an inch of my life one time. My first match was with a kid about three feet tall (I was more than two feet taller), and he ran rings around me as I tried in vain to hit down at him. At the beginning of the second round he popped me on the chin so hard that I went down like a sack of potatoes, right out cold. The end of Round Two saw the end of the match, and the end of Big Tom's boxing career as well.

It may have been just lack of interest in picking myself up and putting the gloves back on, but I think it was more that my utter fascination with country music was guiding me very firmly away from typical childhood interests, whether that meant boxing lessons, or spending a lot of time with the other boys, or playing games for hours after school. It got to the point that I didn't even want to hang around with the old gang at all any more; if the other kids wanted to stand around on street corners or sit in restaurants, that was fine, but I just wasn't interested. I felt that playing and singing and listening to music was all I wanted and needed. Everything I wanted to say, all the emotions and dreams I was too shy to talk to anyone about, came out when I escaped to the privacy of my room and my music. Nothing else seemed to matter, as long as I had that.

So when I talk to you about some of the great songs and legendary performers who influenced me so greatly in my childhood, I hope you'll understand that if it seems my life was totally immersed in music, that's because it really was.

I feel very lucky to have grown up hearing some of the best country and western artists the world has ever known: legends like Roy Acuff, Kitty Wells, Ernest Tubb, Hank Williams, Hank Snow, Red Foley, Little Jimmy Dickens, Bill Monroe, Wilf Carter, Faron Young, Patsy Cline, George Jones . . . the list goes on and on. Many of them I was fortunate enough to see in person at the London Arena; others I got to know in that imaginary concert hall called radio; and still others came alive each time I cranked up our old Victrola and put on a record. Sometimes, I'd hear a singer on the radio, maybe go to my favorite record shop and count out 50 cents for the record, and then read in the newspaper that the very same performer was coming to London . . . What a treat it was to be able to put a face to that wonderful sound I'd been exposed to, and hear the music a whole new way, with all the excitement of a live performance!

But before I get too carried away with talking about radio, records, and concerts all in the same breath, I'd like to tell you a little more about them one at a time, because there was something very special and magical about each of them.

I guess I'll start with radio, which involved a bit of detective work for the listener; finding a station that played country music back in those days was like a game of hide-and-seek. Luckily, I was determined enough to develop the patience for the search. I remember twisting and turning and fiddling with the knobs of the old second-hand mantelpiece radio my dad bought me, hearing nothing but static for what seemed like hours, until at last the very faint sounds of a rhythm guitar or a fiddle would waft into the room, growing gradually clearer and louder. It might last only a few minutes, though, and then I'd start the search all over again. What's more, it always seemed that the best stations came in late at night; no wonder my school work was never much better than average!

Very few stations played more than a few hours of country music back then; not like today, when most communities have full-time country stations, many of them broadcasting 24 hours a day. As a matter of fact, very few stations of *any* kind stayed on the air all day and all night. What happened instead was that a lot of stations had what they called sunup-to-sundown operations, and when they went off the air, a whole other group would come on until midnight, followed by a third group of really powerful clear channels whose signals would just blast out across the continent in the wee hours, when all the other frequencies were cut off for the night. So you really had to be in the right place (the right station, anyway) at the right time if you wanted to listen to country music on the radio: it was a real challenge to fans like me. Fortunately, what I found made the hunt very rewarding.

The stations I remember listening to most when I was a child will probably prompt a smile of recognition from many radio listeners and country music fans. There was XERA in Del Rio, Texas, with its gigantic tower across the Rio Grande in Mexico that beamed its signal into thousands of homes across North America; WWVA in Wheeling, West Virginia; WRVA in Richmond, Virginia; WCKY in Cincinnati, Ohio; WLS

41

and WWJD in Chicago, Illinois, and, of course, WSM in Nashville, Tennessee, home of the Grand Ole Opry. I'll tell you more about listening to those other stations a little later on, but I think you'll agree that WSM should come first.

It might be hard to believe, but even WSM wasn't a full-time country station back when I was growing up; throughout the week they played Eddie Fisher and Perry Como, very sophisticated, middle-of-the-road music for the city folk. Then, late at night, when most people were asleep (except for diehard country fans, like me), they'd broadcast the music I was waiting for. I used to listen so intently that even the names of the sponsors became familiar, like Purina Dog Chow, which sponsored the early-morning syndicated country shows, and RC Cola, which was the main advertiser on Roy Acuff's Saturday morning show.

Naturally, the highlight of my week was Saturday night, and the incredible thrill of the live Opry broadcast, starting at *precisely* 7:30.

I'd huddle close to the radio, my ear practically resting on the speaker, and let my imagination go to work as the broadcast began. It was always the same opening, which I'm sure is as familiar to Opry fans as their own names: the unmistakable sound of a steamboat whistle and the deep, resonant tones of the Solemn Old Judge, George D. Hay, saying: "Let 'er go, boys!" Then, one after another, the singers and musicians would let loose with the most unbelievable, energetic, expressive, heart-stopping series of performances I had ever heard. They all left me just as breathless and astounded as that Roy Acuff show I'd seen, but what was even more tremendous was that they were all different, unique. It was sort of like having a lot of different friends; I felt incredibly close to all of them, but each of them had something that set him apart from the rest. Ernest Tubb was the Texas gentleman who invited you into his private world with songs like "I'm Walking the Floor Over You"; "Warm, Red Wine" and "I'll Walk Across Texas." Hank Snow was our very own Canadian star who gave us all a taste of life on the railroad with "I'm Movin' On." There was Red Foley,

42

who had a great, warm voice and sang some of the best inspirational songs I've ever heard; Eddy Arnold, with his beautiful, smooth voice and Roy Wiggins' steel guitar, his style so unique to Eddy Arnold.

Each of these performers, and many others whom I'll be talking about throughout this book, were sources of great pleasure and inspiration to thousands of country music fans (and aspiring musicians, like me). They were artists; great artists, with so much to communicate about life and its sorrows, joys, triumphs, hardships, humor . . . the whole gamut of human experience. Through their words and music, they painted simple pictures and told stories that stayed with us all our lives. Just hearing them was an education in itself, and I learned a tremendous amount from all of them, not just about music, but about life.

Once I got to know their voices, their styles, their ways of expressing themselves, I could no more get them mixed up than I could confuse a skinny kid with red hair and freckles with a youngster who was dark and chubby. That's how distinctly their musical personalities emerged; even though I couldn't see them, I felt, listening to them on the radio, that I knew them as individuals and friends.

The whole format of the Opry encouraged me to feel very warmly toward all its members, too. There was nothing stuffy or formal about the way the artists were introduced; for example, the announcer, Grant Turner, might say to someone like Porter Wagoner: "Well, Porter, are you all set to introduce us to our next guest?"

"Sure am, Grant, and here's a young lady I'm sure all of you folks will enjoy hearing. We think she's just a great singer here at the Opry, and won't you welcome . . ."

That's what the Opry was like, being introduced to people whose music and personal warmth made them seem like close friends even on first hearing them; and those broadcasts were some of the happiest times I can remember. Of course, when I was really young, I wasn't allowed to listen to the whole Opry program, which didn't finish until midnight, but whenever I got the chance I'd try and sneak in a few extra minutes anyway, because I just couldn't bear to drag myself away. Later on, as I got older, I kept the radio going into the early hours of the morning so I could listen to the Midnight Jamboree, which was broadcast from Ernest Tubb's Record Shop in Nashville, even later, the Eddy Hill Show from Studio A in the National Life and Accident Insurance Building.

Even the names of places where these historic broadcasts came from bring back memories. The Grand Ole Opry wouldn't have been possible without the backing of National Life, which became so closely associated with the Opry that it was almost like part of the show. Same went for the advertisers; names like Martha White Flour, Prince Albert Pipe Smoking Tobacco, RC Cola, Hester Battery, and De-Con Rat and Mouse Killer, were almost as familiar to listeners like me as Roy Acuff, Little Jimmy Dickens and Ernest Tubb. These products weren't advertised the way we know commercials today, wedged in between segments of a program. They were a real *part* of the program; the announcer who introduced Roy Acuff and Ernest Tubb was the same man who told you about RC Cola or Prince Albert tobacco.

The Opry, I soon learned, was where you went when you became the very best, so naturally my youthful dreams of stardom started to point towards Nashville, and, specifically, the Ryman Auditorium, home of the Opry for so many years, before the development of the Opryland complex of today. Of course, I didn't know what those places looked like, but my imagination was greatly stimulated by the sounds, the voices, and the feeling that came through on those live broadcasts. When Grant Turner or Cousin Louis Buck said hello to the folks in the balcony, I felt I was there; when he described the curtain going up, I could *see* that, and when he talked about the performers coming out on the stage, I could picture myself among them, stepping up to the microphone and sending my voice out over the airwaves.

Many of the other stations I listened to also had their share of fine performers, many of whom went on to become stars on the Opry. WWVA in West Virgina was the starting point for artists like Wilma Lee and Stony Cooper, Grandpa Jones, Hawkshaw Hawkins and the Clinch Mountain Clan; and from the Chicago station, WLS, came the likes of Roy Rogers, Red Foley, and Lulu Bell and Scotty. These stations, along with others that the truly determined country fan could find by *really* combing the dial, all had shows that very much reflected the way of life and musical tastes of their listeners.

Take the names of the programs, for instance. The show on WWVA was called the World's Original Jamboree, while WLS had the National Barn Dance. I mean, these terms weren't chosen because somebody thought they sounded appropriately "country"; they grew out of the actual jamborees and barn dances that were regular Saturday night outings for people who lived in hundreds of rural areas and looked to radio to provide another expression of their musical tradition.

For a kid like me, everything about these programs strengthened my great belief in the music they played and the people who lived it.

Again, these were stations I really had to search for, and often couldn't hear clearly until late at night because of interference from daytime station signals. Even when they did come in, the reception wasn't always the best, but what I was hearing more than made up for the fuzzy sound.

A lot of it was the whole atmosphere conjured up by the announcers and performers; just as on WSM, the listener could really fill in the pictures in his mind. Being a youngster with a very active imagination when it came to country music, I just delighted in inventing images to go with all the people and places I was hearing about.

The performers all sounded really down to earth, too; very easy for me to understand, because they didn't act like anything but ordinary people. They even sold products on the air themselves; like Lonny Glossin and Wayne Rainey, who had little 10-minute syndicated programs where they'd play guitar and harmonica, and sing, and then sell harmonicas that you could buy with an instruction sheet showing you how to play "Soldier's Joy" or "The Fox Chase." Or you could send away to WWVA to get lessons on how to play guitar the Doc Williams way. Then there was Don and Earl, The Two Young Christian Singers, who sang gospel music; they sounded like they were being recorded right in their own living room, and they'd invite you to send away for pictures and song books of traditional favorites like "The Old Rugged Cross" and "Lead Me Gently Home."

I didn't see the advertising and promotion as an interruption of the entertainment; to me, it was all very much part of the country show, hearing a song, then the artist telling you about how he'd be giving a show in your area, and giving you an address where you could write to get his picture or a book on how to learn the fiddle, and then going into a commercial. You know, some of those advertisements became country classics in their own right, like the one for baby chicks you could get in the mail. That's right; chicks. You'd get 50 of them, or 500; I don't even remember how many, but the announcer would keep repeating: "Send $4.95 in cash or money order to Chicks, Cincinnati 1, Ohio. That's Chicks, C-H-I-C-K-S, Cincinnati 1, Ohio," and then he'd play a song, and announce it again, until you finally got the message.

I don't know what condition those chicks arrived in, being shipped in a box from Lord knows where, but it was certainly an effective advertisement, which led to many a little anecdote, like this one I heard years later:

Jack: Did you send away for them baby chicks yet?
Bill: Yep.
Jack: Well, how many did you get?
Bill: Oh, round about 500.
Jack: Boy, you must have a real brood goin' now.
Bill: Nope. Ain't got one. They all died.
Jack: Well, what happened to 'em all?
Bill: Don't really know; either I'm plantin' them too deep or too far apart.

Then they'd sell tomato plants that would grow all the way up the side of your house, with tomatoes all the way, and they only cost $9.95 (except that you'd have to spend another

$28.50 on a ladder to get up there and pick them). There were plastic crucifixes that glowed in the dark, and plastic tablecloths; and they'd be selling these things as if to say that the only thing standing between you and complete happiness was the lack of this 100 per cent pure plastic tablecloth, or this glowing crucifix, or this pure white Bible covered in pure white vinyl.

The announcers who told us all about these products were really memorable characters, too; the individual who immediately comes to mind is Lee Moore in Wheeling, West Virginia. I start to smile just thinking about his warm, personal style.

"This is your old coffee-drinkin' night-hawk a-talkin' to you right here," he'd say. "Now Lee Moore's gonna have himself a cup of coffee right now." Sure enough, you'd hear the clink-clink-clink of the spoon in his coffee cup. That kind of personal approach touched everything he did; it wasn't a gimmick. After he got done stirring the sugar into his coffee, it'd be: "Now it's time for old Lee Moore to get ready to sing a song for you and pick the old guitar, and I'll be singin' this for the folks up in Scranton, Pennsylvania on July 23, and then I'll be over at the York, Pennsylvania Park on the 24th for a big jamboree show, so come on out and say hello to your old coffee-drinkin' night hawk Lee Moore."

"By the way, folks," he'd add, "did I ever tell you how I spend a lot of my time at home during the summer? Well, I grow tomatoes right up the side of my house with this plant I ordered right from this station . . .

So here was a very down-to-earth person on this big, powerful station, picking the guitar, drinking coffee, selling tomato plants, pure white Bibles, plastic tablecloths, special chicken feed that would swell your chickens to 687 pounds in two weeks (or maybe it was 688 pounds) and all in the most appealing, simple way that fit in perfectly with the records and songs he was playing. You'd never hear someone like Lee Moore trying to sell a Rolls-Royce while playing Hank Snow records, because a Rolls-Royce wouldn't sell to that audience — God-fearing, church-going people, many of whom lived on farms and appreciated products like tomato plants, all the more because their friend Lee Moore said the products were good.

His very relaxed, neighborly style was what made him so popular at events like jamborees and fairs, where people really enjoyed having him because of the way he came across on the radio, as someone people could identify with.

I appreciated people like Lee Moore very much, not that I ever bought any tomato plants but because of his very warm, friendly approach that reminded me a great deal of the simple style I so much admired in my Sunday school classes and Mrs. Adams' guitar lessons.

Now, you might be wondering why I haven't mentioned anything about Canadian radio so far; that's because there was very little country music programmed on stations in our area when I was very young. But later on, when I got to be in my teens, the popularity of country music was growing at such a pace that all kinds of programs began to crop up on many Canadian stations. I'll tell you a bit later about some of these excellent shows and my involvement with them.

First, though, I'd like to invite you to listen with me as I recall some of the songs I got to know as a child, whether it was listening to the radio or going out to get one of the records to play at home.

They gave him his orders at Monroe, Virginia
Saying, Steve, you're way behind time.
This is not 38 but it's old 97,
You've got to put her into Spencer on time.
He was going down the grade doing 90 miles an hour
And his whisper broke into a scream.
He was found in the wreck with his hand on the throttle,
He was scalded to death by the steam.

That's part of "The Wreck Of Old 97," sung by Vernon Dalheart. It was the first record I ever got to play on our old gramophone, which was basically just a big square box that you wound up on the side. It had little doors that opened in the front, and dozens of needles you'd choose to put in the big round cartridge, and a speaker built right into the machine, which produced a sound that was exactly like a foghorn. But those songs! The stories were better than anything I ever read in school, and the emotion in them was so strong that I played them over and over, trying to capture those feelings so I could sing them the same way myself.

I can even remember what was on the other side of that Vernon Dalheart record; it's a song you will probably recall, too, called "The Prisoner's Song." The chorus goes like this:

Oh, if I had the wings of an angel,
Over these prison walls I would fly,
I would fly to the arms of my darling
And there I'd be willing to die.

I could easily spend an entire book talking about some of the songs I came to treasure, so if I've left out some of your favorites, believe me, they're probably high on my list, too.

There were the Gene Autry records, like "Back in the Saddle Again"; the Sons of the Pioneers with "Tumbling Tumbleweeds" and "Cool Water," probably the two greatest Western classics ever written; all the fantastic railroad songs, like "Tennesee Central Number Nine," "Orange Blossom Special," and of course, "Wabash Cannonball"; Bill Monroe's "Muleskinner Blues"; Eddy Arnold's "Any Time." There were songs about family, church and God; and there were songs about filling up that glass of "Warm, Red Wine"; you'd hear about a boy who'd been killed in the war as in "The Baggage Coach Ahead," and you'd hear about a young child who knows he's going to die and asks his folks to "put [his] little shoes away."

These were songs that touched me to the depths of my soul with their honesty and simplicity, and the more I heard them and learned about the writers and singers who brought them to life, the more I was sure that theirs was a world where I belonged.

These were people who lived the experiences they were telling me about in their songs, like Jimmie Davis, the Louisiana governor and gospel singer. I mean, we all know and love his wonderful song, "You Are My Sunshine," but finding out how he came to write it adds yet another dimension of meaning to it. His wife's nickname was Sunshine; he wrote the song for her when she was dying. If you knew that, then when you heard him sing the lyrics, they took on an almost unbearably poignant significance. It was like that with a lot of the songs I heard; they worked superbly even without that added layer of meaning, but as I found out more about the writers, the words became closer and closer to me.

The writer and performer who most epitomized that level of deep understanding had to be Hank Williams, and I think most country music fans and entertainers alike would probably agree. Whoever thought of calling him "the hillbilly Shakespeare" really hit on the perfect description, because Hank was a great poet who left behind immortal works of art, like "Cold, Cold Heart"; "Your Cheatin' Heart"; "Jambalaya"; "I'm So Lonesome I Could Cry"; and many, many other songs that will live on forever.

He wrote songs as naturally as a bird flies, and all the beauty and pain, sorrow and joy he lived came straight through in those simple, powerful words and melodies. I remember reading something Hank once said about his kind of music: "It can be explained in just one word: sincerity." That was it right there for me, because I knew when I heard his songs that he could never write anything that didn't come straight from the heart, from his real-life experience.

I listened to his songs over and over, and searched through newspapers, magazines and books for every scrap of information about his life. When you're really knocked out by someone, you want to find out everything there is to know about his life.

One of the many stories often told about Hank's incredible natural gifts as a songwriter was related by his mother, who often accompanied him on some of his early shows. On the way back from a show, Hank had apparently fallen asleep in the car while his mother or sister was driving (Hank, for all the fame he eventually achieved, never learned to drive). When he awoke, he asked how far they were from town.

They were just coming into Montgomery, Alabama, and they said: "See, we're nearly home; there's the airport light on the tower."

"I saw the light," replied Hank. Then, suddenly, he sat bolt upright, grabbed a pencil and paper, and began writing:

I saw the light, I saw the light,
No more darkness, no more night,
Now I'm so happy, no sorrow in sight,
Praise the Lord, I saw the light.

Another story concerns Hank's first experience in Nashville before he became a star. Apparently, he went in to see Fred Rose, the publisher who with Roy Acuff had formed the famous Acuff-Rose Publications, and showed him a song called "Move It On Over."

"Well, I really like your song, but how do I know you wrote it?" asked Rose. He then challenged the young songwriter to a test. Hank nodded his agreement, and Rose gave him this story to put into a song:

"There's a girl who marries a rich boy instead of a poor boy who lives in a cabin," he said. "Go in that room over there and see if you can make that into a song."

According to the story Hank came out 30 minutes later and sang the following:

Tonight down here in the valley,
I'm lonesome and oh how I feel
As I sit here alone in my cabin,
I can see your mansion on the hill.

Do you recall when we parted,
The story to me you revealed,
You said you could live without love, dear
In your loveless mansion on the hill.

The scope, insight and depth he had were unforgettable. One moment he could be singing a song that sounded like a page from the Bible, the next minute he could be describing joyous times on the Louisiana bayou, and the next instant it would be a story of lost love that could tear you apart. I was also crazy about the little recitations and stories he told as Luke the Drifter.

What was all the more amazing was that he was able to accomplish all this in a few brief years. To compare him to some of the great classical composers, he was like Mozart, who wrote such a tremendous amount of music in such a short life. Hank made it big in country music, and after he was fired from the Opry for his drinking problems, he was heading out on the road again, trying to make a comeback.

It was winter, and Hank was in the back seat of a rented limousine as he and Charles Carr drove through Kentucky in a blinding snowstorm headed for a booking they had in Canton, Ohio. Hank had found this unregistered doctor to give him a shot of something for his back, which had bothered him ever since he had fallen from a horse. Carr was letting him have only an occasional drink, keeping the whisky bottle in the front seat and rationing it out to him in small amounts when his shaking got really bad. He finally fell asleep, and somewhere in the middle of the night, when he hadn't heard him move for several hours, Carr decided to stop and check on him. He opened the back door as the snow whipped across the road, and gently nudged Hank to wake him, but he just slumped over, and by the time he was rushed to the hospital, it was already too late.

It was New Year's Eve, 1952, and Hank was only 29 years old.

I remember being at a friend's house when my dad suddenly called me to come home. "What's the matter, Dad?" I asked.

"It was just on the radio, Tommy," he said. "Hank Williams is dead."

I felt shocked and deeply hurt; Hank Williams meant a heck of a lot to me. I guess I'd also always hoped against hope that I would someday be able to see him in person, but that just wasn't in the cards. I've always felt regret at missing that experience, because I felt so close to him, whether listening to one of his songs, or just looking at his photograph and feeling such compassion for the sorrow and loneliness, as well as the great pride, that shone out of his eyes.

Everyone I've ever met who had the opportunity to hear Hank Williams in concert told me he was the most magical, mesmerizing performer ever to grace a stage. I think that Minnie Pearl, an outstanding performer herself, put it best when she said Hank was the only artist she'd ever seen who "never failed to stop an audience in its tracks." Just listening to his records stopped me in mine; I think they might have had to scrape me off the floor after a live performance.

However, I did get to see just about every other country and western star of the day, since I was lucky enough to live in a city, London, that attracted most of the major performers from the Grand Ole Opry. There were lots of fans who came to the show, but I don't think anyone was ever in the lineup for tickets ahead of me; I would have been up at 5 a.m. if it meant being first in line for Ernest Tubb, or Hank Snow, or Little Jimmy Dickens, or the many others I was so fortunate to hear.

That first show I saw, with Roy Acuff and the Smoky Mountain Boys and Girls, pretty much set the standard for what I expected from Opry stars. I don't mean to say that none of the others were as good; far from it. I guess it was just that, being the first show, it was such a revelation to me that I went to see all the others with that first experience of country music in mind. I was never disappointed, either; every single one of the performers I heard when I was growing up seemed to take their rules from the same book as Roy Acuff: honesty, sincerity and respect, for themselves and the audience. They all had that in common.

The performers didn't talk too much; just a short introduction, and they'd start right in playing their songs; after all, that's what the audience had come for. If they said something about London, or talked about how nice the streets were, or the good weather, we felt that was terrific, but we were even more delighted when they played and sang. They'd maybe introduce the other musicians, sing some more of their hits, then gather around one microphone and sing a gospel song, always taking off their hats first. After a last song, they'd thank us all, perhaps mentioning some of their upcoming shows, and that would be it. Very simple; no fancy costumes or dancing, no spotlights lingering on the fingers of the lead guitarist, nothing but the pure pleasure of the music and their very straightforward, uncluttered style.

If that sound like a strict formula, that's exactly what it was. Nobody expected Ernest Tubb to suddenly throw off his cowboy hat and launch into an elaborate dance number. Or if Carl Smith suddenly started twirling his guitar in the air and going into a long, complicated discussion of his picking technique, well, we all would have thought something was very seriously wrong; and that sort of thing just never happened.

Even the clothes they wore and the way they acted on the stage was part of keeping things simple. Many musicians just wore a plain western suit, cowboy hat and boots; very basic, and well-groomed. Some of them, like Porter Wagoner, wore more stylized suits, but this was completely in line with his image. The audience (myself included) would have been shocked had he walked onstage in a pair of grubby jeans.

The only thing that really would have turned us off would have been for one of these performers, whom we respected and admired, to have done something insincere that didn't fit into the context of their music and their identity. I can honestly say that none of the artists I saw and heard in those early days ever did anything like that.

I wouldn't want anyone to get the idea that all these people sounded alike, though; nothing could be further from the truth. Without exaggeration, each of them had a style and approach that was as individual as a signature. You know, if I'd been brought into the London Arena blindfolded, I could have told you within the first four notes of the opening of a song whether it was Ernest Tubb's band or Faron Young's, just by hearing the sound of the lead guitarist, and I could pick out Carl Smith's steel guitar style from Billy Bird's (Ernest Tubb's steel guitarist) in a matter of seconds.

Same for the singers; each was unique. I already knew all their songs by heart from radio programs or records (my folks patiently endured even the 38th repetition of songs like "I'm Movin' On") and I'd gotten to the point of playing and singing many of them myself, stretching Mrs. Adams' guitar instruction to the limit, warbling along in my own untrained voice, and trying my best to sound like the artists I loved as I waited for the day when I could hear them at a show and find out how they'd sound, compared to their records.

They were never disappointing; they sounded just like their records, only better. I thought I was going to come unglued when I heard Eddy Arnold sing "Bouquet of Roses" while Roy Wiggins, his unbelievable steel guitar player, coaxed that absolutely unique, ringing sound out of his steel. I still marvel when I remember that there were only three of them: Eddy Arnold, Roy Wiggins and the bass player; together, they sounded like a whole orchestra.

What's more, you'd never see the star, whether it was Eddy Arnold, Ernest Tubb, Hank Snow, George Jones or anyone else, suddenly wander offstage in the middle of the show and leave the band to do an instrumental number. They knew the audience wanted to hear their hits and their new songs, so they stayed right there all the time. There was always a wonderful interplay and communication between all the band members and the singer, and we could tell from their smiles and the way they looked at each other as they played that they were having fun; that just added to our enjoyment of the show.

I guess if there was a star from Nashville in town, I was going to be at the arena somehow. I can't even remember how many shows I went to (that's how many there were), but apart from the ones I've already mentioned, there was Hank Snow, Cowboy Copas, Lonzo and Oscar, Little Jimmy Dickens, Wayne Rainey, Tex Ritter, Gene Autry, Grandpa Jones (who wore a false moustache at the time!) and many, many others, all of them fantastic performers.

Seeing these people was like a dream come true for me; I can't tell you how many times I'd listen to a Hank Snow record and try to imagine what it might be like actually to *see* him playing those notes and singing those melodies. Then I'd go to the show with my dad and it would be ten times better even than my imaginings. I'd watch him close his eyes and sort of bend one of his guitar strings to get more sound, and it would be like a revelation to me: oh, so *that's* how he does it! Or he'd add a little something to a passage, with a little smile, and the next time I heard the record at home, I'd remember the smile, like a special little gift for fans whose love of country music made them listen to every last note.

The songs they sang, like their way of performing, were all unique; but just as they never strayed far from the underlying simplicity of their presentation and stage appearance, the songs also had in common an honesty and sincerity which could be understood equally by an adult who went to the show to relax after a hard week's work, or by a starstruck kid like me. When Ray Price sang "Talk To Your Heart," it was entirely different from Hank Snow singing "Rhumba Boogie," yet they shared a quality of straightforward, sincere emotion; they told simple stories in a universal way, without ever talking down to their audience.

There couldn't have been a better place (other than the Ryman Auditorium, of course!) to see those shows than the London Arena. Most arenas probably make you think of hockey games, but this one was more like a theatre, a sort of art deco look, with recessed lighting, drapes along the sides, a beautiful dance floor, great big pillars surrounded by seats, and a big stage with wings and a gathered curtain. The lighting was good, and you could hear clearly wherever you sat. Just about any kind of show came to the arena: the circus, stage shows (other than plays put on at the London Little Theatre), and even roller skating and dances were held there. Naturally, I had a one-track mind about the kind of entertainment I wanted, and I've always felt fortunate to have experienced it at the old London Arena.

Even the end of the show was exciting for me, because that meant I'd be able to meet some of the performers. They almost always made time for their audience afterwards; they played their music for us, so they weren't about to turn their backs on those same people who just wanted to shake their

56

hands and get close to them, if only for a moment. I can't remember a single performer who refused to sign an autograph for me; they were all warm and friendly people who always smiled at my eagerness and enthusiasm and were very kind to me.

One of the greatest thrills I ever experienced was going backstage to meet Hank Snow. I don't think I was more than 11 at the time, and I was terrified to ask him if I could hold his guitar, but I finally mustered the courage. "Sure, go ahead, son," he urged, encouragingly, and I gingerly picked it up, like it was made of gold (which, to me, it was) and played a few chords before handing it back to him and standing there utterly awestruck and completely tongue-tied.

(It is a mark of Hank's great sensitivity that he recalled that incident, and very kindly related it to me a few years ago; by then, I was able to tell him in greater detail just how much his kindness had always meant to me.)

I remember, too, that the stars would always tell us to come and say hello if ever we were in Nashville. To me, that sounded like the most fabulous, faraway place; a magic kingdom I conjured up in my imagination while I listened to the Grand Ole Opry on the radio. Actually to get there seemed impossible.

Well, the impossible finally happened, thanks to Dad. Canadian National railway employees could get passes to travel on foreign railroads, but only once a year, and they had to put in a request far in advance. So Dad put in for a pass on the Louisville and Nashville Railroad, and it finally came through just about the same day our long-awaited tickets to the Opry arrived. I remember staring and staring at the return address on that envelope: WSM, Home of the Grand Ole Opry. We were really going!

Everything about that trip was exciting; even the travelling, because all the records and shows and radio programs I'd been listening to were suddenly coming to life in the most wondrous way. The train itself was part of all those songs; there was even a song about one of the Louisville and Nashville's passenger trains, The Hummingbird, recorded by

Johnny and Jack and the Tennessee Mountain Boys. When the train stopped at a little junction (and that train stopped often!), I'd look around eagerly at all the farmhouses and old mountain homes and my mouth would fall open as though I'd seen a vision or something. I mean, just imagine spending your life looking at beautiful photographs of a land that intrigued you more than anything else, and suddenly you were placed right in the middle of that country for the first time. Well, that's how it was for me, seeing those places described in the songs.

We'd be rolling through Kentucky at night and the moon would come shining through the train window, and I'd think about the song, "Blue Moon of Kentucky." Then we'd stop in a town, and I'd head for the general store to just look at the people. I mean, the man behind the counter looked like any of the performers I'd seen at the London Arena, and even sounded the same; I half-expected him to leap over the counter and start singing: "We were waltzing one night in Kentucky. . . ."

That may sound a bit far-fetched, but for me, it was confirmation that everything about those songs was true to the lives of the people I was now seeing for the first time. Even the products they were selling in that store were the same ones that were on the Opry: Martha White Flour, Jefferson Island Salt, Prince Albert pipe-smoking tobacco (which I bought, not that I could smoke at 12, of course, but just so I could stare at the label on that tin).

When I say I was enthusiastic about the trip, I think anyone aboard that train with me could certainly attest to that, after hearing my piercing yelp of delight as we crossed the border into Tennessee and came in sight of the Smoky Mountains. Roy Acuff territory! I could just see the boys out in front of a cabin with a fire going, gathering around with their fiddles and banjoes and guitars while the fog hung like a cloak over the rugged hills. When the train actually did pass an old grey wooden shack, with a guy out back in his field, I could just about see him finishing his ploughing, getting cleaned up, and driving into Nashville in his truck to do the Opry.

When Dad and I finally got to Nashville, on Thursday night, we spent all of five minutes in our little hotel room; I couldn't wait to go find the Ryman Auditorium just so I could see where all my idols performed. The place was closed until Saturday night, but we managed to coax the commissionaire into letting us have a look (I probably would have gone down the chimney to get inside if he'd said no!). Anyway, we went inside.

I stood there, transfixed. There was the balcony they'd talked about on the radio, and the big clock they used so they'd know when to sign on and off the air, and the seats that looked like big church pews, and the wooden stage facing all the curved rows of seats like a star circled by a half-moon.

Without even thinking what I was doing, I walked straight up to centre stage and laid my hands down on it. I just wanted to feel my hands on that stage where all those performers had stood.

On Friday night, Dad and I went to the famous Studio A at the National Life and Accident Insurance Building, where they used to broadcast a live radio show with the Opry stars who happened to be in town that night; it wasn't called the Friday Night Opry or anything, and there weren't any backdrops or stage settings, just some chairs set up right in the radio station where you could see the performers doing the live show. Then, on Saturday night at 7:30 p.m., we were back in the Ryman Auditorium for a night I'll remember for the rest of my life.

I never budged from my seat (except to jump up and down with excitement) from the moment that show started to the end, at 12 midnight. Those 4-1/2 hours seemed more like 4-1/2 minutes; that's how fast the time slipped by, and that's how much fun I was having. It was as if I had been set loose in a gigantic candy and toy store and told I could have anything I wanted.

Finally, I was *seeing* the Solemn Old Judge, George D. Hay, and watching him blow the steamboat whistle: "Let 'er go, boys!" There were the Jordanaires, singing in harmony on the Jefferson Island Salt commercial: "Puuuuure Saaaaalt," and the announcer presenting the Martha White portion of the show, and there was the old microphone bearing the magic words: WSM Grand Ole Opry, and the performers in the background, waiting their turn: Red Foley, Hank Snow, Ernest Tubb, Roy Acuff and the band, Lonzo and Oscar, Bill Monroe, Minnie Pearl, Carl Smith, Ferlin Husky, Marty Robbins, Johnny and Jack and the Tennessee Mountain Boys, Sam and Kirk McGee from Sunny Tennessee, the Fruit Jar Drinkers, Moon Mullican, Lou Childrick, Lester Flatt and Earl Scruggs . . . Everybody was there, and I mean *everybody*; if you had made it, you were on the Opry, and you were there on Saturday night.

I loved watching them all mill around the stage like that, so much at ease and natural. I mean, it was a show and they all performed in a very professional manner, but it wasn't a staged sort of event; the Opry was a radio show, and made no apologies for that. For an audience, that meant they were part of the show, and they loved it. *We* loved it. It was very exciting, being right there while this broadcast was going out all across North America. And we were seeing it all happen.

When they started to play and sing, I just about came out of my seat; one hit record after another, coming alive as the performers stepped right up to the microphone and gave it all they had. The guitars rang and the fiddles sang and the old banjoes honked in the background . . . I couldn't believe how great it was!

I think the man sitting next to me must have had black-and-blue marks for weeks afterwards from me poking him in the ribs: "Did you hear that? Wasn't that *great?*" I'd say, every five seconds. I mean, the man was listening, but I couldn't figure out why each time I turned to him he wasn't coming out of his skin the way I was, and I just wanted to make sure he didn't miss anything.

Well, there hadn't been any doubt in my mind before, but now my resolve was even more firmly fixed: Someday, I would perform here, up on this stage, in front of this microphone.

You'd think that after almost five hours of music, I'd be ready to pack it in for the night; but, no, instead I dragged Dad down Broad Street to the Ernest Tubb record shop and stood there until 1 a.m., watching the radio show being broadcast. Finally, we went back to the hotel.

"Now, come on, you've had a long day," Dad said, as I regaled him with my interpretation of "Warm, Red Wine." "It's time to go to bed." Well, I waited until Dad had fallen asleep and then took off out of that hotel like a shot, racing as fast as I could toward the WSM Studios, way at the other end of Nashville. When I got there, the disc jockey was kind enough to let me sit there while he spun country records for that late-night show.

You know, when I think about it now, it was crazy for a kid of 12 to be out in a strange city at 1:30 a.m., not to mention coming back at 4 a.m., when the broadcast was finally over (or maybe it was actually 5 a.m.).

It was perfectly natural that Dad was worried and upset with me. But I think he knew I wasn't being deliberately disobedient; it was just that everything to do with country music was so incredibly important to me that I don't think anything or anyone could have stopped me from making that early-morning trek across town.

All too soon, it seemed, we were on our way home. But there was one final treat in store for us in Cincinnati, where we had a four-hour stopover before changing to the train that would take us home. While we were waiting, I asked Dad if we could try to find the radio station I'd listened to at home, WCKY, and maybe meet some of the people I'd heard all those times. He agreed once again (Dad is a *very* patient man), and we finally found the building after taking only two wrong turns.

As it happened, one of the announcers I'd often heard, Marty Roberts (Nelson King being the other), was right there when we arrived, and he was very nice to us. We saw the studio and watched him spin some records, and then, to our complete surprise, he suddenly started to talk about us on the air.

"Well, folks," he said, "we've got a couple of fellows here from London, Ontario in Canada; Jim Hunter and his son Tommy, just on their way back from the Grand Ole Opry, and they decided to drop in and say hello."

When we got home, Mom was almost beside herself with excitement, because she just happened to have the radio on while Marty Roberts was introducing us, and she'd heard the whole thing!

That trip to Nashville really got me thinking about ways to get started in a music career; I mean, my only experience had been playing the guitar with the other kids in Mrs. Adams' recitals, and I knew that wasn't going to be enough to get me on the Grand Ole Opry. But I wasn't at all sure how to get started, so I began asking some of the performers I heard at the London Arena for some guidance (when I got brave enough, that is!).

Not too long after the trip, Ernest Tubb was performing in town, and I remembered his friendly, straightforward style so well that I got up the courage to ask him. He was extremely nice to me, and after signing his autograph in my copy of *Country Song Roundup* (every aspiring country singer's Bible of classic hits), he gave me what turned out to be the most solid advice I could ever have heard: "Well, son, I think you should get known in your home town first," he said. "That's always a good start."

Above I took this photo of Bill Monroe and the Blue Grass Boys on my first visit to the Grand Ole Opry with my father.

Left 1958, age 21.

Below 1960, age 23. This is my first, only, and definitely last white suit.

1955

1956

1961

Shirley was, and always will be, the only girl for me.

Right There wasn't a happier guy in the world than I was when Shirley agreed to be my wife.

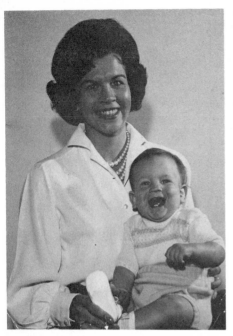

Proud parents of our first-born, Jeff.

Greg, Mark and Jeff in 1974.

Above The Hames Sisters, Jean, Marjorie and Norma, tempting me with candy in a Valentine's Day promotion shot.

Right Country Hoedown, 1956. King Ganam, Tommy Hunter, Bill Kuinba and Gordie Tapp as Cousin Clem.

The cast of Country Hoedown.
Front Row: Gordie Tapp, Tommy Common, Norma Hames, Marjorie Hames, Jean Hames, Tommy Hunter, Johnny Davidson.
Back Row: Ray Marlow, Sandra O'Neil, Barbara Barlow, Billy Van, Laura Berkley, Stephanie Taylor, Gordon Lightfoot.

In Resolute Bay in 1959.

In the Gaza Strip in 1970
with Mike Ferly, Jack Jenson
and Marc Wald.

With Shirley in Frankfurt,
1971. We are greeted by the
official German chimney
sweep.

With Johnny Cash in 1961. Johnny came by to visit
me when I was doing the Tommy Hunter Radio
Show.

With Ruffy our dog.

CHAPTER 3

Early Career

Garden parties, strawberry socials, peach festivals, fall fairs, Christmas parties, church socials, town hall dances . . . Ernest Tubb wasn't exaggerating when he said that getting known in your own home town was a great way to start.

I can't even recall whether it was a strawberry festival or a dance in a church basement that launched my career, but I do remember that I was 13 years old when I received my first dollar as a professional performer. That's exactly what I earned, too: $1, which was just fine with me. Heck, I would have paid *them* for the chance to sing and play in front of a real audience!

Luckily, there was a lot of opportunity for an eager young performer; those small community events and gatherings, many of which don't even exist today, were extremely popular get-togethers when I was growing up, and they provided me with very valuable experience. I remember times when I did three or four shows on a Sunday alone, singing "Happy Birthday" at a child's birthday party, or "Rudolph the Red-Nosed Reindeer" at a Christmas party in a church basement, and then one or two other shows where I'd be able to do more of the country songs I'd been practising so hard.

All of us in the London area knew each other, and we were always helping one another by passing on information about upcoming events where there might be a chance of getting hired.

For example, one guy who did a juggling act at a garden

party might hear that they were looking for a country singer for their next party, and he'd let me know about it; then, if I was at some other show where the organizer mentioned he was interested in finding a juggler, well, I'd just pass that along.

The variety of audiences at these early shows was very good for me; I was beginning to learn what different kinds of audiences wanted and expected. If I were playing a town hall show, I might pick my favorite country songs right off the Hit Parade of 1951, but if I were playing for the Knights of Columbus or the local women's church league, I'd be much more general in the music I picked, because that audience might not know the Number One country song. So instead, I'd do something like "Cold, Cold Heart" or "Bouquet of Roses," which I felt they'd be more familiar with. I'd really learn to *watch* the audience's mood, and try to sing and perform in ways I thought that particular group would enjoy.

By the time I was 13, I was just about as tall as I am now, six feet four inches; my pride and joy was the bright yellow cowboy suit, cowboy boots and hat that Dad and I bought at Hank Williams' Western Corral that time we went to Nashville.

One job I had, playing in the Capitol Theatre in Woodstock, Ontario, reminded me, in a way, of how young I really still was. I got the job through my teacher, Edith Hill Adams, who convinced the theatre manager, Tommy Naylor, to hire some of us to go down there and put on little shows in between the first and second features. It hadn't been that many years before that I was a kid in such an audience, paying out my 15 cents to go and see the Saturday afternoon westerns, the classic films like *Twelve O'Clock High*, and of course all the Gene Autry and Roy Rogers movies. Even my absolute idols had movies out; Ernest Tubb in *Hollywood Barn Dance* and Roy Acuff in *Night Train to Memphis*, which I sat through from noon on Friday until the projector stopped running at 1 a.m. on Saturday.

But now, even though I was still just a kid, I was the one up on the stage who was expected to provide the show, and that

72

was an altogether different feeling; standing there after the news and cartoons and the first feature, and trying to figure out what could possibly get their attention as much as the shoot-'em-up movie they'd just been cheering from beginning to end: "Yaaaaaay!" Well, I'd try to do songs that fit in with the movie they were watching, usually western songs, and maybe talk to them a bit. Then it'd be the same kind of show during the evening movie, and that was it.

It must have gone fairly well, because Mr. Naylor always asked me back, and I guess I played and sang at that theatre for a couple of years, until I started getting other shows in little communities outside London, like Ilderton and Delaware.

When I wasn't working as a performer, I could usually be found in my room, practising.

School, as you can probably imagine, was not that high on my list of priorities; most times, I couldn't wait for the day's classes to finish so that I could rush home and practise for my next show, or just learn some new songs. But the fact that I managed to earn average marks is proof that I had a number of fine teachers, who I still remember with great fondness. One of them was an English teacher who used to get us to read only a short passage at a time from whatever we were studying; say, Sherlock Holmes, and then we'd discuss and analyze that section in the class the next day. That way, we really got a good sense of how the writer was developing the plot and characters, and the whole book seemed to make a lot more sense.

Another really terrific teacher was the track and field coach, who also taught us in gym. Yes, that's right; the kid with the one-track mind on country music actually got excited about competitive sports! Because of this teacher's faith and exuberance, I got so enthusiastic about track that I even managed to place in the top five in several of the events. I'll never forget the way he talked the day he presented me with an award as the most improved athlete on the team. "Here's a youngster who never even heard of the high hurdles three weeks ago," he said, "and yet he went out and qualified and got into the finals and placed second, third and fourth in his events. That is a real accomplishment." (Of course, as far as I was concerned, it was his ability to motivate me that was the real accomplishment.)

But more often than not, when I was in school, my mind was really elsewhere. If I saw a limousine go by outside the classroom, I was completely lost to what the teacher was saying; I was too busy trying to imagine who might be in the car, and if I'd seen a Tennessee licence plate on that car, I'd have been out the door and gone before anyone could blink an eye. I might not have known the answer to the algebra question my teacher was asking, but nobody had to tell me that all the stars from the Grand Ole Opry travelled in those big black limousines!

Of course, there were times that my love of country music actually worked to my advantage in school, and once it even got me out of trouble in an unexpected way. I had this one English class in which we had to memorize something like 500 lines of Shakespeare during the course of the semester, and the teacher informed me in no uncertain terms that I was way behind in the assignment.

"You'll just have to stay after school and catch up, Hunter," he told me.

Well, I came in, but I just knew it wasn't going to work. I could no more memorize 500 lines of Shakespeare than I could fly to the moon. Now, if it was Hank Williams or something, that would be different, but . . . Suddenly, the old light bulb went on.

Tommy: Sir, do I have to memorize Shakespeare or is the idea just to be able to memorize something?

Teacher: Hunter, if you can memorize your own telephone number, I'd consider it a miracle.

Tommy: Well, here, sir (handing him my *Country Song Roundup* book). Ask me anything out of that. Anything at all.

The teacher started with "Don't Let the Stars Get in Your Eyes," worked through "Bouquet of Roses," "Cold, Cold Heart" and at least a half-dozen other songs, with me rhyming them off, absolutely letter-perfect. Finally, he set the

74

book down, a little bewildered.

"Just how many of these songs do you know, Hunter?" he asked, gesturing toward the book, which probably contained close to 70 songs.

"Oh, I guess about 50, sir," I answered.

I guess he figured that added up to more or less 500 lines, because I passed that course.

For the most part, though, I can't say I got that much satisfaction out of school; it was something I went through because I had to, not out of any great pleasure or aptitude for academic work. I just couldn't wait to get home to my guitar, my radio, my music.

It was around the same time, when I was about 14, that I began to notice that there was a lot more country music on Canadian radio stations. I really enjoyed listening to these programs; for one thing, they were a lot easier to pick up on the dial than some of the American ones I'd been tuning in.

Some of the stations in our area included CFCO in Chatham, which broadcast country as well as a live show called the Newberry Barn Dance Gang; CHLO in St. Thomas, which broadcast some country music; and the ones I became most familiar with: CKNX in Wingham, CFPL in London, and CHML in Hamilton.

Each of these stations had its own unique identity, but what they had in common was that they were all basically non-country stations that set aside one or two hours a day for country music.

Let me tell you a little about each of these programs, and the people who were involved with them.

Let's start with CKNX, Wingham. Now, Wingham was a very small town in those days, but in a way, it was the focal point for even smaller communities, and the radio station drew on that close link in an extremely effective and successful way. W.T. "Doc" Cruickshank, the announcer, was always very aware of his audience; he didn't set out to try to prove a point or compete with other stations, and as a result the show included elements like auction sales, swap shop announcements, and farm reports that really interested the listeners in these mainly rural areas that the station served.

The entertainment also very much reflected the region; the station started the CKNX Travelling Barn Dance Show, with a group of performers who went on to become some of Canada's most popular and successful musicians: Earl Heywood, Jack Kingston, Don Robertson and the Ranch Boys, Al Cherny and of course, the late Maurice Bolyer, whose great contributions to Canadian music will long be remembered. Thousands of people would come out to see them on Saturday nights in little towns like Lucknow and Clinton, and during the week, they'd be kept busy playing town hall dances anywhere from Wingham to Seaforth. ''Coast to coast, Canada's largest travelling barn dance,'' the announcer always said on the air. Well, maybe it wasn't quite coast to coast, but they sure had the right idea, and as a matter of fact, the CKNX Barn Dance eventually did end up being syndicated on the national network, courtesy of the CBC's old Dominion Network.

A number of performers from CKNX went on to join the very successful Main Street Jamboree on CHML, Hamilton. Matter of fact, one of the CKNX performers, Jack Kingston, helped start the Jamboree, which developed into another top country music show.

For people like Jack Kingston and the Mainstreeters, and Maurice Bolyer, who had served their apprenticeships on the CKNX Barn Dance, coming to Hamilton opened up much wider careers. Jack was the man who set the whole tone of the show, and Maurice, who started out as lead guitarist with the band, began to develop more of what was just a sideline for him at first: the banjo, which of course is the instrument he became famous for in later years. Then there was Wally Traugott, a great fiddler, Gordie Tapp, who had been the staff announcer at CHML, and the Hillbilly Jewels.

The third station I heard a lot as a teenager was CFPL, right in London, which broadcast a country show featuring Lloyd Wright and his Radio Rangers. What I really liked about Lloyd was the way he brought a wide variety of musical styles into his 15-minute show and really tried to appeal to a whole range of tastes, while keeping a very folksy appeal, with musicians like an old-time fiddler and a singer who yodelled very well.

I also enjoyed the way Lloyd performed and talked, in a friendly and relaxed way that sounded so natural that I never suspected he had actually spent hours working out precise script for every second of that 15-minute show.

But before I get a little too far ahead of myself in talking about Lloyd's radio script, let me tell you a bit about how I happened to cross paths with him and some of the other performers I met in the early days of my career.

Back in those days, remember, country music wasn't something that was programmed all day and all night, as it is now. The radio shows basically grew out of the popularity of the little dances, variety shows and other events featuring performers like Lloyd Wright.

Many of the shows in the London area were like town hall dances, or variety shows at places like the Centralia air force base or any number of legion halls, and I'll tell you, just mentioning some of these places sure brings back fond memories of some of the terrific people I met.

There'd be maybe five or six acts in these shows, and a typical lineup went something like this: first, a magician like Evward Myers, a juggler like Anne Mae, a dancer like Joey Hollingsworth, who became a close friend of mine; next, a guy by the name of Bill Howell, who did pantomime to music; then I'd go out with my guitar and sing three or four country songs; then a tap dancer; then Lil Gibbons, who would do a couple of songs in the style of Sophie Tucker; and then Lloyd Wright and his Radio Rangers or Bern Conway and the Continentals would be the main band, and they'd also play for the dance later that evening.

I also remember Gladys Cornell and Myrtle Armstrong, who used to do absolutely wonderful routines. Gladys would do the "Laughing Song"; she'd sit at the piano very sedately, accompanying herself as she sang: "Ah-ho-ho-ho-ho-ho-ho-ho-ho, ho-ho-ho, ho-ho-ho," all in perfect rhythm. Well, after about three of those ho-ho-hos, which got progressively

77

louder, somebody in the audience would let out a chuckle, then another, and pretty soon everybody would be just rolling in the aisles, absolutely rocking with laughter.

Now it would be Myrtle's turn, and she'd come out dressed in this elegant evening gown, carrying her violin very properly at her side, like a lady from the symphony orchestra. She'd walk very slowly to the centre of the stage, carefully tuck a cloth under her chin, then the violin; all very proper, you know, tuning up the violin while everybody waited expectantly. Then, when she was sure she had everyone's undivided attention, she'd suddenly whip around, spit into a spittoon, and break into a real foot-stompin' hoedown. I mean, that audience just *roared*!

They were both really great gals, and they were extremely kind to me. I didn't have a car in those days, of course (I was still only 14 years old), so very often Myrtle and Gladys would give me a lift to some of the shows we were doing all over southwestern Ontario. I'd take a bus into downtown London and meet them in front of the Hotel London, and then we'd take off from there.

Well, one time we were all performing in Port Perry, a little resort community where they held a lot of shows. I arrived downtown just in time to see their car pull up; at least, it *looked* like their car, although I couldn't see Myrtle or Gladys at all for the mountains of boxes and suitcases and pots and pans heaped up in the back seat. It turned out they had a cottage nearby the place where we were performing, so they decided to bring all their stuff along; and I ended up squeezing into the back seat with my guitar and my little suitcase (which I used to carry my outfit).

You know, it was a miracle I got in there at all, and as it was, I had to just about wrap myself up like an accordion to get my long, gangly legs into the car. That's the way it was all the way to Port Perry, for two agonizing hours, wedged in against all this stuff in the back seat, and listening to Myrtle trying to teach a few new words to her pet mynah bird, which somehow got out of the cage and started flapping around the car and tweetering to beat the band. I'll tell you, there's no business like show business!

That's how it was, though; I'd travel for two or three hours, or even longer, do the show, turn around and head back, sometimes not even arriving back in London until way past midnight. So after all this effort, travelling with mynah birds in cramped cars (or even hitch-hiking if I couldn't get a ride) and coming home in the wee hours, if I got paid $3 or $4, well, I never really questioned it. I'd never even ask if I was going to get paid at all, for fear that the people who hired me might be offended and not ask me back. I just considered myself lucky if I got a job at all.

We all got shows through each other back in those days; there weren't promoters or talent agencies, so everyone was basically a booking agent for everybody else. Gladys and Myrtle would both arrange some shows, and another performer who did quite a lot of booking was Bern Conway.

Well, Bern knew a number of places, like the Knights of Columbus annual dinner, where he'd been working for years and years, and where they were always looking for new acts. He'd be talking to the organizer about getting the ventriloquist who had performed the year before, and the guy would say: "No, let's have something different this time."

"All right," Bern would say, "I can get you a magician and a cowboy singer."

"Sounds great."

So the cowboy singer was me, and the magician might be someone like Roy Head, who performed with his wife, Doris (they called themselves the Royal Heads of Magic). Then, Roy booked shows himself; someone would give him a small budget and ask him to put together a little hour-long show. He'd call someone like a girl singer who worked with a pianist, and me with my guitar, and then he'd do a routine himself. One of my favorites was a really funny sequence in which he'd produce all these rubber masks out of nowhere, and then get audience members to come up on stage and put them on; there were Frankensteins and Indian chiefs and all kinds of characters running around. Then he'd hand them all tom-toms and candles and get them all jumping and leaping all over the stage; just the sight of all those housewives and businessmen up there cavorting around in masks was absolutely hilarious, and no one laughed harder than the participants themselves!

Another performer I worked with quite often was Anne Mae, who used to do acrobatics as well as juggling; you know, balancing acts and tumbling, that sort of thing. I really enjoyed working with her, even though our shows were sometimes in fairly basic environments; I mean, most of the time we were performing on the back of a truck out in the middle of a field somewhere, at a fall fair or other kinds of outdoor events. That got to be a bit precarious at times; I'll never forget the one night when Anne Mae was doing a balancing routine on the back of the truck. She set a board on a round wooden cylinder and, holding two glasses of colored water, climbed onto the board to rock back and forth. Everything was going just fine until the cylinder somehow knocked into a steel rivet on the flatbed . . . Colored water went flying everywhere, all over her hair, on the audience, and just narrowly missing my one and only cowboy suit.

As I said, I liked Anne Mae a great deal, but the same cannot be said of her dog, Rifles. Now, Rifles was supposed to be a trick dog, but the best tricks he seemed to do always ended up sticking to the bottoms of my boots, and as for personality, well, that dog was like a cross between a cobra on a bad day and the meanest junkyard mutt you ever saw. If I even came close to where he was lying, tied up (luckily!) he'd spring up and start growling, snarling and baring these ferocious looking, long, yellow teeth.

Well, the way it worked in those shows was that you went around the other side of the truck to change into your outfit, because there just were no dressing rooms, and of course, the one relatively private place was (you guessed it!) right within chomping distance of dear old Rifles. I put off the dreaded event as long as I could, but finally I had to face the music; or, rather, the teeth . . . Every move, as you can imagine, was done very, *very* carefully, inching out of my travelling clothes and into my cowboy suit, my eyes never once glancing away from Rifles. Then came the moment of truth; I had to bend over to pull up my pants.

I'm sure it wasn't my imagination that I could just hear Rifles straining at his leash for the chance to plant his fangs right on the target, but by some miracle, he couldn't reach far enough. All I can say on the subject today is that I sure hope Rifles is now in doggie heaven, because that's about the only place I can think of where his disposition might be improved.

We didn't *always* have to change right out in the open, of course, but the dressing room situation was often, well, limited. It's only now, thinking back on those days, that I remember that most times, the guys and gals used to change in the same room. Basically, there usually wasn't more than one dressing room in most of the places we performed, so we just went ahead and changed, not really thinking about it much. We were just trying to get into our costumes as quickly as possible so we could get on stage.

As for my shows, they were always just me and my guitar, usually up on stage for 15 or 20 minutes, which doesn't sound like a lot of time, but believe me, it sure seemed like an eternity to a kid of 14, up there trying to hold an audience's attention with as many country hits as I could collect. But I didn't let my apprehension get in the way of really enjoying the music I was playing and singing, and I guess part of that must have gotten across to the audiences, because they always seemed to give me a really kind, warm reception.

At home, I practised songs I liked, and on stage, I would try to alternate different kinds of songs, like slow ballads and more up-tempo numbers; I even changed the order of the songs in the middle of the performance if I thought the audience liked a certain style better. I didn't do a lot of talking, keeping in mind how the performers I really admired did their shows at the London Arena. I just got up there and went for broke; gave every one of those five or six songs everything I had.

After the show, if it wasn't too late, there was a whole group of us, like Lil Gibbons, Joey Hollingsworth, Bern Conway and some of the other people I've told you about, who used to get together for a drink or a bite to eat at a place called The Wheel, out on Highway 2 near London. We'd all be coming from some of the surrounding towns and villages; Joey might be on his way back from Stratford, Bern might have been playing Komoka, and maybe I'd just got done in Strathroy, and we'd all meet at this little roadhouse on a Saturday night, just to sit and talk about our shows.

There'd always be a local band playing there on Saturday nights, sometimes Lloyd Wright and his Radio Rangers, and often Lloyd would ask us to come up and perform one of the numbers we'd done that evening. It inevitably turned out that everyone who had done a show that night got to recreate every moment of their performance again, up on that little stage at The Wheel; it was great fun for us, and the audience didn't seem to mind the whole thing, either!

You know, even being exposed as I was to all these different styles and types of performers whom I worked with, I never found myself wavering in my loyalty to country music. I very much appreciated my fellow performers professionalism, and I sure hope they felt the same way about me, but as far as being influenced by anyone, my influences were the same as they'd always been: Roy Acuff, Ernest Tubb, Hank Williams, and all the other great artists who'd come to symbolize music to me. Working as a performer, and learning to respond to an audience professionally, served only to enhance my particular musical ideals; if anything, I was even more enthusiastic about country music than before, to the point of single-mindedness, as the following incident reveals.

One time, when I was doing one of those little out-of-town shows, I remember the announcer asking a man from the audience to come up on stage for a moment. When he got there, the audience started wildly applauding and cheering. I couldn't understand this at all. I mean, the man wasn't doing anything; just standing there. Well, anyway, we just got on with the show, and afterwards, when we all went across the street to a little coffee shop, there he was again, with a crowd clustering around him, clamoring for autographs; if the restaurant owner'd had a red carpet, it would have been stretched three times around the block. Finally, curiosity got the better of shyness, and I went over and asked him, very politely, what his name was.

"I'm Turk Broda," he said, smiling.

"Oh, I see," I said (not really seeing anything at all except that I still didn't know who this guy was). "Um, well, could you tell me what you do, sir?"

Well, Mr. Broda naturally looked a little confused; after all, didn't every red-blooded Canadian kid know that Turk Broda was the greatest goalie ever to stand in front of a net? Well, not this kid, apparently. I'd heard about hockey, of course, but that was about as far as it went. Nashville stars, not hockey stars, where the ones on my mind.

Now, you might have thought that performing in all those shows was enough to satisfy a kid of 14 in his desire for a career, but I was always trying to think up new ways of getting experience in singing and playing. One time, when I was visiting a friend, I noticed that he had one of those little disc recorders they were making then so that people could make their own records right at home. It was a big machine with a cutting groove, and you'd put the record on, push the needle down, and record your voice or play the piano or whatever you wanted. You couldn't stop and start or anything like that, as you do when you're using a tape recorder. I mean, most of us were still getting over the shock of Alexander Graham Bell's new invention, let alone know anything about tape recorders.

Anyway, when I saw this gadget, I suddenly had a brainstorm: I'd make a record, take it into a radio station, and maybe they'd hire me! Well, I made the record (which I wish I still had as a memento) and decided that the station to hear it was going to be WJR in Detroit, which was a big station with a country show called Casey Clark's Jamboree.

So off I went to Detroit, alone, at the age of 14.

How did I get there? The only way I knew; the same train Mom and Dad and I used to take to go visit my aunt and uncle. Some of the men who worked with my dad at the train station recognized me and let me ride the train.

"Now, you just stay real quiet, right in this corner here," the one guy said, then looked at me a little suspiciously. "Now, does your dad know you're here, out of school and everything?"

My heart pounding, I tried to sound as calm as I could. "Yeah, well," I said, crossing my fingers behind my back, "we've got the day off school and I just thought I'd surprise my uncle."

He peered more closely at me. "Well, all right," he finally said. "Now just remember to stay out of sight."

All I had to go on when I arrived in Detroit was that WJR was located in the Fisher Building on Woodward Avenue, which was about like saying the place was somewhere on Yonge Street, which goes right through downtown Toronto and out the other side for a couple of hundred miles. But I got on the streetcar and just rode and rode until I found the building at last.

What happened once I got inside made the trip getting there seem easy. It went something like this:

Tommy: Excuse me, I'd like to see Casey Clark.
Receptionist: He's not in at the moment.
Tommy: Oh, well, when will he be in?
Receptionist: I really couldn't say.
Tommy: Could I see the program director?
Receptionist: What is it about, please?
Tommy: Well, I've come all the way from Canada to see if I could get a job on your radio station, and. . . .
Receptionist: We're not hiring right now.
Tommy: But you don't even know what I do.
Receptionist: I told you; we are not hiring at the moment.
Tommy: But I sing and play the guitar.
Receptionist: Well, we're not interested in any singers or guitar players at the moment.
Tommy: But I sing country music.
Receptionist: Well, we're not really interested right now.
Tommy: But it's good music . . .

It was only when she started to talk about phoning the

police that I finally took no for an answer, and even so, I still managed to convince her to take my address and my little record (not that I really thought anyone would ever hear it, let alone start combing the streets of London in search of me).

To say the least, I was feeling a bit low when I walked back out onto Woodward Avenue and got on the streetcar to take me back to the station, but my spirits lifted pretty quickly as we passed a little bar with a sign advertising a singer: "DIRECT FROM NASHVILLE," it said. I was off that car in a flash and into that bar; I mean, the word Nashville was like a beacon to me. I walked up to the bar, asked for a bottle of Schlitz, and put the dollar down; "Yessir," the bartender said, like I was a full-grown man instead of a boy of 14. Well, I suppose I had done a lot of growing up in the past year, but I had no idea that passing for 21 was going to be that easy.

Up on the stage, the performer from Nashville (I can't remember his name) was just finishing a set, so I walked over and started asking him about some songs I knew. "Hey, do you pick guitar?" he asked. I nodded. We introduced ourselves, chatted a bit more, and then he went back to do his second set. But after he'd played the first song, he suddenly set the guitar down.

"Folks," he said, "there's a young man down in the audience who's here all the way from Canada, and he sings and plays guitar. His name's Tommy Hunter, and maybe if you folks all give Tommy a big hand, he'll come on up and do a song for us right now."

So up I went, and he handed me his guitar. I was so happy with the turn of events after that big letdown at WJR that I really gave it everything I had, and after I'd done a couple of songs, the audience was all yelling and applauding.

"Go ahead; finish the set," the guy from Nashville said. So what started out to be just a few songs ended up as the longest performance I'd ever done: a whole hour. I just stood up there, playing all the songs I knew, and just having a fantastic time. After I finished, it seemed like everyone in the place was gathering around me, shaking my hand, wanting to buy me drinks, asking me where I was working and if I had any records out. I just couldn't believe how enthusiastic and friendly they all were, and I felt that the trip had been worthwhile, after all.

Getting back home proved to be quite an adventure, though. I was okay getting the night bus that went through the tunnel to Windsor, Ontario and the conductor on the train, luckily, knew my father and let me sneak onto one of the cars again. But I guess all the excitement of the day finally caught up to me, and I fell so soundly asleep that the next thing I knew, the train was way past London and headed east into Woodstock. By the time I jumped off, raced toward Highway 2, and got a lift in a transport truck heading back into London, the sun was coming up.

My parents had been up all night, of course, worried sick about me. "Where have you been?" Dad shouted as I walked in the door. "What happened to you?" (Those were the *polite* things he said!)

"Well, Dad, I was in Detroit . . ."

"DETROIT?!"

"Yeah, Dad, I was trying to get a job on Casey Clark's Jamboree, and then I saw this guy in a bar from Nashville, Tennessee, Dad, and I got up and played guitar, and geez, they thought I was really good . . ."

The way I saw it, I hadn't really done anything wrong. I didn't mean to worry my folks; I was just out fulfilling my dreams and that was all I was thinking about. My parents naturally saw it a little differently, and to them it was cause for concern. But, you know, although they were quite upset with me, I think that at the same time, they understood that the whole trip really meant something to me and wasn't just a teenage prank. I don't remember my folks ever forbidding me from trying to get jobs as a performer, even after that little episode (although I *was* urged, in the strongest possible terms, to keep them aware of my schedules from then on!).

There were plenty more little excursions like that one as time went on. I'd hitch-hike, try to get on the train, even walk, if there was the slightest chance of a job waiting for me at the other end. Often, it would turn out to be a dead end I was chasing, like the time I hitch-hiked to St. Thomas to try to get a job singing on the station there; CHLO, The Voice of the Golden Acres, it was called. I talked a blue streak trying to convince the program director to give me a chance, but it seemed the golden acres just weren't going to hear my voice, at least for the moment.

Sure, it was tough to have my youthful enthusiasm turned away time after time, but I never really became discouraged by the rejections because I felt sure that eventually, someone would say yes and let me do a radio show.

In the meantime, I kept on with the small variety shows in the London area, and started to branch out a bit into playing with bands. Now, when I say bands, that didn't mean four or five musicians of similar backgrounds who get together and develop a sound over a number of months and years. These were more pickup bands; if I heard a guy playing the guitar or fiddle in a certain way and I thought we could play together, I'd suggest getting together. One of the guys might have a car, and we'd get some posters made up and spend a few hours nailing them on telephone poles; then we'd maybe do a little show on a Saturday night, with the audience mostly composed of friends and relatives.

I was really enthusiastic about the possibilities of the small groups we got going, and I wouldn't think anything of riding the bus or my bike 30 miles out to the farm where one of the guys lived, so we could spend some time practising. I mean, if I thought there was the slightest chance of achieving that country sound I was always aiming for, I'd work for three hours, just on the introduction, to try to achieve it. I'd show the guys anything and everything I knew about harmony or phrasing and go over it with them so we could all get it right; I guess I always figured it was worth the effort.

Trouble was, they usually didn't want to take it that far; I mean, we were only playing at little shows that didn't really pay that much, and while I saw it all as good experience, it didn't quite mean the same thing to them. Most of these guys were in their mid-20s or older, and they often had families, jobs and other responsibilities that I wasn't really considering when I kept trying to push them more.

So these small bands never really seemed to go anywhere; as soon as I thought we were starting to get a good sound, one of them would get a steady job in a factory, or another would get married and give up music. I guess they just didn't figure it was worth the effort when all we were paid was $15; that wasn't going to put supper on the table for their families. Thinking back on it now, I can certainly understand their point of view, but for a kid of 15 with big dreams, it was a bit of a disappointment.

Anyway, I soon learned that the only way to play steadily with a band was to join an established group, maybe one that was playing all summer long at a beach resort and needed a singer or guitar player. There were a few groups like that at places like the Belmont Arena, near London, where we did dance music.

That was a whole new experience for me, learning to play in the very strict, rhythmical dance tempos that would get people up and moving to some of the old-time steps like polkas, minuets, waltzes, fox trots and schottisches. (Does anyone remember dancing to some of those steps?) I soon learned, playing rhythm guitar and singing in a dance band, that I had to be careful to keep the beat nice and solid, otherwise it just wouldn't work for dancing. I mean, it was altogether different from playing and singing by myself, when I could slow down, speed up, and otherwise interpret the song. But playing dances was a discipline that really gave an added dimension to my rhythm that has stayed with me to this day; and from time to time, I enjoy playing for a dance even now because of the fond memories I have of playing with those bands back then.

Not that any of us could afford to get really sloppy and start wandering around the stage talking to each other because we thought the people were too busy dancing to notice us. If it were a three-hour dance, we treated it as a three-hour stage show; we stood there and played and looked at each other like we were having fun, which we were. Otherwise, the audience would have thought we didn't care, and they wouldn't have enjoyed themselves much.

There was only one dance band I worked with in those days that I really didn't like, although they were a sharp group in their own way, well-rehearsed, solid musicians. You'd always know exactly what you were going to get at one of their dances: two fox trots, a ballad, a square dance, three polkas, a schottische, two more polkas, three waltzes and so on, with absolutely no variation. Well, I lasted with them a grand total of two nights; I just couldn't stand the deadly routine, and the way everyone performed, looking as if they just didn't have anything better to do. It was too much of a blow to my natural exuberance.

I was learning all the time from watching the performers I worked with, and I was also learning what not to do. For instance, if the audience shifted uncomfortably when a performer told an off-color joke, I made up my mind never to try that (and I never have).

So when it came to this one unfortunate experience with the dance band in London, the fact that they had the discipline to rehearse a lot certainly caught my attention in a positive way, but I didn't feel I was going to learn much about stage presence from guys who spent most of the show staring down at the floor, looking like they wished they were someplace else.

Lloyd Wright really helped me a lot, by explaining how he did his radio show and also in a much more direct way. You see, one of the people he worked with at CFPL, the women's commentator, named Mary Ashwell, also happened to be actively involved in the London Little Theatre; she was the producer and director of a play they were doing called *Dark of the Moon*. One day, she asked Lloyd if he knew a tall, skinny kid who sang and played guitar; she'd cast all the other roles, but couldn't find the right person to portray that one character.

"I know just the boy for you," Lloyd said. "His name's Tommy Hunter."

Naturally, I just jumped at the chance, especially when I found out that the play was all about the hillbilly folklore of the Carolinas. I figured all the actors would be real country music fans who were as enthusiastic as I was about the music, and I happily made my way over to the theatre to meet them.

I don't think I'd played and sung more than two bars of a song in front of this group when suddenly I heard a muffled titter, then a chuckle, and finally they were all chortling away. They were laughing at me, at my music . . . Well, I just finished, packed away my guitar and walked out, vowing to myself that I'd never return.

The next day, I got a phone call; it was Lloyd. He wanted to talk to me face to face, so we met in a little coffee shop.

"I want you to go back, Tommy," he said, firmly.

"Go back?" I asked, astounded. "Mr. Wright, they *laughed* at me! They think country music is funny. I mean, they're supposed to be doing a hillbilly folklore play and they think the music is funny. Why should I go back; just to let them laugh at me again?"

Lloyd stared thoughtfully into his coffee cup for a second, then met my troubled gaze squarely. "Now, look," he said. "I'll tell you why you should go back. That experience you gain will teach you something, and mark my words, you'll appreciate it further down the line. The makeup, the lighting, the timing, the curtains going up . . . some little part of that is going to rub off on you, and you'll be glad it did. So don't you close your mind to it. Go back and give it a fair shot."

That got to me. I took his advice and returned to the theatre, and you know, the first thing that happened was the director came over, apologized, and explained that most of the cast just didn't know anything about that kind of music. They weren't trying to be rude, she said; it just struck them as funny because they didn't know any better.

From that moment on, the whole mood changed; the rest of the cast even began taking some advice from me, because of my background in the subject. First, I'd rehearse my part, which was very natural to me, since the person I was playing was a singer and guitar player, just like me. So I'd sing my song, "The Ballad of Barbara Allen," which basically tells the

90

story of *Dark of the Moon* at intervals all the way through the play (it's a folk song, but I always managed to give it a country sound), and after that was done, I'd try to help out some of the cast if I could. Mostly, it'd be little things, like showing them how to clap on the right beat while they were doing a gospel song, or how to pronounce certain words.

"And now, folks, it's time for the revival hour," an actor would say. "How's that sound, Tommy?"

"It sounds pretty good," I'd say, "but I think what they'd say is revival *ahr*. Ahr, not hour."

The little theatre system is really a series of competitions, first local, then regional and finally, national. We won our local competition in London, and then the Western Ontario one, and finally beat all the other plays in Ontario; so that meant our play now advanced to the Dominion Drama Festival, competing against all the other provinces in Canada. What's more, that year the festival was being held in Victoria, British Columbia, which would mean my first trip right across the country!

I celebrated my 16th birthday on the train going out west, and what a wonderful birthday it was! By this time, we were all as close as a family, and we had a whole car to ourselves on the trip out. Every night, I'd get the guitar out, and we'd be singing "Don't Let the Stars Get in Your Eyes," "Jambalaya," "Bouquet of Roses" and dozens of other songs. Instead of laughing, or turning up their noses at what they'd once thought country music was, they were now having a great time. We'd all sing in harmony, and Walt Townsend, who played banjo in the show and had always complained that he couldn't play "that music," was now pickin' that banjo like a real country boy.

By the time our last night on the train rolled around, our car was so packed that you couldn't move; people from all over the train, the conductor, and the stewards, all gathered in there to join in the fun. It was great; absolutely terrific.

Unfortunately, our standings in the Dominion Drama Festival were not equally terrific. I think it was basically that the adjudicator who was judging the plays didn't really understand *Dark of the Moon*. He was looking for a Shakespeare tragedy to sink his teeth into, like *Macbeth* or *King Lear*, and our play, with its South Carolina folklore, didn't quite fit the bill. It was one of those plays that was either going to be critically acclaimed or else killed at the start. We got killed.

To be fair, the adjudicator did say some nice things about us individually, so it wasn't that he disliked us all, personally, as performers; he just didn't care for the play.

But there was a man in the audience who, unbeknownst to me, was making some very particular judgements about my performance, and after we finished, he came to the reception to find me. "My name's Norm Pringle, and I'm with CKDA Radio here in Victoria," he said. "I enjoyed the way you did that ballad, and I was just wondering . . . Are you a country singer? I mean, that's a folk song you were singing, but you sound more like a country singer."

"That's right," I said, delighted. "Definitely country."

"Well, fine," he said, smiling. "How'd you like to stop by the station tomorrow morning and do my radio show?"

I guess my jaw dropped about six feet. "Are you kidding?"

"We'd be pleased to have you," he said. "See you about 8."

Needless to say, I hardly slept a wink all night for sheer excitement. I went over every song I knew, trying to imagine which one he'd want me to do. Finally, it was morning.

Well, when I came in with my guitar, it turned out he didn't want me to do just one song; he wanted me to play and sing for a full 30 minutes. I'd never expected that, but before I could say a word, he was already introducing me, and then whispering, "You're on," flipping a key and pointing the microphone in my direction.

I was scared to death, but I sang every song I remembered from the *Country Song Roundup* and tried to talk as best I could, recalling the few words I'd heard the Nashville performers say to the audience between songs. All the while, I kept trying to forget about this very powerful-looking microphone right under my nose, and all the machinery that was carrying my voice out to, I don't know, the *world*, as far

92

as I could tell. When it was over, I was drenched with perspiration, but I felt fantastic. I turned to Norm, and he beamed approvingly. "Real good, Tommy," he said.

I didn't find this out until later, but it turned out that Norm had taped a bunch of those songs I'd done on his show. Months later, he'd put on one of the tapes and tell his listeners: "Well, folks, here's our boy from London, Ontario who visited us a couple of months ago, and we've had a number of requests since then, so we'd like to introduce him to you again." It seems some of the listeners enjoyed my singing, because Norm sent me all these fan letters, and that's how I found out that he'd replayed that show.

It looked like radio was finally giving me a chance.

CHAPTER 4

On the Road

"**H**ow'd you like to come and do my show?"
It was Lloyd Wright on the phone, just a couple of days after I returned from Victoria after doing *Dark of the Moon*. It seemed that our participation in the Dominion Drama Festival had been quite a source of pride for London, even though we didn't win any awards; there were all kinds of articles in the local newspaper and people were talking about the play. That made me an interesting guest for Lloyd, because we'd have something else to talk about in between my playing the guitar and singing.

I was really delighted; after two years of trying just about anything to get on the radio, here I was, getting on a second station in less than two weeks!

It was a real pleasure doing Lloyd's show. I was very comfortable with him, since I already knew quite a bit about his style and format, which suited me just fine. Lloyd had me on the show several times, each time doing just one or two songs, some of them with Lloyd's band, the Radio Rangers. I was very comfortable with their music, after all those community shows we'd done together over the past few years.

Just getting the chance to do radio made me want to work twice as hard, practise even longer every day, and find just as many fairs, dances and variety shows as I could. I felt that getting those few breaks on stations like CKDA and CFPL gave me something more to work towards.

Because of those radio shows, I did get more jobs, but it also played havoc with my obligations to my school work, considering the number of times I returned home at 3 or 4 in the morning after doing those shows.

I guess it had been coming for years. I'd known since I was nine years old what I wanted to do, and I'd been performing since I was 13. I still remember walking a girl home from school one day, just kicking up the autumn leaves as I talked about some of my hopes and plans. Suddenly, I whirled around and blurted out: "I'm going to be a country singer when I grow up. Just you watch me!"

"I believe you will," she said, looking at me as if she were seeing me for the first time. "I really do believe it."

Well, fulfilling the dreams I talked about that fall day was getting in the way of my school work, and, it seemed, the reverse was also true. More and more, I felt that a choice had to be made, and as so often happens when there's a difficult decision to be faced, it was a single event that provided the final push in what I hoped was going to be the right direction.

Grade 10 was the year I had to take physics, whether I liked it or not, and to be perfectly blunt, I was not looking forward to it at all, especially with all the talk going on around school about one particular physics teacher, who had a reputation as an especially tough taskmaster. "If you get him," whispered one of my classmates, just before we were assigned to our various teachers for the semester, "just watch out!"

Naturally, my physics teacher turned out to be none other than this man everybody had been discussing, whom for discretion's sake, we'll just call Mr. Carmichael.

Mr. Carmichael was certainly true to his advance billing; very demanding. But for some reason, maybe because of the challenge he presented, I got it into my head that somehow I would do well in his course. When our big mid-term exam rolled around, I buckled down and threw myself into my studies. I worked so hard that I knew that textbook inside out; all the experiments and formulas flashed before my eyes in my dreams, and if anyone had asked me about a particular theory, I could have cited it word for word, including the page number it appeared on in the book.

95

For the first time in my life, I picked up an exam paper and felt that wonderful sensation of knowing, even before I started to write, that there was not one question on that test that I couldn't answer. I just knew I was going to score top marks, maybe even 100 per cent.

The next morning, Mr. Carmichael handed us back our graded papers. I eagerly reached for mine and then stared, dumbfounded, at the mark: sixty-one. I just gazed and gazed at the big red number, and couldn't believe it. Not after all that work. There had to be a mistake.

"Mr. Carmichael," I said, walking up to him at the end of the class, "are you sure you marked my paper right?"

He looked through my test for a few moments. "Yes," he said. "That's right; sixty-one per cent."

"But Mr. Carmichael, what did I do wrong?" I just couldn't figure it out. "I'm sure I knew the material very well."

"Well, Hunter, you see, the drawings you did to accompany the experiments. They just weren't very good. That's where you lost your marks."

"But didn't I get all the answers right?"

"Well, yes, you did . . ."

I just stared at him for a very long moment. If he'd thought that my drawings were good, I'd probably have scored in the high 90s. Before I could even think about what I was going to say, I shot back: "You know, I thought this was supposed to be a physics course, not an art class," and walked straight out of the classroom.

A short time afterward, just after Christmas, I went into the principal's office to tell him I was quitting. He tried to talk me out of it, of course, but my mind was made up. If I'd worked as hard as I did and could only succeed in barely passing this physics course, I told him, I didn't see much point in continuing. He tried again to change my mind, and we talked a bit more, but I think he finally realized my course was set, because he did wish me good luck and shake my hand.

Looking back on it now, I realize that it wasn't just my experience with Mr. Carmichael that signalled the end of my academic career. My path had been heading in a different direction anyway, and it was just a matter of time before I would have given up school, even without that extra little shove. I guess I just wasn't destined for higher education, even though, years later, I managed to catch up on at least some of what I'd missed through independent reading.

(I tell this story with one *very* strong caution: I would absolutely never counsel a young person to leave school, because I feel an education is essential to anyone starting out in today's world.)

What was my parents' reaction to all this? Well, they'd both told me many times before that if I wanted to be a doctor, or an architect, that they'd help me as much as they could. But that's not to say they were bitterly disappointed in my decision; Mom and Dad saw it coming. They'd been living with the sound of my guitar playing endlessly into the night for nigh on seven years, not to mention the more recent late-night returns from the shows I was playing all over the countryside.

Besides, they could remember all too well from their own teenage years (in fact, they had begun work even younger than I had) how strong the need could be to work full-time, and I think they knew I wasn't quitting school to run away from responsibility, but to accept it in the work I had chosen so many years earlier.

Not too long after my decision to leave school, I saw a notice in the newspaper that the whole cast of Main Street Jamboree was coming to London from Hamilton to do a Saturday night show at the London Arena. I had a little money left over from doing a variety show out in Ilderton, so I decided to go see the show, which I'd heard on the radio so many times. They were good, too. Gordie Tapp was the announcer, and there was Jack Kingston and the Mainstreeters, a very talented banjo player by the name of Maurice Bolyer, and a fine group called the Hillbilly Jewels.

After the show, I stopped in at The Wheel to say hello to the owners, Billy and Frankie Ford. I thought I'd just stay for a quick coffee, but as usual, I ended up borrowing a guitar from one of the regular band members and started to play some of the songs I'd learned recently.

Right in the middle of my spur-of-the-moment show, who should walk in but a group of musicians who'd been on the Main Street Jamboree show over at the arena: the Hillbilly Jewels, they were called. They sat down and listened to me play, and when I'd finished, one of them, Randy Stewart, came over to talk to me, and asked where I'd been playing.

We talked for awhile, and then, completely out of the blue, he slapped the table and said: "Hey, I think you'd be good on the Jamboree. What do you say I write a little note for you to take down to Hamilton?" With that, he ripped a page out of a little notepad he had in his pocket, and scribbled down a little message to Russ Eastcott, the program director, recommending me for the show.

I was delighted by Randy's kind gesture, and didn't lose any time following up on his suggestion. Bright and early Monday morning, I presented myself, guitar in hand, to the receptionist at the offices of CHML in Hamilton, handed her the little piece of paper with Randy's note on it, and asked to see Mr. Eastcott. Then, I sat down to wait . . . and wait . . . and wait. Must have been a good three hours later that Randy happened to walk in and notice me sitting there.

"How's it going?" he asked.

"Fine," I said, "but I hope I'm going to be able to see Mr. Eastcott today; I handed the receptionist your note to give to him."

Randy told me to hang on a second and disappeared around a corner. A few minutes later, he located Mr. Eastcott and I was directed to Studio A.

I never even got through my second song before Mr. Eastcott stopped me. "How would you like to be a guest on our show?"

The following Saturday, I went back to Hamilton and rehearsed for a short while at CHML before driving with Wally Traugott to do a show at the Sanford racetrack near Niagara Falls. It was just starting to rain when we left Hamilton, and by the time we arrived at the track, it was pouring cats and dogs.

98

"Hey, look at that stage!" yelled Wally, pointing. The stage was on a sharp slant, and with all that water pouring down, it looked just like a sloped skating rink. Felt like one, too; at one point, I slid down to the front so fast I almost fell off. I just managed to catch myself at the last second, and by some miracle, didn't miss a single beat of the song I was doing. The audience cheered and broke into loud applause; they thought I'd done it on purpose!

Right after the show, we did a dance, which was broadcast on the radio station as well. By then, I was dead tired, since I'd been up at the crack of dawn to catch a train; still, it was a great relief to be inside that dry, warm high school auditorium, and my spirits picked up as soon as we started playing. The band had a great country sound, and I'll never forget one moment, when Wally hit a particularly good fiddle run and glanced immediately over at me to see if I'd got it. I grinned back delightedly, and answered him with a little guitar run of my own on the next chorus of the song; when I looked over at him, he was beaming twice as happily as before.

The next morning, there was a great big, huge envelope in the mail for me, from the musicians' union headquarters in New Jersey. Oh, that's nice, I thought. There wasn't time to initiate me properly into the union, so this is my letter of brotherly welcome.

But when I opened the envelope, there was no friendly greeting awaiting me; instead, I read with horror a list of some 25 rules and regulations I had apparently broken. The words just swam before my eyes . . . did appear on a radio station without permission for same . . . did without proper authorization unlawfully appear in an unauthorized performance, thereby being in violation of sub-section 2296-C, sub-clause 84-B . . . and so on, page after terrifying page. I was in absolute shock. If this was Wednesday, I figured the firing squad would be waiting for me at dawn Thursday; I'd never work again. In a total panic, I rushed to the phone and made by first-ever long distance phone call (there wasn't another one for a long time!) to the station in Hamilton, hoping they might be able to sort this mess out.

As it turned out, the whole thing was a misunderstanding between CHML and the union, and all of us got that same horrifying letter. CHML told me not to worry, and the whole matter was very quickly rectified.

I never did become a regular on Main Street Jamboree, although I did numerous guest appearances on the show, and really got to enjoy working with so many professional musicians at shows all over Ontario that were going coast-to-coast on the CBC. It was really the whole idea behind the Opry coming to life in rural Ontario instead of rural Tennessee: people out on a Saturday night to relax and enjoy the music they felt comfortable with: fiddle tunes, country ballads, old-time waltzes.

I guess my name must have been circulating quite a bit more after those guest appearances on the Main Street Jamboree, because I was invited to come to St. Thomas to do a spot on CHLO, which was essentially a middle-of-the-road station that devoted a few hours to country music.

It was around the same time that I got a call from a guy in Wingham (not too far from London) who introduced himself as Slim Boucher. He tuned in the Main Street Jamboree whenever he was in the Hamilton area because one of the regular Mainstreeters, Maurice Bolyer, used to play in his band, the Golden Prairie Cowboys. "I've heard you on the radio a couple of times, and you're pretty good," he said. "How about coming up to Wingham?"

I was in Wingham the next afternoon, and I guess the audition must have gone fairly well, because the next thing I knew, Slim and his partner, Lucky Ambeau, had joined me, and we were all singing and playing together. Nobody even mentioned whether or not I'd been hired; Slim just started talking about where we might do our next show.

"Um, Slim," I said.

"Eh?"

"Am I hired? I mean, do I get the job?"

"Hell, yeah!"

There were only three of us, but between us, we had

enough instruments to set up a music store! Slim played bass and banjo, I sang and played guitar, and Lucky, who was one of the most versatile musicians around, played guitar and fiddle, sang, did some comedy, and could even play the bass when Slim was on banjo.

We hardly had a day or two to start getting used to each others' styles of playing before Slim announced that he'd managed to get the Golden Prairie Cowboys an audition in Toronto at a club called the Bermuda Tavern, right downtown on Yonge Street (the club is still there today). We went down there on a Friday, got the job, and started work Monday night. Just like that, almost overnight, we all landed in Toronto, and to be perfctly honest, it was quite a shock to my system. I'd grown up in a relatively small, quiet community, and Toronto seemed crowded and pretty frightening to a 16-year-old who'd never lived away from home.

Mom and Dad were a little worried about me going away, of course, but they respected my need to try my wings away from the nest. In fact, despite my youth, I had been travelling around in search of work as a performer for more than three years, without any serious repercussions. Still, the hug they gave me, and the look in their eyes, let me know beyond any words just how deeply felt was their love and concern.

Our first couple of weeks in Toronto were incredibly hectic, as we raced around practising almost every day. We didn't even have suits that went together, and we couldn't buy new ones until we got paid. But finally, we managed to get matching outfits, rehearse our act, and even find a place to live!

Lucky, his wife Gloria and their children lived with her parents in Toronto, so they were all set. But Slim and I had a heck of a time trying to find a place to stay; rents seemed very high, and so many of the places we could afford were miles away from where we were working downtown. A few of the other musicians told us about an old house on Pape Avenue, in the east end of the city. I can still see the sign over that house:

MRS. POPOVICH'S ROOMING HOUSE.
WEEKLY OR MONTHLY. REASONABLE.

Well, it *was* fairly reasonable, but we had so little money that we could afford to pay for our room only a week at a time; besides, we figured we really didn't know how long we would be in Toronto. The room didn't have much furniture; only our beds, a couple of chairs and an old beat-up sofa. The place was so small that we couldn't have fit much more in there even if we'd been able to buy a few more pieces of furniture.

We shared the kitchen with a young couple who lived at the other end of the house, and we all had to use the same bathroom, too, which required a good deal of careful planning. This couple had a small baby, which of course meant that the bathroom was occupied a *great* deal of the time, throughout the day and well into the night. Coming home after the show was finished was also a tricky business, with a baby in the house. I can't even remember how many times Slim and I would tiptoe up the stairs at 2 a.m., shoes in hand, shushing each other all the way up to our room, only to step on a creaky old floorboard just a step from our door and hear the inevitable wail of protest: "Waaaaaaah!"

I was always terrified of running out of money before we next got paid, so I used to go to a little grocery store at the corner and stock up on a huge jar of peanut butter, strawberry jam and a quart of milk. None of us could have afforded a restaurant even if there'd been one in the neighborhood, and buying some of the essentials for real cooking, like meat and potatoes and vegetables, was less expensive than a restaurant.

At least we didn't go hungry, and even after eating all that peanut butter back in those days, one of my favorite lunches to this day is a peanut butter sandwich!

Playing at the Bermuda Tavern was quite an experience; the audience came to expect a very energetic, peppy kind of show. We did a lot of good western songs, the real hard country material right off the Hit Parade, and some of the classic fiddle tunes.

102

Performing at the Bermuda actually aged me five years overnight; or, more to the point, I aged *myself* five years in a single night. You see, I was a little worried that a liquor inspector would come in one night and check the place out, only to find that one of the performers was a 16-year-old boy.

So my solution was to give myself an older look, and I don't think I'm far wrong in saying that I'm one of the few males in the western world who has ever actually gotten a receding hairline on purpose. In those days, country performers used to wear their hats pushed back, with the front part of their hair combed forward in a wave; what I did was shave the sides in such a way that it looked like I was losing my hair.

After a short stint at the Bermuda, the three of us got a job playing at the Corsair, another Yonge Street club. Nice place, too, except for one minor difficulty; it was a jazz club. Must have been quite a shock for the regular audience to settle down for an evening of Miles Davis and get Bob Nolan and the Sons of the Pioneers instead! To make matters even worse, we were hired December 29 and were expected to provide the entertainment for a New Year's Eve party; I don't think that hard-bitten jazz crowd ever rang in a New Year in quite that style ever before.

Strangely enough, though, we started to change the whole audience around at the Corsair. A lot of very enthusiastic country fans, who'd been going to the Bermuda to hear us, started moving down to our neck of the woods when they found out where we'd gone; and pretty soon, the jazz fans started to drift uptown to clubs that played music just a little closer to their tastes.

It wasn't too long afterward that we found out we'd finally been hired at *the* Toronto club, the Olympia, probably better known as Le Coq d'Or, which years later became the territory of the great rockabilly star Ronnie Hawkins, but at the time was mainly a country and western club. We were all delighted at this turn of events, and Slim decided to go out and hire a few more people, just to round out the band a bit. He hired a girl singer from Hamilton by the name of Billie Cake, and decided to get in touch with his brother, Bernie, an electrician who played great steel guitar on weekends in his home town of Bathurst, New Brunswick. Bernie joined us just prior to our opening at Le Coq d'Or.

Slim, Lucky and I went down to Union Station to meet Bernie's train, and when we got there, we went over to wait by the arrival ramp; the Toronto train station has a gigantic, very impressive-looking main lobby all covered in stone and marble, and we were afraid we'd lose him in the crowd unless we were very close to where all the passengers were coming up from the trains. While we waited, I leaned up against one of the huge pillars at the top of the ramp so that I could rest my legs, and watched all the people going by, trying to figure out which one was Bernie.

Suddenly, there appeared an unbelievable vision coming up the ramp. I couldn't even tell if it was a person at first, because all I could see was a billowing, ankle-length raccoon coat topped by one of those Russian fur hats with the flaps that come down the sides. In one hand was an amplifier that had to weigh a good 300 pounds, in the other was a case containing a three-necked steel guitar, and under each arm was a large suitcase. I mean, the guitar alone was enough seriously to hamper the takeoff of a DC-8 jet!

Suddenly, Slim shouted: "Hey, Bernie!" and started down the ramp.

When we all got back to the rooming house, we were in for another little surprise, because Bernie started peeling off all the layers of clothing, an operation which must have taken a good 20 minutes; first the coat and hat, then an overcoat he had underneath the raccoon job, then a sweater, thermal pants, a flannel shirt . . . and there before us stood a happy little guy who couldn't have weighed more than 90 pounds soaking wet.

Bernie was an extremely nice, kind person whom I liked very much. He had a wonderful way of expressing himself: "Hey, you with the face in front and the hair in back," he'd say to me, and I'd just break up. He was also a talented steel guitarist, and I enjoyed performing with him.

Only one problem he had on stage; well, it wasn't really *his* problem, exactly. Slim had this theory that we needed a lot of show business in our act, a lot of moving around and twirling the bass in the air. Bernie was the guy he was always going after: "Get moving!" he'd shout. But poor Bernie just wanted to sit on a chair and play steel, and besides, he had such skinny little legs that by the end of the night, he'd just be shaking from head to toe from the effort of bending over that steel guitar and rocking back and forth from foot to foot. Finally, after a couple of nights of this, Lucky and I convinced Slim to let Bernie sit down while he played. (Most steel guitarists play sitting down now, so maybe we started something!)

The Golden Prairie Cowboys really made the rounds in Toronto; after Le Coq d'Or, we played the El Mocambo (another club that's since gone the rock 'n' roll route), the Concord and the Famous Door, as well as a short stint at the Jockey Club in Hamilton. Then, Slim got this idea that we should audition for the Arthur Godfrey radio show in New York.

The train ride to New York was great, and I really enjoyed watching the countryside roll by outside the window, but the city was another question. It wasn't just the sheer size, but the endless crowds rushing along the streets; pushing, shoving, and yelling. I was utterly overwhelmed by it; just like Toronto at rush hour, only 10 times more crowded and at least 100 times nosier. The four of us shared a room at the Chesterfield Hotel, right in all that downtown noise and traffic, and we struggled over to our auditions; first at the Village Barn in Greenwich Village (which didn't work out) and then to the CBS Studios, where the Godfrey show was broadcast.

I guess we were pretty nervous, because when we got done, the director who handled the auditions thanked us and spoke those familiar words: "We don't really have a spot for you right now, but why don't you think about trying another time?" (A gentle way of saying we hadn't made it.)

Besides, our particular style created a difficulty of its own as far as radio was concerned. We were basically a show group, and on a radio program, of course, nobody could see our costumes and movements.

So once all the visual aspects were taken away, what remained was the music; and while we were fairly good in terms of a live show, we really hadn't taken enough time to fine-tune our sound to meet the demands of a radio broadcast. We were jumping from one environment to another, and we were jumping too fast. We learned from that experience, and decided to work on perfecting our sound.

Suddenly, Lucky called a halt. "I'm hungry," he announced. "Hey, lookit, there's Jack Dempsey's Restaurant. I've always wanted to see him; maybe he'll be in there."

So in we went, and we did get an autograph from the great heavyweight himself. The restaurant was a little pricey for us, though; the cheapest item on the menu was pie with ice cream, and it was still too expensive for us to get more than two orders for the four of us. Meanwhile, Bernie came back upstairs from the washroom utterly baffled at having to pay an attendant 50 cents for the use of a towel after washing his hands. I mean, you could *buy* a towel back home for less than that! (Clearly, none of us was really cut out to be a big-city sophisticate.)

After we finished our coffee, we headed back outside and onto Broadway; we must have looked like a real bunch of country bumpkins, pointing and gawking up at all the skyscrapers, and staring, open-mouthed, at the passing parade. Suddenly, a scrawny-looking man in a dirty raincoat grabbed my elbow: "Hey, buddy," he muttered, "wanna buy a diamond ring?"

"No." I tried to walk away.

But he was right behind me. "Hey lookit this ring," he persisted. "It's worth $5,000 and I can let you have it for only $500."

"Forget it," I said. "I haven't got that kind of money." Just then, a policeman walked by and I looked right at him, trying to get across to him through my pleading eyes that this guy was bothering me. But I couldn't bring myself to say anything, and the officer just moved along.

"Listen, let's just make it $200 and we'll call it a deal," the guy said, hauling this giant rock out of his pocket. "Look, I'm not kidding you; it's a real diamond," and he ran the stone down a shop window. Sure enough, there was a deep scratch.

"I don't have $200," I said. "I've only got $10, and I've got to get through today and tomorrow on that."

"So we'll make it $5," the guy said, pleadingly. "Look, I ain't got much money . . . you don't realize what you're getting . . . I mean, this really *is* a diamond!"

Finally, just to get rid of the guy, I gave him the $5 and took the ring. The other guys had walked on ahead, but Bernie had lingered behind to wait for me and when I caught up, he asked to see the ring.

"Oh, Tommy," he said, "you better watch out for the police. That ring she's stolen for sure."

With that, the guilt of a stricken conscience took over. A stolen ring . . . All the way back to the hotel, I kept looking behind me, certain that the entire New York police force was out hunting for me; and when we reached the hotel, I had visions of a dozen burly officers bursting in to haul me off to prison.

That night, we were doing a show in New Jersey at a place called the Copa Club, owned by Smokey and Shorty Warren, with whom I'd once performed for a couple of weeks at the Brass Rail in London, Ontario. When we got there, I pulled Shorty into the office and showed him the rock: "Am I going to get in real trouble?" I asked, telling him the whole story.

After he'd finished laughing, Shorty tried to explain the facts of life to me. "Tommy, the whole city of New York is full of these guys," he said. "They've got suitcases full of these things that they run off on an assembly line for 50 cents; they just wait for guys like you to come along and unload them. You haven't got a worry in the world, except that you're out five bucks!"

We did our show, went back to the hotel for some sleep, and then headed back uptown to catch our early evening train.

As the train pulled out, leaving New York City far behind, it was a great relief to hear the familiar sounds of the wheels on the rails instead of all that noise and traffic.

It got me thinking about what we had accomplished in New York, and what lay ahead for us as a group. It got me thinking that a group like ours could begin to create a sound, how we could develop something different from the average, run-of-the-mill Western performer.

What were the elements it took for Hank Williams to express himself musically and lyrically; to paint such a dramatic picture? How did someone like Hank achieve his sound? Was it an accident, or was it something you could learn to do? How did other artists, like Hank Snow and Ernest Tubb, each achieve the sound that was so distinctively his, and no one else's?

The train rolled on, into the night.

After a few weeks back home, we were able to get a guest appearance on the CKNX Travelling Barn Dance Show, which broadcast just what the name suggests: shows and dances in high school auditoriums or little local arenas near Wingham, a beautiful little town in southwestern Ontario. The regulars on CKNX were very popular, as I've already mentioned, and we all loved performing up there. I've got to say that while there were some things I liked about working in Toronto and New York, I felt much more at home, at the time, in those small towns around Wingham, because they have always suited my pace.

Whenever we went to Wingham, the regular Barn Dance fiddler, Al Cherny, was always kind enough to let me stay with him in the rooming house where he lived at the time, and I'll always remember how he and I devised what had to be the world's most economical method of dealing with socks that had been stuck in a pair of cowboy boots all day. *Much* easier than washing them; we just stuck them out the window to air out overnight. Only flaw in our perfect system was that those socks would be frozen stiff as a board by the time we hauled them inside in the morning, and we'd have to thaw them out over the hot-air register.

Al cooperated with me beautifully one time when I decided to liven up an uncomfortable car ride to Toronto from

Wingham one time. We were just heading out to a Sunday night show at a jamboree show in the Crang Plaza auditorium: there was Earl Heywood, a great guy, well known as a Western performer and mainstay of the CKNX Barn Dance, along with Al, Slim, me, and all our instruments and equipment. Lucky was going to meet us in Toronto.

Slim was the only guy with a car, so we made arrangements to meet at his place and proceed from there. We all showed up right on time, dressed in casual clothes; we'd all made a point of packing our outfits because Slim was forever telling us it was much more classy to change in the dressing room rather than show up in what we were going to wear onstage.

But after all that, guess who answered his front door all dressed up in his stage outfit? That's right; Slim. We didn't have time to banter about it right then, so we all piled into the car and headed out. That car was packed to the gills; Earl in the back with all the stuff, then Al and Slim in front, with me in the middle, knees up to my chin. We just seemed to crawl along, and my mind was wandering over a million thoughts . . . Suddenly, I glanced at Slim, all dressed up and humming happily to himself at the wheel.

I just very carefully slid my left knee over to the steering wheel and pressed against it as Slim turned a corner. He started fighting the wheel: "What's wrong with this car?" The instant he turned his head, I pulled my knee back and stared straight ahead like nothing was happening; when he turned back to the wheel, I nudged Al in the ribs and he nodded enthusiastically. Earl perked up right away, too, and leaned forward in the back seat.

Once again, I brought my knee forward the same way. The third time, Slim started to worry. "I think there's something wrong with the car," he muttered.

"I don't know, Slim," said Al, absolutely poker-faced. "Maybe it's the steering or something."

Well, Slim wasn't taking any chances, so he decided to pull over to the side of the road to check things out, and before we could stop him to say that it was all a joke, he was lying flat out under the car, poking around for problems. When he emerged, breathless, his nice suit was completely covered in dust, gravel and oil from under the car. "I think I got it," he said proudly.

None of us had the heart to tell him what he'd *really* got, so after we got back on the road (the wheel was behaving remarkably well by then!), I turned to Slim: "Hell of a job you did there, Slim," I said. "You're as great a mechanic as I've ever seen." Slim beamed happily, and Al did a great job of pretending to be choking on a mouthful of the apple he was eating.

(That's just by way of introduction to Al Cherny; I'll tell you a lot more about him later on.)

Another car trip I remember very well was coming home late from a dance we'd played one night, during the summer. This time, the fiddler was Ward Allen, another regular on the CKNX Barn Dance, and then there was Slim, Lucky and me. We'd all had a couple of drinks after the show, but I think Ward either had more than a couple, or else he just had a very low tolerance for alcohol, because he wasn't exactly steady on his feet.

Once we all piled into the car, he just fell dead asleep and started snoring loudly; but every few minutes, he'd sort of snort, and mumble: "Are we home yet?"

"Soon there Ward, sure," one of us would answer.

This kept up all the way back to Wingham, and by the time we reached town, we'd worked out a bit of a welcome-home plan for Ward. "Let's just test his eyesight a bit," Slim said, stopping the car in front of the town cemetery.

"Are we there yet?" This was Ward again.

"Sure Ward; have a look," I said, pointing across the field. "See? That's your house, right over there."

"Oh yeah, right, I can see it," and Ward stumbled out into the night. (I doubt he slept out there, though, because I talked to him the next morning, and he never mentioned a word about it!)

If it sounds as if all we did was get into hilarious scrapes and practical jokes in those days, that's probably because we were all just struggling to make ends meet and survive in a pretty tough and demanding business; and the hijinks we indulged in were really to help keep our spirits up. I can honestly say, however, that none of us ever got into any serious trouble; it was all good fun, of the kind that makes you look back and chuckle at those great memories.

About the only really serious situation I can recall us encountering was one time when we were all going to Toronto from London. It had nothing to do with me putting my knee against the steering wheel this time; in fact, no one had any idea what was coming, which was what made it all so frightening.

A young lady who sang with us sometimes was driving the car, with me in front and two of the guys from the band in back. I recall that we'd just passed Clappison's Corners, a little town whose name is firmly etched on my memory because of what happened next.

One moment, we were just going down the road; and then, in a flash, the car started spinning out of control and off the highway, rolling down an embankment with dust and gravel flying up in a huge cloud. Suddenly, the driver's door flew open as we skidded sideways, and I saw the girl start to slide down her seat . . . she was going to fall right out of the car!

It all seemed to be happening in slow motion; there was all the time in the world for me to reach out, grab the collar of her fur coat, and haul her back inside the car. But it must have been only a split second, because the instant I got her safely back inside, there was a terrible crash and that awful sound of crashing glass and metal. That open door had just sheared right off as it smashed into a tree on our way down the slope.

"Oh my God," she sobbed, as we came to a thudding halt. "That could have been me!"

We were all pretty badly shaken up, and the car was a complete write-off, but we all walked away from that accident. Any country performer can tell you at least one story like that; or, unfortunately, even worse. Thank God we were among the lucky ones.

It was shortly after that sobering incident that the Golden

Prairie Cowboys started to drift apart. Bernie went back to his electrical business in Bathurst, New Brunswick; Billie returned to Hamilton, and Slim did some work on television in the Maritime provinces and finally settled down in Chatham, Ontario (not too far from London). I'm more than sorry to have to write that we lost Lucky a couple of years ago.

In 1954 I had just turned 17. Work was scarce and I just did the occasional radio program on some of the stations I've mentioned, along with the dances and fairs I'd been doing all along. One afternoon, when I was home practising, a girl I knew, who was dating a friend of mine, dropped over to see me. She'd brought along a girlfriend of hers who worked with her as a Bell Canada operator. "This is Shirley Brush," she said, introducing her friend. "I've been telling her all about how you sing and play the guitar."

The three of us sat in the kitchen and talked, and I found myself asking Shirley all kinds of questions about herself. She turned out to be a year younger than me, and had left school just that year to go out to work, just as I had, at the end of Grade 10. She had three sisters, one older and two younger; her father's name was Ernie Brush, and he worked on the railroad same as my dad, only Mr. Brush was a conductor on the Canadian Pacific Railroad, while my dad worked for the Canadian National. Her mom's name was Clementine (although she'll probably smack my knuckles for giving her full name; Mrs. Brush prefers to be called Thelma!).

I felt extremely comfortable with Shirley; I didn't feel obligated to put on any airs or try to impress her in any way, and there was none of that awkward, nervous feeling I so often got when I was talking to girls. We just seemed to get along as if we'd known each other for years.

After we'd chatted for an hour or so, the other girl suggested that the four of us go to a drive-in movie that evening (her boyfriend had a car). "Love to," Shirley and I answered, almost in the same breath, and we laughed at the coincidence. It was right about then that I noticed how blue her eyes were . . .

Shirley and I saw each other almost every day after that first double date; either we went for supper at my house, or spent the evening over at the Brush home, where I quickly became a familiar sight to Shirley's folks. Matter of fact, I was often at the house so late in the evening (because of my peculiar schedule) that Mr. Brush frequently resorted to rousting me out of there; it even got to the point that he laid down an 11 p.m. curfew for me. Many's the time that Shirley and I would be sitting in the living room just a bit past zero hour, and hear her dad's car pull into the driveway after he'd finished a late shift. Well, if he came in the back, I was out the front door so fast that I even surprised myself with my speed!

Mr. Brush never got *really* angry with me, though; he seemed to understand that Shirley and I meant a lot to each other, and I think he considered me a fairly responsible person. Shirley always used to tell me that with a house full of girls, her dad looked on me a bit as the son he never had. That made me feel great, because I liked and respected him.

One day, after Shirley and I had been going together for a few months, Mr. Brush sat me down in the living room and asked me, quite straightforwardly, what I did for a living.

"Oh," I said. "I sing and play guitar."

Long pause.

"Much of a future in that, son?"

I considered his question for a moment, then answered him just as straightforwardly: "I sure plan on having one."

I could tell by the way he nodded that he believed what I'd said, and his look of approval really clinched what Shirley had been saying about his feelings toward me. That meant a great deal to me.

Besides spending time at each other's homes, Shirley and I really enjoyed going to movies together, or taking long walks, or going down to the beach at Port Stanley on that same little train I'd taken to go to those church picnics as a child. Neither of us had a car, but we both liked walking, and there was always the bus or the train if we had to go any distance.

About the only interest we didn't share was dancing; I had

113

never really learned how to dance and was not especially good at it, while Shirley's dad had taught her all the steps years before. She was forever asking me to take her dancing, and I'd always find some excuse not to go: either I had to practise, or I had a show, or I was too tired. Anything to get out of it.

One day, just after Shirley's sister Marlene started dating a guy named Johnny, Shirley asked me if I'd like to double-date with them one evening.

"Sure," I said. "That sounds like fun."

"Well, we'll pick you up around eight, then," she said. "Johnny has a car."

"Sounds great." I pictured a nice evening at the drive-in.

Well, wouldn't you know it; we all headed out to Springbank Park, where all the big bands played, and absolutely *everybody* was dancing. (It wasn't so bad, really; I only stepped on Shirley's toes six or seven times.)

Everything we did together seemed to be fun, even just talking on the phone. Christmas and our birthdays were very special, and we'd split the day between our two homes, exchanging our gifts and feeling really at ease with each other's families.

Not long before my 18th birthday, I got a call from the manager of the London Arena, who knew me through some of the shows and radio programs I'd been doing around the area. "Hi, Tommy," he said. "Guess who's been looking all over town for you?"

"Who?"

"King Ganam, that's who!" he said, triumphantly. "What do you think about that? Tommy? Hello?"

King Ganam was one of the most popular fiddlers in Canada; he'd been on television, doing a show called Holiday Ranch, and he had his own extremely good band the Sons of the West. What on earth could he want with me?

The manager explained that Ganam had left the TV show and was looking around Toronto for a new band member; someone who sang and played guitar. At most of the places where he'd asked for suggestions, they'd given him my name, remembering me from the Golden Prairie Cowboy days. But it seemed he'd lost the piece of paper with my name on it, and all he remembered was that I was a tall, skinny kid who lived in London. So the next time he was playing the London Arena, he decided to ask about this elusive kid who he wanted to audition for his band.

"I knew right away that he meant you, so I said I'd give you a call," the manager told me. "He'd like you to come down here after the show and do a few songs."

I couldn't believe what a great opportunity that was, and I raced right down there. After the audience started filing out of the arena, I went backstage and asked for Ganam.

"Glad to meet you," he said, shaking hands. "Well, let's see what you can do."

I sang two songs, finishing with a lovely ballad called "The Kentuckian," the theme song from the Western movie by the same name. I guess I must have done fairly well, because when I finished, he nodded and smiled: "That's great."

I looked at him expectantly, waiting for the verdict. "Okay, here's what we'll do; I'll call you tomorrow and let you know," he finally said.

That was Friday night, and by Saturday afternoon I decided to go out to a movie just so I wouldn't have to hang over that phone any more. While I was out, I phoned home to check if he'd called after all.

"Mr. Ganam called, Tommy," Mom said the instant she heard my voice. "He wants you to call him back."

I didn't wait to get home; made the call from the nearest phone booth.

"Tommy, I think you should move to Toronto as soon as possible," he said. "Now, I can't promise anything, but I'll try to steer as much work your way as I can."

Well, it wasn't quite the same as a firm promise, but it sounded like a real chance. That evening, at The Wheel, I told Shirley what had happened and how Ganam had suggested that I move to Toronto.

"What about that disc jockey job you applied for over at CFCO in Chatham?" she asked. (What a memory! I had completely forgotten it in all the excitement of my audition.)

"Oh yeah," I said, feeling a bit confused. "I don't know what to do about that now; maybe I should wait to go to Toronto . . ."

We talked a bit longer, and just as we were getting on our coats to leave, in walked Joey Hollingsworth, who'd worked with me on so many of those variety shows. I hadn't seen him in ages.

"Hi, Joey," I said, introducing him to Shirley, and we all sat down to have another coffee. "So what's been going on with you lately?"

"Tonight was my very last show in London," he announced, dramatically. "I'm moving to Toronto to try and make it."

Suddenly, my head was completely clear. "When are you planning on going, Joey?"

"Monday morning."

That was the day after tomorrow! Well, no time like the present, I told myself. "You suppose I could get a lift with you, Joey?" I asked, to everyone's complete surprise. "I think I'm moving to Toronto."

Shirley and I talked it all over again as we went home; she was a bit upset at first, since we'd been inseparable for the better part of a year, and now we didn't know exactly when we'd be seeing each other again. That bothered me, too, but I felt that I just couldn't pass up this chance; I tried to explain my feelings to her as well as I could.

"I think I understand, Tommy," she said.

"Well, do you think you still want to be my girl, even though we're going to be in different cities? I mean, I want you to; don't you?"

Shirley just smiled and nodded, and gave me a kiss. I felt about 10 feet tall.

Mom and Dad and I had a good talk on Sunday, and I felt so close to both of them when they told me not to worry about a thing, but just to come home if anything at all went wrong. We all knew, without saying a word, that this good-bye was different from the last time I went to Toronto, and it was

116

about that time when Mom beat a hasty retreat out to the kitchen. I was pretty close to tears myself, and Dad's voice sounded a bit hoarse, too.

"Here, Tommy," and he pressed a couple of bills into my hand. "Just to get you started." With that, he joined Mom in the kitchen and I sat there on the couch, watching the snow fall outside the window and thinking about the three of us opening presents on Christmas morning. The tears weren't far behind.

Next morning, Joey and his dad picked me up in Mr. Hollingsworth's Nash, a beautiful old car with a passenger seat that reclined so anyone who had to be on the road a lot could just pull over and get some sleep. As we pulled away from the house, I turned around to wave and wave at my folks standing out on the front steps. Then we turned the corner, and I couldn't see them any more.

CHAPTER 5

Lean Years and Country Hoedown

I had half-decided to find another rooming house, the way I did the last time I was in Toronto, but Joey said he had a better idea.

"I've heard of a great place to stay in Toronto where you could maybe get a room, and it isn't even that expensive," he said, as we made our way into the city. "It's called the West End 'Y'."

The West End YMCA, right in the middle of one of Toronto's oldest neighborhoods, at College and Dovercourt Streets: what a lot of warm, fond memories that old place conjures up, even when I recall some of the difficult times I went through in those days. Even now, I occasionally go for a bit of a walk past that corner, just to remind myself of what it was like. Just being there brings it all back again, although the building doesn't look at all the same; it's been completely renovated and expanded to nearly twice the size it was when I lived there.

Back then, the "Y" was just a simple, solid old brick building, with all the sports facilities downstairs and the rooms on the upper floors, where we all stayed. Joey had a lot of shows booked in the Toronto area (yes, he was still tap dancing), so he had enough money to get a private room.

So I was assigned to a room with a guy by the name of John Pettigrew. It was just a long, narrow little room with a bed and dresser at either end, and not much else besides our clothes and few other possessions, like my guitar and John's books.

John and his friend Leonard Hart, who lived just down the hall from us, quickly became my closest pals at the "Y." Both of them had unusual backgrounds; John was a former Greek Orthodox priest and Leonard was once a physicist, who used to tell us that he helped develop the formula for the atom bomb.

The two of them used to get together sometimes, in the room John and I shared, for endless discussions about science and religion; since their points of view were pretty much at opposite ends of the spectrum on just about every issue, those talks could get rather heated, to say the least. At first, I tried to be the peacemaker and settle things down between them, but after a while, I used to get an almost irresistible urge to encourage them to get into it. "Hey, you guys; you know, I was reading the other day in the newspaper where this scientist says there's no God," I'd say, perfectly straight-faced — and off they'd go, hammer and tongs.

Sooner or later, though, some of the other guys along our hall caught on to my little technique, and when the noise level started to climb, they'd come and pound on our door: "Hey, Hunter, quit provoking those two, eh? I gotta work in the morning and I wouldn't mind getting some sleep in the meantime!" (Or words to that effect, anyway.)

Of course, we all had to work the next morning, so eventually we'd quiet down and go to sleep.

I'm not exactly sure what Leonard and John did for a living after their previous careers ended. Neither of them ever seemed to have much money, so maybe they washed dishes part-time, or else had some sort of sales job, like I did.

I had a job selling paint at the Eaton's department store downtown. I didn't dare look for any work singing and playing guitar until my union membership had been transferred from the London local to Toronto. In the meantime, I had to find some sort of work, because what little money I had was almost entirely gone.

I worked in what they called the tunnel, which ran from the main store to the Eaton's Annex; they had all the different kinds of paint stored there, along with other supplies, like trim and sandpaper. Today, a salesman can make a pretty good living, but then, I was earning about $32 a week, which literally left me with only a dollar or two to live on after I'd paid my rent at the "Y" and the streetcar fare from the west end of Toronto to my job downtown.

Of course, there was a commission paid on top of that salary if you sold a certain quantity of Eaton's house brand paints, called Eatonia and Teco, if I remember correctly. But I didn't quite catch on to that system for the first little while, and I was forever trying to sell the more upscale brands of paint, figuring that was the way to earn points, both with the customers and management.

So although I never gave up practising my guitar, singing and listening to my favorite country stations on John's little radio, a good deal of my life became consumed with the endless search for ways to make ends meet, whether it was figuring out economical ways of getting my clothes cleaned, or just trying to scrape together enough money to have a bowl of soup once in awhile.

The clothing problem was easily solved; I did my own washing and just didn't buy anything new. I had two rather old suits, and to keep them clean I'd take the pants and lay them between the box spring and mattress at night so they'd come out all nice and flat, with the crease in the proper place. Then I'd get the jacket and hang that up in the shower, with the water running real hot so the steam would rise and get the material all nice and pressed. The shirts all had those French cuffs that were really popular in the 1950s; that made things very convenient for my purposes, because when one side of the cuff got dirty, I could just turn it over! So it didn't really matter if I only had two shirts; at least I could keep the cuffs looking all right, and even if my suits were all shiny with age, at least they were clean and well pressed.

Now, as for my shoes, I had two pairs; one black and one brown, both of them far from new, but they were as sturdy as

Sherman tanks and I made sure to keep them in good shape, because I just couldn't have afforded to buy new ones. Besides, if I was lucky, on the way back from steaming my jacket in the shower room at the end of the hall, I might run into someone out there shining their shoes (the smell of polish *really* lingered if you did your shoes inside those small rooms!) and I'd ask, as nonchalantly as possible, if I could borrow a bit of their polish. I'd never press my luck, but if the guy happened to mention that he had brown polish too, I'd just jump at the chance to get both my pairs of shoes nice and shiny.

The food problem wasn't quite so easy, although I did learn some pretty effective methods of extending my rather limited menus. For instance, if I ordered a bowl of soup in the Eaton's employee cafeteria, and the girl behind the counter gave me some crackers to go with it, I'd just wait until her back was turned and then ask the other girl, the one at the cash register, if I could have a second package of crackers. Or I'd keep my eye on the guy sitting next to me, and when he'd finished his meal, I'd ask him in a very casual way if he planned to eat his bread, or the rest of his cake. I'd eat anything that wasn't nailed down!

If I'd had a proper kitchen, I might have been able to scrape together enough money to cook my meals, the way I did sometimes when I was in Toronto with the Golden Prairie Cowboys. But there weren't any fridges and stoves in our rooms at the "Y" (although some of the guys kept little hot plates in their rooms) so I wasn't able to recreate that unique stew I used to make when Lucky Ambeau and I shared a place in Toronto the year before. Unique? Well, just let me give you the recipe.

Stew à la Tommy Hunter
First, you open up the fridge and take out anything and everything you see (except the chocolate milk and strawberry jam), paying particular attention to that package of stewing beef you bought on special the other day. Sure, grab that half a tin of pork and beans; it'll go great, thicken things up a bit,

121

you know. Carrots, potatoes, onions, parsnips . . . any kind of vegetables you see hanging around in there. Salt and pepper; very important. Ketchup, too: absolutely essential for that extra added something.

OK, so now you get your beef, cut it into nice, even cubes, (hey, watch it there; I said *even* cubes, not great big hunks!) and get it smoking real good in the pan, see? If it looks like it's starting to burn, just pour a little water in there; it'll be fine. Now, while the meat's cooking away, you get your onions, whack away at a couple of those, and throw them in the pan.

I guess that pan's getting pretty full by now, so you better dump the whole thing into a big pot and make room for all the other vegetables. Don't forget the parsnips, now. Get it all in the pot, and then throw some more water in there so it won't all stick to the bottom.

Now, you've got your stew simmering away on the stove, but the color probably doesn't look so great, so there's where the ketchup comes in. Just dump it in until the whole thing looks a bit more colorful, and lots of salt and pepper. Don't worry if it's too red from the ketchup; just go on over to the cupboard and grab a bottle of HP Sauce. A few shakes of that should just blend the colors a bit better so it looks more like stew, you know?

After it's been simmering for a while, maybe you can mix up some of that leftover Tea-Bisk you didn't make into pancakes last Sunday, and just stir up a couple of dumplings. Don't worry if they plummet right to the bottom of the pot; that just means they're going to be *real* substantial when the whole thing's ready.

After cooking it for about three hours, try it out; it's not going to kill you and it might even taste pretty good. Best part is, it'll last all week long if you cook it on Sunday, although I wouldn't let it go past Friday, because it might be a little ripe by then.

Bon appétit, as Lucky always used to say before digging in (he'd mutter something else that sounded like some kind of prayer, but I never could make the words out).

Anyway, I could have used some of that stew during those

122

first few months at the "Y." It was getting so I couldn't even afford a bowl of soup any more. One week, what I'd been dreading finally happened; I ran out of money three days before I was supposed to get paid.

The first day without food wasn't so bad; I'd kind of gotten used to going hungry from time to time, and 24 hours was just a slightly longer time, that was all. But by the end of the second day I was feeling kind of light-headed, and on the third day that gnawing sensation in my stomach became a very sharp pain. I felt terrible, but I didn't know what I was going to do; we weren't going to get paid until the end of Friday, which was still a whole other day away. I just couldn't ask anyone for help. Finishing off someone's leftover apple pie in the cafeteria was one thing; borrowing money was quite another.

Well, I decided to go out for a walk just to get my mind off food for a few minutes, and when I returned, I noticed Leonard walking down the hall, away from the room I shared with John. When he saw me, he very casually said, "Hi, Tommy," but I could tell from his tone of voice that he'd been up to something; it was just a bit too casual. Inside the room, John was lying on his bed, apparently very absorbed in the book he was reading. That was a bit unusual, too, because John almost always had something to say when I first came home. A bit perplexed, I walked over to my own bed and sat down. It was then that I noticed, on the top of my dresser, a huge jar of peanut butter, a loaf of bread and a quart of milk.

"What's all this, John?" I asked.

"What's all what?" He barely looked up from his book.

"All this food."

He finally glance over at the dresser and shrugged. "I don't know," he said. "Maybe somebody was trying to save you a trip to the grocery."

Well, I could see that he wasn't going to own up to it, and neither was Leonard, but it was clear to me that the two of them had seen my predicament and decided to help me out. What touched me even more than their kind gesture was their sensitivity in trying to conceal what they'd done so I wouldn't be embarrassed and refuse their help; they knew me well enough to realize that I'd never ask on my own. I'll never forget how wonderful that food tasted to me, and I'll never forget the generosity and understanding of my two friends.

Now, you might be wondering why I didn't just call up my folks in London and ask them for help; after all, they'd both said repeatedly before I left home that I should let them know if there was ever anything I needed. Besides, asking your parents for a hand isn't the same thing as asking strangers, is it? Maybe not; but nevertheless, I just couldn't do it. I felt that if I was going to make it, I'd have to make it completely on my own. It was sort of the same kind of motivation as wanting to do my work with my own two hands. Even if calling on someone who was well-connected might give me the kind of break that would get me there faster and easier, that wasn't the kind of break I ever wanted.

I really hope that Mom and Dad, who always put so much value on making their way in their own lives, can understand that being truly self-sufficient has always been just as important to me as to them.

By the time that bread and peanut butter was gone, I felt determined never again to let myself get to the point of going hungry for days. I'd been having a lot of trouble trying to earn any commission on top of that $32-a-week salary, so now I set out very strongly to find out what the other salesmen were doing that I had somehow missed. I learned, finally, that you got extra money by selling more of the house brand paints, and once I found out that those house brands were just as good quality as some of the more expensive varieties, my natural enthusiasm took over and I started to sell can after can of the stuff. Some of my other old habits started to go, too, like spending 15 minutes looking after one customer while three or four others wandered in, looking for help. If the other salesmen could wait on two or even three customers at the same time, so could I.

As the weeks went by, and I became just a little less preoccupied with where my next meal was coming from, I started getting better acquainted with more of the people who lived at the "Y," many of whom I still remember with great fondness.

There was Murray O'Hara, a really pleasant and good-natured man from the Windsor area who worked for a bank and later became a bank inspector, travelling all over Canada in his work. Murray has since died, but I had the opportunity to meet Mrs. O'Hara and the children not too long ago, so that I could talk with them about some of the fun times Murray and the rest of us shared at the "Y."

There was another guy I liked very much; Stu Henderson, a bright, sharp, well-educated individual who worked as an accountant. Now, Stu worked hard, but he also liked to enjoy himself: he really appreciated good food and fine wine, and he was a sharp dresser.

"Whewwww. . . really doing it, eh, Stu?" we'd all chorus, as he emerged from his room and flicked a tiny trace of lint off the shoulder of his well-cut suit before going out for a night on the town. (I ran into Stu on a plane flight about eight years ago; he looked just as natty as ever!)

Perhaps it seems strange that such people as accountants and bank inspectors would live at the YMCA rather than getting their own apartments, but you know, the "Y" was a terrific place to live. The rooms weren't all that big, but they were clean and comfortable, and there was the added element of having lots of interesting people next door or just down the hall; everybody seemed very friendly and there'd always be somebody to talk to if you felt like company.

There were guys like me, just getting started, as well as some people who'd already made it, such as one distinguished gentleman from England, I can't recall his name, but he was the president of a large tea company who used to stay at the West End "Y" whenever he came to Toronto on business trips. I guess he just found the atmosphere more conducive to getting his work done than going to a fancy hotel, which he certainly could have done if he'd wanted to. Instead, he'd get a phone put in the room, and a desk; everything he needed would be right there. There were all kinds of athletic facilities if he wanted to get some exercise, and even if the rooms didn't have private bathrooms, there was a huge, spanking clean shower room right at the end of the corridor.

There was at least one occasion when I wish I'd been somewhere other than the shower. One day, I was happily scrubbing away, trying very hard not to laugh at the guy in the next stall, who was howling away (I'd never call it singing!) at the top of his lungs, in a very out-of-tune voice that could be heard all too clearly over the running water. Suddenly, in the midst of all that din, I heard the very faint sound of what sounded like a bell ringing.

"Hey, John!" I shouted. "Did you hear that?"

"Hear what?"

I figured I was hearing things, so I kind of shrugged and went back to my shower; when I was just about finished, there it was again. John had (thankfully!) stopped his serenade, and I could hear it clearly now. Definitely a bell.

"John, hey, turn your shower off for a second," I yelled again. "I'm sure I heard something."

We both turned off the water, and, sure enough, there was a loud clanging noise: it was the fire alarm! Without even thinking about clothes, I wrapped my skimpy towel around my waist, dashed to my room, grabbed my guitar, and made a mad lunge for my cowboy boots and hat — the only belongings that really meant something to me.

Taking the stairs three at a time, I came to a skidding halt directly in front of the reception desk, where the clerk was sitting absolutely dumbfounded at the sight of me.

"Where's the fire?" I shouted, one hand clutching my guitar for dear life, the other hand frantically trying to straighten my hat, which was tilting dangerously askew. (By then, I'd completely forgotten what I was wearing; or, rather, what I *wasn't* wearing.) "We gotta get out of here!" I made like I was going to run right out onto College Street.

"Um, just a second, Tommy," the clerk said. "I don't think there's any need for that. It was just a false alarm."

I tried to sneak back upstairs quietly, but all the guys were waiting for me in front of the room, shrieking with laughter.

"Hey, Hunter!" one of them bellowed (I think it was Murray). "Is that a new act you're trying out?"

Well, things eventually quietened down and got back to normal, and I finally got dressed and headed off to Eaton's, thinking to myself along the way that I'd really found out through that little episode just what my real priorities were; and clothing certainly wasn't one of them.

When I got to Eaton's, the supervisor told me they were taking me off sales for awhile and I was going to work in the storeroom. I was a bit disappointed, but I could understand the reasons for the decision; I mean, I was as skinny as a rail, and my suits (such as they were) looked at least three sizes too big for me. Not exactly the ideal image to present to the public.

But to my surprise, they put me back on the sales floor just a couple of days later; it seemed a few of my regular customers had been asking for me. Maybe appearances weren't so important after all!

At about the same time, a message was left for me at the front desk of the "Y," asking me to get in touch with King Ganam; I phoned right away and found out he wanted me to do more shows with him and The Sons of the West. At first, I played only in the shows they did in small towns around southwestern Ontario; Ganam would hire someone else in my place to do the Toronto dates, such as his regular Saturday night dances at Casa Loma, while I waited for my Toronto union membership card to come through.

The shows I was part of were in the same kinds of places I'd gotten used to playing as a kid. (I keep saying it was when I was a kid, but even by the time I joined King Ganam's band, I was still only 18 years old!)

We had a lot of fun playing those small towns, and there were big crowds because of King's popularity on television. One thing I noticed right away was King's very natural approach to his shows. It was great, because he was always so spontaneous; whatever happened on any given night, well, that was the whole show right there.

I really liked the naturalness, but I thought it might

enhance the show even more if there was a little bit of format, like doing an opening routine to warm up the crowd, and then having Ganam come out as the star of the show.

Even after I started playing with the band, I kept my job at Eaton's, because I never knew exactly how much I'd be making on those out-of-town shows in any given week; it could be $60, or even $90, but then again, it might be only $30. You never really knew. So it didn't seem like a great idea to give up a steady income.

Pretty soon, though, my union card came through, saying I could now appear in the Toronto area. As a result, I pretty much was forced to give up my promising career as a paint salesman; there seemed to be a better chance for me if I pursued the profession I was really interested in!

I didn't know exactly how to break the grim news to my supervisor, but as luck would have it, I didn't really have to. The very day I made up my mind I was going to tell him about it, he happened to be in our area making one of his inspections.

"What's this?" he demanded, running a finger over some cans of paint on a shelf in my section. "These are supposed to be kept clean, you know."

"Well, sir, I thought I was a salesman," I retorted. "If I spent all my time cleaning, there wouldn't be much paint sold, would there?"

One thing led to another, words were exchanged, and pretty soon I was turning in my color chart for the last time. I don't even recall whether I quit or he fired me; let's just say that we came to a parting of the ways.

A few weeks later, in early June of 1956, we were on our way back from playing a show when King told me that the CBC was looking for a summer replacement for Holiday Ranch. It was to be a pilot first; and if the pilot was successful, we'd be on for 13 weeks across the entire CBC network.

I can't tell you how excited I was to do that pilot; there was all the thrill of what we were doing, as well as our anticipation: where would we be going beyond that stage? We made the pilot in the studio (it never did go out on the air) and I went home to cross my fingers and wait. Then came the phone call from King Ganam.

"Well, Tommy, run a comb through your hair and polish up your teeth," King said. "You're going on television!"

The CBC decided to call the summer series Country Hoedown, starring King Ganam; and I think they made a great choice in both the name and the concept.

My own television experience had been extremely limited up to this point. I'd done some local television in London; after Lloyd Wright branched out from doing his Radio Rangers show on CFPL, he got his own TV program and invited me on there as a guest a couple of times. I can still remember that very first show; all the lights, the camera wheeling around, and that half-terrifying, half-exhilarating feeling of knowing you're going out live to all those people, only now they're seeing you instead of just hearing you. I wore my favorite (and only) cowboy suit, the one I'd gotten in Nashville years before, and as for makeup, it was mainly Clearasil, since I was at the height of the teenage acne stage at the time.

But when I finally got to singing (it was "Sixteen Tons") I forgot all about the cameras and lights and just felt great. It didn't even bother me afterwards when a friend who'd seen the show told me I had what looked like black patches all over my face; that was the pigmentation left by the Clearasil!

I didn't know at all what to expect when I walked into CBC's Studio Four on Yonge Street for our first rehearsal of Country Hoedown, but it certainly didn't take long to get to know the other cast members, who were all fantastic and helpful people. I don't especially make a habit of speaking for other people, but in the case of the Hoedown cast, I don't think any of them would mind very much if I said we were very much a family, especially in those early years of the program.

Let me introduce you to them, and tell you a bit about their various backgrounds:

Of course, there was King Ganam (his actual first name is Ameen), who played the fiddle and was the star of the show.

He was born in Swift Current, Saskatchewan, graduated from the Royal Conservatory of Music in Toronto, made records, and did radio, before joining the cast of Holiday Ranch and forming his own band, The Sons of the West. King had done radio and performed all over Canada and the United States.

Gordie Tapp was the emcee for Hoedown, and he also brought his very funny and popular Cousin Clem character to life on network television, after many years of fine-tuning the routine on CHML Hamilton.

The featured singers were Tommy Common, who worked in an automobile plant before being discovered on the CBC talent show, Pick the Stars; Lorraine Foreman, who had done tours all over Canada and England before coming to Hoedown; and the Hames Sisters (yes, they really *are* sisters), Marjorie, Norma and Jean, who came from a very musical family. Lorraine's experience was primarily as a pop vocalist; and Tommy concentrated more on the Western styles.

So as you can see, we all brought very varied experiences to Hoedown with us from our individual performing careers, but we did have something in common: none of us, with the exception of King Ganam, had ever worked on regular network television before. I guess that element we all shared at the beginning had a lot to do with the way we all banded together and really pulled for each other; and our enthusiasm and eagerness must have been infectious, because all the cameramen and other crew members very much joined in the feeling of togetherness that made Hoedown so much fun and such an instant success.

That first week, we came in Monday and Wednesday, during the afternoons only, to get ready for our first show, which was scheduled for that Friday night. (As it happened, that turned out to be pretty much our regular schedule; afternoon rehearsals on Monday and Wednesday, and all day, as well as most of the night, on Friday.)

Our set was a very simple, authentic old-fashioned barn, and we had a very straightforward country format. Each of the singers did solos; King played the fiddle and conducted the band, and Gordie did all the introductions, except when it came time for his Cousin Clem routine, in which case one of the singers would introduce him. The show was only a half hour long, so there just wouldn't have been time for much else, except of course the commercials, many of which were done live.

Those Monday and Wednesday rehearsals were just basically for us to get familiar with what we were going to do on the Friday night show, which would be a live broadcast, as so many programs were in the fifties.

Hoedown got its start in the early days of Canadian network television, which resembles the TV of today just about as much as an automobile of the 1950s looks like one of the cars you might see out on the road these days. The very idea of color television was many years away from becoming reality, and everything, including most of the commercials, was done live on the air. Nowadays, no one does their own commercials and almost all programs are taped in advance, although some of them are taped before a live studio audience.

There was also a whole different feeling in the TV industry; it was a heady time for all the networks, and the CBC was right in the middle of this beehive of activity that was sweeping across North America. Toronto was pretty much the hub of activity in Canadian television in the 1950s, and is still today a major world centre for television, New York and Los Angeles being the others.

An immense array of talent in every conceivable field was being let loose on a delighted viewing public. Actors who were to go on to brilliant careers around the world, like Christopher Plummer, Lorne Greene and William Shatner, were making their first television appearances on new shows like Ford Theatre, General Motors Theatre, and Performance. Among the singers just making their start were Paul Anka and Giselle Mackenzie, a classically trained vocalist, and a violinist whose hilarious and entertaining duos with Jack Benny were to become classics of their kind.

Insightful and trend-setting public affairs programs, for which the CBC would become known around the world, in-

131

cluded Tabloid, Almanac, Closeup, Newsmagazine, and Front Page Challenge, which remains one of the most popular series on Canadian television to this day.

Live entertainment shows offered a dizzying choice to viewers, including the Wayne and Shuster Show, the Shirley Harmer Show, Cross-Canada Hit Parade, the Bob Goulet Show, the Jackie Ray Show, the Howdy Doody Show, the Juliette Show, and the Billy O'Connor Show.

So it was into this very vital, lively atmosphere that we got together to do our first broadcast of Country Hoedown, on June 30, 1956.

In all the excitement of doing our very first show, I can't really remember *exactly* what it was like, but I do recall Gordie's terrific ad-libbing, which added to the spontaneity and enjoyment we all felt.

Changing the script turned out to be a pattern of things to come, at least as far as Gordie was concerned. Gordie enjoyed ad-libbing, and I never remember him coming out with a single word that was quite the same as it was on the script. It was always a real guessing game for the rest of us to try to figure out what he might do next; if he was singing a song in the rehearsal, the one thing we could all be sure of was that it would be an entirely new song by the time Friday night rolled around. There was no way he would be able to remember the lyrics that long.

But Gordie always had a way of making up new words, even down to the rhymes, and some of the songs ended up *so* funny that we'd all be shrieking with laughter, even though we knew that the whole thing was going out on the air, live, coast-to-coast! I guess the fact that Gordie was so closely associated with the Cousin Clem character made it seem like it was all being done on purpose, so no one ever discouraged him.

Matter of fact, I remember one time when somebody printed up a bunch of cue cards for Gordie, and the rest of us got together and planned a little joke.

Tommy Common and I did the deed; we set fire to the cue cards, and watched as the flames licked away at all those carefully chosen words. Well, Gordie just stared calmly past the smoldering cue cards and proceeded to ad-lib the entire number, as perfectly as always. I guess that joke was on us!

A great sense of fun always seemed to be part of life on the set of Hoedown. I recall another time that Tommy Common was practising a song called "Gotta Travel On." He was wheeled out on a huge steamer trunk, carrying all his belongings in a suitcase, and then he finished the song.

There was a long pause.

"Hey, where's Gordie?" demanded the floor director. "He's supposed to knock on the inside of the trunk and then come leaping out."

"Heck," said Gordie, who didn't much like being shut up in small places, "I'm not getting in there *now*. Wait till the dress rehearsal; I'll do it then."

So they finished doing the rehearsal, and Tommy shouted: "Hey, Tapp, I hope you'll spend the evening practising how to get in and out of that trunk. Gotta get it right, eh?"

"I'll get it; don't worry," Gordie replied. So off went Common, and Gordie and I just sort of stared at each other for a moment. All of a sudden, this *very* wicked grin started to spread across his face, and he motioned a couple of the other guys over to where we were standing. "Hey guys, here's what I think we should do. . ."

Well, finally Friday came and it was time for the dress rehearsal. Everything went very smoothly; Tommy sang the song just beautifully, and the trunk didn't squeak or creak or anything, just rolled along absolutely great. Finally, Tommy jumped off the trunk, and there was the knock from inside, right on cue. "Is that Gordie Tapp?" Tommy asked, just like it said in the script.

"Yep," came Gordie's voice, clear as day.

Very confidently, Tommy pulled open the trunk . . . and froze in complete shock as a scantily dressed burlesque dancer pounced out onto the stage, to the raucous accompaniment of the band playing the well-known number that usually comes just before the shouts of: "Take it all off!"

Tommy just stood there for another second, then let out a

133

horrified shriek and took off for the backstage area as if he was being chased by a posse. In the wings, he smacked right into Gordie, who was holding his sides with helpless laughter as I tried, without much success, to hold him up.

Well, between loud guffaws, Gordie and I told Tommy what we'd done. Tommy was managed by Ian Reed, who also booked dancers at the Victory Burlesque, so we called him up and asked him if he could find us a dancer who wouldn't mind being part of this little practical joke for 15 minutes or so. Then, we got the band to learn an appropriate melody, and finally, while Tommy was putting his makeup on, we rushed Gordie upstairs to hide and got the dancer into the trunk in his place.

Well, by the time we got done explaining, Tommy was laughing just as hard as the rest of us. "Say, Tommy," Gordie asked, "how come you were so scared when you saw who was inside the trunk?"

"Hell, I thought they were filming some episode of This Is Your Life," he replied, "and I couldn't figure out where she fit in."

Of course, doing Hoedown wasn't just one laugh after another; we all worked very hard to put together a show we hoped the audience would enjoy. It seemed that the combination of good fun and good music that so much characterized Hoedown in those early days was also a hit with the viewers, because the fan mail just came pouring into the studio, at the rate of almost 2,000 letters a week.

At the end of the 13-week summer season, we got the good word: Hoedown's contract was being renewed for its first full season on the CBC network.

A few months into the season, the new producer, Len Casey, came over to tell me that from then on, I'd be singing my weekly solo down in front of the stage along with the other regulars. You see, during the summer, our budget was so tight that I was doing my solos right from the bandstand, going back to playing rhythm guitar after I'd finished singing. When Len came on the scene, he decided it made a lot more sense to have me sing in the same area as the other regulars, so he got another guitar player to replace me on the band-stand, and brought me down front with the others.

That really gave me a boost, and I felt very grateful to Len Casey for seeing some possibilities in a shy, skinny, nervous kid who also happened to have an abiding love for country music.

The change didn't affect my relationship with the other cast members, either; we were all just as close as before. I remember that Marjorie, Norma and Jean all came over to me after my first rehearsal off the bandstand and said some very nice things about the song I'd done; Lorraine added her own words of encouragement, as did Gordie and Tommy; and King Ganam was also very happy for me.

Now, the fact that Tommy Common and I had the same name got an idea going in the audience of trying to choose which one of us they liked better. I was tall, Tommy was shorter; I had a rough, natural sort of voice that fit straight-ahead country, while Tommy's beautifully trained voice really suited dramatic production-type numbers, like "The Streets Of Laredo." It amounted to: "Which of the two Tommys do you prefer?" and I guess the audience figured there had to be some kind of contest going on. Nothing could have been farther from the truth; Tommy and I were good friends, and we saw a lot of each other after rehearsals. Either we'd go and have a quick bite somewhere, or, if there was time, he'd invite me home to have dinner with his wife and family, which I always enjoyed very much. Both of us were also very happy with the kind of material we were doing and we had no desire to compete with each other.

None of us on the cast was ever out to imitate or to outdo anyone else; we were just very young, enthusiastic per-formers who loved working together and wanted to do the best for our audiences.

As for my lifestyle outside the studio; well, we had a year-long contract now, and I was making more money in my new job on the show, but that still didn't mean I was going out on any spending sprees. Just the pattern of what had happened on Hoedown so far gave me a very clear idea of one important aspect of television: Nothing is forever. Sure, the audience liked us during the summer, and that's why we got a full season after that; but there were no guarantees. If the CBC management decided at the end of the year that we weren't working out any more, we could all be out of jobs, just like that. So I felt I had to be as practical as I could about money and try to build things up a bit, so I wouldn't suddenly be up the creek without a paddle if Hoedown ended.

Basically, I didn't change my way of life; after all, a kid of 20 from small-town Ontario isn't exactly clamoring to dine at the most luxurious restaurants and wear $500 suits! I continued to take the streetcar to work (except when Tommy Common happened to be in the area and offered me a lift), and I kept up my little room at the West End "Y," where I remember spending many late nights listening to the radio and writing replies to all my fans.

Every once in awhile, I'd go for an occasional swim in the "Y." Each time I went down to the pool, without fail, I saw an elderly man in there, swimming lap after lap after lap, with incredible energy and determination. He'd be in there when I came in, and he'd still be swimming by the time I was on my way out.

One day, I happened to come down later than usual, and he was just climbing out of the pool, so I went over and introduced myself.

"Glad to know you, Tommy," he said. "My name's Fernleigh Wheatcroft."

We chatted for a few minutes, and it was just as I suspected: Mr. Wheatcroft told me he swam three hours every day.

A few days later, I happened to be listening to the radio; the news was on, and the announcer was giving a live report on a man who was making an attempt to swim across Lake Ontario (this was just after Marilyn Bell's successful crossing of the lake, and a great number of experienced swimmers were trying to get across themselves).

"We've just gotten a bulletin," the announcer said. "Fernleigh Wheatcroft, a 60-year-old swimmer from Toronto, is

136

attempting to swim Lake Ontario and is only seven miles from shore. . . . He could well become the oldest man ever to conquer the lake! No, wait . . . our reporter says now that Mr. Wheatcroft is being pulled into the boat that's been following him throughout his gruelling 29 hours in the water. Apparently, the roughness of the waves was just too much for him. . . . A very brave attempt by Fernleigh Wheatcroft of Toronto, a local aircraft mechanic who's been a marathon swimmer for many years now. . . ."

I sat there absolutely stunned. So *that's* why he'd been doing all those laps! Well, I was sure he wouldn't be home for awhile; they'd probably want to give him some little plaque or something, and they'd certainly want to have a doctor check him out after swimming all that distance.

I decided to go get something to eat; I'd be able to go over to his room and congratulate him a little later on, when he got back to the "Y."

On my way back from the restaurant, I had to stop for a red light while I was crossing the street; as I was standing there waiting, a streetcar came along, and who should come very slowly and painfully down the steps but Mr. Wheatcroft! It couldn't have been more than an hour before that they were all talking about him on the radio, and now here he was, probably just right out of the water and onto the streetcar without so much as a word from anyone. I raced across the street calling his name, and enthusiastically pumped his hand. "Congratulations, Mr. Wheatcroft! I just heard all about you on the radio, and I think what you did was just fantastic; really great!"

Mr. Wheatcroft nodded and smiled his thanks, and as we walked back over to the "Y," he told me what had happened. In the last stretch of that unbelievable swim, he'd gone underwater at one point. "There wasn't anything wrong; I felt fine, and I was just dipping down to get more power into my stroke," he explained. "But the people in the boat thought I was in trouble, what with the waves and all, so they insisted that I come out. I really think I could have made it, but that's the way it goes."

137

"But didn't anyone say anything to you afterwards, or do anything for you?" I asked, incredulous.

"Well, no, you see, I was disqualified because I didn't finish," he said, without any trace of resentment in his voice. "I guess there wasn't very much *to* say, or do."

I felt terrible that no one had at least taken Mr. Wheatcroft to see a doctor, just to make sure he was all right after 29 hours in the water! On top of that, I was kind of worried about him, too; he was walking with difficulty, probably because his muscles were all stiff and sore, and his face was badly sunburned. So I saw him up to his room and then ran across the street to the drugstore to get some sunburn cream and a bottle of Wintergreen lotion, which I'd used myself for aching muscles when I did track and field as a kid at school. At the grocery, I bought a can of beef bouillon that I figured would help him get his strength back.

"Thanks so much, Tommy," he said, after I finished rubbing him down with the lotion and getting him to drink some of the bouillon, which I'd heated up on the little hot plate he had in the room. "I really appreciate it, but you know, you didn't have to go to all that trouble on my account."

"It's my pleasure," I said. "I think what you did was tremendous!"

Imagine Mr. Wheatcroft thinking I was going to any trouble . . . To me, he was a real hero, and I'll always remember him.

CHAPTER 6

When It Rains It Pours

Back on the set of Country Hoedown, everything was perfectly normal, which is to say that everyone was their usual zany selves. There was never a dull moment, whether we were just clowning around on the set, or else laughing our way through those odd accidents of fate that always seem to occur in the wrong place at the wrong time.

Take Gordie's pig, for example. (I wish *somebody* had taken Gordie's pig before it arrived at the studio, but those are the breaks, as we sometimes say in the business. . .)

How did a pig ever get on Hoedown in the first place? Well, Gordie was doing some kind of song about a pig, so he decided it'd be a great idea to bring the genuine article along, just in case any of our viewers didn't already know what one looked like. In those days, Gordie had just moved onto his own farm, and was full of all kinds of interesting and impressive information about agriculture, pigs included. So we were all fascinated to see some real evidence of the knowledge he had been able to accumulate in his newfound career as a farmer.

Anyway, we were convinced that Gordie had this pig very much under control, so when the two of them turned up to do the routine, we weren't a bit worried. But it seemed that the pig didn't quite share our confidence; when it came time for Gordie to emerge as Cousin Clem, the poor critter literally had to be dragged out on stage, squirming and squealing all the way.

Well, Gordie got through the first verse and the chorus, and the band did the turnaround all right (that's when the instruments briefly play the melody of the song before the singer starts another verse). Then, just as the camera turned to get a shot of the pig before Gordie started singing again, nature took its course, and the terrified animal let go with a shot of his own: it was as if someone had fed him about 10 pounds of prunes!

At this point, Gordie desperately started ad-libbing. He had a cane that he used in the routine, so he twirled that thing in the air, up-ended it, took aim, and finally wound up in an absolutely magnificent golf shot. Unfortunately, the handle slipped as he made his swing, and guess what ended up spraying in one enormous wave all over every single member of the band? Well, they were right in the middle of playing the Hoedown theme (we'd sing it at the start of the show and then the band would take over the melody at the end), and let me tell you, we never before said goodbye to the folks in such an unusual manner. The piano player couldn't bring himself to touch the keys that bore the marks of Gordie's tee shot, so he just skipped those notes entirely and played the ones next to them. That was fine for him, but it didn't do much for the song, which ended up sounding like a real dog's breakfast; or should I say a pig's breakfast?

Not all the little incidents on our show were accidents, though. I remember one time, after I'd proudly gotten through a really difficult guitar solo without missing a single note, I was happily basking in the applause and feeling rather pleased with myself. Well, they say pride goes before a fall . . . Out of the corner of one eye, I saw Gordie and Tommy Common approaching me, all smiles but with the glint of mischief in their eyes. Before I could figure out what they had planned, they'd whipped out a couple of pairs of pliers and cut every one of my guitar strings!

140

You'd think all this carrying on might get us into a bit of hot water with the viewers, or with our producers; after all, hi-jinks aren't exactly a conventional part of the production of a television show. But instead, our spirited personalities turned out to be a major part of what made Country Hoedown appealing to audiences, and as we went on through our first couple of seasons, the response from viewers seemed to get stronger. It was the same sort of thing that used to happen with Gordie's hilarious ad-libs of songs when he couldn't remember the words; he had fun making up new lyrics, we got a real kick out of his improvisations, and the audience really enjoyed being part of it all.

Len Casey, who was our producer in those early years of Hoedown, appreciated that our sense of enjoyment contributed to the show's success, and being a talented violinist himself, understood what made a good show. He knew there was nothing more important than a simple format, good songs that the audience would enjoy, and most of all, that feeling of sheer pleasure that the performers shared, with each other and with their viewers.

Although Len's knowledge of country music was limited, he never tried to put a damper on our enthusiasm for it; he trusted our perceptions and never asked us to do anything to our presentation that would make us feel uncomfortable. In fact, Len added to our enjoyment of working on the show (and, I think, the audience's pleasure) by introducing a number of good new features on Hoedown.

One of his very successful innovations was a fiddling contest, with participants from all over Canada, with winners getting the chance to make a solo appearance of their own on the show later on. One of the most talented fiddlers I remember from that contest was a man by the name of Roy Renwick. He did so well that he was invited back on the show for several weeks running. That didn't seem to disrupt Roy's regular job too much, although none of us ever quite knew where he'd be arriving from. Roy was a pilot for Trans-Canada Airlines (better known today as Air Canada), whose greatest love next to flying airplanes happened to be playing the fiddle. One time, after finishing a terrific solo that just knocked everybody out, Roy turned to me and whispered: "Hey, Tommy, maybe I should give up this airplane stuff and get a real job!" and you know, for a while there, we all thought he might just do it.

Of course, the contest also brought its share of very unusual characters; many of the competitors would use just about any gimmick they could think of in order to draw a little extra attention to themselves.

For instance, one guy would stop right in the middle of a fiddle run and suddenly jump straight up in the air. I mean, we'd have to shade our eyes and gaze toward the ceiling; that's how high he went.

Then there was another fellow whom we all called the little whisky-taster because he worked in a distillery somewhere and brought us these little jars that looked like maple syrup containers, only you can bet there wasn't anything inside that ever came from a maple tree! Well, he planned to do a number which some of you may know, a famous fiddle tune called "Hot Canary"; he decided that he was really going to do it up right, so he bought a tiny stuffed canary which he stuck right on the end of his fiddle. It really caught the eye; we were all very impressed.

While he was waiting for his turn to compete, he started getting real nervous, so he grabbed a box of resin and started running it back and forth across the bow, over and over, just for something to keep his mind off his stage fright. Well, he must have gotten enough resin on there to keep the string section of a symphony orchestra going for several weeks, because when he started to play, this huge cloud of resin flew up and totally engulfed him in a thick, white fog.

Nobody could even see his face, let alone the canary he'd stuck on the fiddle to illustrate the tune; and the cameraman had to come over to check if the guy was still there, because all he could see on his monitor was this white cloud. Despite all this, the guy played very well, and he ended up coming back on the show another time (minus the box of resin!).

Another great feature that Len introduced on Hoedown

was a series of ethnic dance segments, with groups represent-
ing the Polish, Russian, German, Ukrainian and many other
ethnic communities from all over the country. One time, Len
thought it would be a nice idea to invite a group of native
Canadian Indians on the show. He asked an excellent group
of traditional dancers to come to the studio on the Wednesday before the show so they could have a chance to rehearse.

Well, I've got to say that I've never seen such an absolutely
perfect rehearsal in my life. Everything went right; the
dancers were just fantastic, and the whole scene was very
dramatic. To begin their performance, six dancers, in very
elaborate and beautiful costumes and headdresses, all sat on
a bench, absolutely still; meanwhile, the leader of the group,
a man who had to be in his 90s, beat out a haunting rhythm
on his drum and chanted at the same time.

The crew decided to keep the camera on the leader while
he was playing and then very slowly track across each of the
dancers' faces. Just as the camera reached the last dancer, all
six of them jumped up and began doing this circle dance
around their leader.

Well, the whole performance was just stupendous, and
when they'd finished, everyone on the set broke into spontaneous applause; we'd never seen anything like it!

Come time for the show on Friday night, they all walked
out silently, and we all waited. The dancers sat down and the
leader began to beat his drum slowly. Then, the chant finally
started: "Heyayaya . . . Heyayaya . . . Heyayaya . . . Hack-
hackhackchokecoughhack . . ." Somehow, he'd gotten a frog
in his throat and started coughing uncontrollably. So he
stopped, cleared his throat *very* loudly, and, as we all watched
in consternation, began again. Same thing happened; he
never got beyond the first few notes of his chant, and this
time, the coughing was so bad that we were afraid he was
going to collapse.

What could we do? I mean, we were live! As you can
imagine, the whole backstage area was complete pandemonium.

Len: What the heck's going on?

Gordie: Sounds like he's got something stuck in his throat.

Me: I hope he's all right.

Len: What are we going to do? . . . wait a second . . . no, if we pull the camera back to the other dancers, that'll spoil the whole effect of them sitting there . . . they'll just be regular dancers . . . hang on a second . . . No, I guess we'll have to pull the camera back . . . (Len said a few other things, but we won't go into any details!)

So the cameramen pulled back, and lo and behold, instead of sitting impassively on their bench, the dancers were all poking each other in the ribs and talking; we could see their headdresses bobbing up and down as they shrugged and gestured toward their leader, clearly asking each other just what we'd been asking: what's going on? Finally, after looking around helplessly for some sign of what they were supposed to do next, they all jumped up and started dancing. Of course, that threw the crew off even more than before, and general chaos descended, as Gordie and I staggered off to the dressing room where we cried with laughter.

At times, it seemed that even if everything on our show went exactly the way we expected, there had to be some sort of humorous twist later. I recall doing a song called "Detroit City" one time on Hoedown; it was a difficult song for me, because of one intricate section in which the key changed down and the singer was supposed to make this transition by tuning the guitar string down in a sort of sliding sound while keeping in the rhythm of the song at the same time. Well, I practised this technique for hours at home, but I still wasn't absolutely sure I'd get it right on the show.

Friday night rolled around, and what do you know? I did the song perfectly, both tuning down and then going back to the original key. I could hardly believe it; the band was impressed, the producer was delighted, the rest of the cast was slapping me on the back, and I was on Cloud Nine.

I was so happy that I decided to phone my parents in London that night to find out if they'd seen the show.

"Yes, I saw it, Tommy," Mom said, sounding a little tense.

"What's wrong, Mom? Didn't you think I was good?"

"Tommy, I think you ought to be ashamed of yourself," she said, "not taking the time to tune your guitar before going on television in front of the whole country!"

Somewhere around the end of my second year on Country Hoedown, I finally decided it was time for me to get an apartment of my own, so I packed up my few belongings and moved to a small one-bedroom apartment just on the outskirts of west-end Toronto. It wasn't that I figured I'd made it so big that I could now afford to live in the lap of luxury (I mean, my place was far from being a penthouse suite!), and I certainly didn't feel I was now above living at the YMCA. In fact, I was very sad as I walked out that door at College and Dovercourt for the last time; I was leaving behind a lot of good friends, and a lot of fond memories of the four years I had spent there. I guess I just felt I wanted a place where I could cook my own meals once in awhile, and where I had a bit more space to roam around.

Now that I was living out in the suburbs, I pretty much had to get a car to get back and forth from the CBC studios, especially since our working hours didn't exactly coincide with the normal 9-to-5 working day.

But my sense of practicality came into play once again; I didn't rush down to the local Cadillac dealer and order the top-of-the-line luxury model. I could certainly afford a car now, but I still felt I had to be careful with my money; even though Hoedown was such a success, none of us could ever really predict what might happen next year, or at some point in the future.

The car I picked out was an Oldsmobile, but instead of going for a straightforward color like cream or blue, my eye was caught by this new shade the salesman showed me. It was called Heather, and it was pretty close to being pink, with a nice pearly finish that made it really stand out; I mean, you could see this car coming 100 miles away. To this day, I still don't know why I chose that colour.

Anyway, less than a week after I got the car, I was in London to visit Shirley and we decided to visit a friend of hers from Bell Telephone. As soon as we pulled up to the house, I could hear dogs yapping, and when we got inside, there were six or seven of the cutest little balls of white fluff you ever saw in your life, all squirming and jumping around like crazy. Shirley's friend and her husband raised poodles, and this was their latest batch of pups. Well, one of them took a real liking to me, and I completely succumbed; had to have this puppy. Even though I knew an apartment probably wasn't the best place for a dog, I figured I could make it nice and comfortable.

I picked up my new puppy early Monday morning and drove straight to rehearsal; there wasn't enough time to go home first, and I thought somebody on the set would probably be able to look after the pup for me. I pulled up in front of the building, climbed out of the car with the puppy carefully tucked under my arm, and closed the door, only to hear behind me the sound of the most uproarious laughter coming from the opposite sidewalk.

"Hey, Hunter," somebody shouted (I think it might have been Gordie). "Whaddya call that dog — Fifi?" and there came another burst of raucous chortling.

I guess it hadn't really occurred to me how I looked, but of course it must have been quite a sight to see a six-foot, four-inch cowboy clambering out of a pink car and clutching a tiny white poodle. Needless to say, that was the first and last time I took my dog to rehearsal.

(As for the car, it didn't fare too well, sad to say. None of the windows or doors ever sealed tightly, so every time I drove down a dusty country road, I'd have to get my suit cleaned. Then, there were the power windows, which came down but never went back up; open-air ventilation, summer and winter. I finally sold it, and the new owner did the most humane thing; he wrapped it around a bridge abutment and put it out of its misery, luckily while escaping any injury to himself.)

After its first few seasons, Country Hoedown became a familiar fixture in Canadian entertainment, both among viewers and in other segments of the television industry. Eventually, members of our cast began to receive invitations to do guest appearances on other shows. One such production that I recall vividly was a spoof on the Broadway musical *The King and I* that was done by the Jackie Rae Show.

The people who produced the Jackie Rae Show decided it would be a great idea to have the spoof focus on King Ganam, so they planned this huge, lavish production with great sets and singing and dancing, all building up to the grand finale, when Ganam would walk out in his cowboy suit, wearing a crown on his head and a long train, while all these attendants came in carrying his fiddle and bow on fancy silk cushions. Well, this all appealed to Ganam very much, and the rest of us thought it was terrific, the idea that King was suddenly going to become the King of Siam.

Aside from walking over to centre stage in a very dignified manner, the only thing Ganam really had to remember was one line. Once they were all gathered together at the end, Jackie Rae would turn to Ganam and say: "Well, King, what do you think of that?"

In response, Ganam was supposed to say: "It's a puzzlement!" which is actually a line from the original musical, and which the writers thought would be a hilarious climax to the production.

Even though that was his only line, Ganam had a lot of trouble remembering it during the rehearsal, and he got so worried that he decided to write the words on the palm of his hand before the live broadcast of the show.

Well, the production went superbly; all the set changes were perfect, the costumes were fantastic, and everything was going along just great. But right in the middle of the broadcast (the spoof lasted 15 minutes, with the King of Siam making his appearance only at the end), Ganam started getting nervous again, so he went into the washroom and washed his hands. When he came out again, it was just about time for him to come onstage.

Very confidently, he set his crown on his head, walked very royally over to the middle of the stage and stood there, beaming, as Jackie Rae asked: "Well, King, what do you make of that?"

147

With all the confidence in the world, he looked down at his palm. There was nothing there. He'd totally forgotten about washing his hands, and, of course, that line had gone right down the drain with the soap and water! Panic-stricken, he started looking around; on his shirt, in his pocket, on the other hand . . . Nothing. Where did it go? Finally, Jackie came to his rescue: "Guess it's a puzzlement, eh, King?" he prompted helpfully.

"Oh, right. It sure is a puzzlement!"

Not too long afterwards, I heard that the Arthur Godfrey Talent Show was holding auditions in Toronto; I figured I had a better chance by now than that time when the Golden Prairie Cowboys tried to get on the show, so I decided to go along and see how it went. Well, I made it through the audition and was all set to fly to New York to do the show, but I had to miss both the dates they arranged for me because I'd already made prior commitments.

I thought that probably put an end to my chances of ever doing the Godfrey show, but just a short time later, Godfrey himself accepted an invitation to open the Lord Simcoe Hotel in Toronto and broadcast his show all week from the Pump Room in the hotel. As it turned out, he used Canadian entertainers for those broadcasts, and I happened to be one of them.

At the end of my number, to my great shock, Godfrey turned to me and asked, right on the air, if I wanted to come to New York for a week and do his show! I accepted very promptly, and about two weeks later, I got a call inviting me to New York for an entire week. The Arthur Godfrey Show was the biggest thing in American radio in its heyday; Godfrey himself was one of the best-known personalities on the continent, and it was a great honor for me to be invited to participate.

Of course, there was one problem to contend with; how was I going to do my Hoedown rehearsals? Well, I got permission to do only the Friday afternoon rehearsal before the live broadcast, which gave me just enough time to work everything in, although it made for a pretty jam-packed schedule: Saturday and Sunday I spent with the musical arranger of the Godfrey show, going over the week's material; from Monday to Friday, I did the show; and on Friday morning, right after Godfrey said goodbye to his listeners, I was out the door of the CBS studio and in a cab to the airport so I could rush back to Toronto in time for the Hoedown rehearsal.

The only thing was, instead of one week, this pace lasted for almost two months (luckily, I had a lot of stamina!).

Godfrey always seemed to enjoy my performances and, I suppose, my enthusiasm and willingness to work hard. Arthur Godfrey was *not* one of those individuals who allows a performer to just slide along on their talent; he insisted that everyone around him had to give 100 per cent.

The way Godfrey saw it, he had the responsibility to make sure that he had interesting people on the air, and that the format of his show was appealing to his audience; so he made it his business to ensure that absolutely everyone on his show, from the producer to the arranger to the writers, were doing their jobs. There was never any question of whose show it was, or what direction it was going; Godfrey was always in charge.

He was great to work for, and I admired him greatly. At the end of my first appearance, I noticed the way he questioned the other guests, and I was so scared of being asked something I couldn't answer that I rushed out to a newsstand and picked up copies of every newspaper I could find, from New York to Los Angeles, Chicago, Denver, and especially the Canadian papers. Then, I spent the rest of the day going through them, so that if he threw a question concerning current events at me the next day, I'd have some knowledge of what he was asking and have something to say. Godfrey always felt a great respect for his audience, and I've got to say that I had a tremendous amount of respect and admiration for his dedication to the high standards he maintained on his show.

Godfrey didn't demand excellence only from others, though; he gave of himself totally. Along with his morning radio program, he had two television shows, one that ran every day from 11 to 11:30 a.m. and a Wednesday night show called Arthur Godfrey and Friends. I worked on all three of these broadcasts with him, and from my experience, it was certainly clear that all the expectations he had of others were no more than what he demanded of himself.

I'll always remember that although he talked very easily and well on the air, he seemed to have very little to say between shows. A few times, I happened to be outside the CBS studios when Godfrey pulled up in his Rolls-Royce (he was always behind the wheel, with the chauffeur in the back seat!). He'd grab his cane and his briefcase and start briskly toward the door. "Good morning, Mr. Godfrey," I'd say, and he'd just nod and continue on his way. Not rude, just thinking about something else, and probably saving all his energy for the show. It seemed that very little else mattered.

So, yes, Godfrey was tough, but he was also extraordinarily motivated, and extremely perceptive. One time, when I was rehearsing for the Wednesday night TV show, I was running into trouble with a song in a medley I was doing with Godfrey, Johnny Nash and Carmel Quinn at the piano. It was a very up-tempo Broadway type of song, and I knew that if I stayed in that studio from now until Doomsday, I wasn't going to get it. I was literally shaking with fear at the idea of what Godfrey must have thought of me, when suddenly he came over and stopped the rehearsal.

"Hold it right there," he said. "Tommy, do you know this song?"

"Not exactly, Mr. Godfrey," I said, quaking in my cowboy boots, "but I'm trying to learn it."

"Learn it?" he said, incredulously. "Why, you're a country singer; I have no idea why anyone would give you a song like this. It's just not your kind of song." With that, he turned to the others. "Why would anyone give this kind of song to a kid who does country and western songs? It just makes him sound awkward."

Quick as a flash, he turned back to me: "What kind of song do you think would fit?"

Well, about 20 different titles flashed through my mind, and I mentioned one. "Perfect," he said. "Let's try it."

Just like that! He perceived instantly that the Broadway show tune was all wrong for me, so he instinctively knew how to find out what was right, instead of trying to force me into a mould that I'd never, ever fit. I mean, just imagine telling an opera singer to warble his way through "Back In the Saddle Again"; that just sounds ridiculous, right? Well, it makes about as much sense to ask a country singer to do a Gilbert and Sullivan aria, or a hit tune from the latest Broadway show.

Godfrey's remarkable perception extended to everything on the show, including the commercials. When he got on the air to talk about Sara Lee coffee cake, you just *knew* that he sat there in the morning and ate it; and if he described the great taste of Lipton's Tea, you could be quite sure that he had a cup of it right next to him. It wasn't that he flogged these products into the ground, either; he had a subtle approach that reflected real knowledge of human psychology.

I'll always remember the approach he used in talking about Chicken Noodle Soup; instead of going on and on about it, he'd say there wasn't much chicken in it, just a lot of noodles, and that would get twice as many people going out and buying package after package just to see for themselves how little chicken was in there. Or else he'd say something like, "Let's see, we're running out of time and I really should have mentioned something about Lipton's Chicken Noodle Soup. Oh well, let's all go out and buy some anyway; we wouldn't want to annoy Mr. Lipton." It worked, too!

About the most harrowing (but at the same time, exciting) experience I ever had on the Godfrey show was one day when I was doing a song called "North Wind" on both the radio and TV programs. We'd finished the radio show, walked downstairs to the TV studio and met the other guests. We were just doing our first commercial when Godfrey leaned over to me and whispered, "How long does your song run, Tommy?"

Luckily, I had that one memorized: "Two minutes and 23 seconds exactly, Mr. Godfrey."

"Hmmmm." He offered no explanation.

Well, a little bit later in the show, I happened to glance at the clock and noticed that we were getting toward the end of the program; there wasn't going to be time for me to do my song. Oh, well . . .

Suddenly, with just over a minute to spare, Godfrey turned to me. "Before we run out of time, why don't you do your song?" *Before* we ran out of time? We *had* run out of time!

I had no other choice; I'd have to wing it somehow. So I started the song, sang a verse and a chorus, then yelled to the band: "Let's try that one more time!" and we did the chorus again. Just as we reached the last note, I glanced up at that clock again. Two seconds to spare!

Without a blink, Godfrey said goodbye to the viewers, right on cue; and I flopped into a chair, completely soaked with perspiration. After a long moment of silence, he turned to me with a big smile on his face. "Thatta boy," he said. "You'll be in this business for awhile."

After my experiences on the Godfrey show, I was invited on a number of radio programs back in Toronto, including a very popular series called The Happy Gang. The program had been on the air for more than 20 years, and the long list of regulars included some of the best-liked performers in the country, including Bert and Joe Niosi, Kathleen Stokes, Bobby Gimby, Eddie Allen, Jimmy Namaro, and Lloyd Edwards. They didn't normally have guests on their show, but for some reason they invited me on their program.

Ken Dalziel, the producer, walked out with me to my car afterwards, and I thanked him for allowing me to appear on the show. "You enjoy radio, don't you?" he asked, smiling at my enthusiasm.

"Oh, it's terrific," I said, telling him all about the Godfrey show and some of the programs I'd done as a kid in London, Hamilton and Wingham. "I've always wanted to have a radio show of my own if I ever got the chance."

"Really?" Ken asked, egging me on. "How do you think

you'd do a show of your own?"

Very innocently, I just told him my idea of a show, which was basically the same concept of the radio programs I'd grown up listening to: there'd be a four or five-piece band, an announcer and myself; we'd sing some songs, talk a bit, and that would be it.

Well, a few months went by, and I'd forgotten all about the conversation with Ken when one day, he called, right out of the blue. "Remember you were saying how much you'd like to do radio?" he asked. "Do you still feel that way?"

"Oh, sure I do; of course," I said, a little confused.

"Well, how would you feel about doing a 30-minute show this summer?"

Totally bewildered by now, I asked him what he was talking about, and he finally filled me in. The network needed a half-hour summer replacement show for the Happy Gang; it would be for only 13 weeks, till the Gang returned in the fall, but it would be broadcast every day, Monday to Friday.

To tell you the truth, the whole idea seemed a bit frightening, especially since it was going to be five days a week; but after talking it over with Ken, I decided to go ahead. It was only going to be for the summer, and since I didn't have any Country Hoedown rehearsals or shows to do until the fall, I'd be able to put all my energy into the radio show.

We sure had a great bunch of people collected to work on the show, and that really made a difference as far as my slightly shaky confidence was concerned. I mean, I was so apprehensive about it (and at the same time, determined to make it work) that I don't even remember feeling excited about the fact that, at the age of 21, I was now going to be on the CBC network in a radio program called The Tommy Hunter Show. All I could think about was trying my best to do a good job, and I was really happy to have people around me like Ken and the wonderful performers who became our regulars.

Our guitar player, Al Harris, who also played steel, was a very good all-around musician who had originally worked on the TV show Holiday Ranch. Then, there was a great singing group called the Rhythm Pals, including Mike Ferby on bass, Marc Wald on accordion, and Jack Jensen on rhythm guitar; the Pals had just arrived in Toronto from Vancouver, where they'd done extensive work on radio and TV.

We started out with Bruce Smith as announcer, an extremely professional yet very warm radio personality, who was also the morning man on the local CBC radio station. Bruce was well-educated and knowledgeable, but with all his knowledge, he never lost the ability to communicate with ordinary people, which is really what an announcer's job is all about. (Later on, when the show was well into the summer, he used to get on his early morning show and work in a little message during the weather, which I always enjoyed: "Now folks, the weatherman tells us the roads are pretty slippery, so just take care, and Tommy, if you're coming back from visiting your folks in London, watch those curves; we'd really like to see you later on your show!")

After a short time, Bruce was joined by Bill Bessey, another very good and experienced radio personality who also happened to know a great deal about country music; he had a show on CBC for years called Ontario Roundup, and I remember hearing it a number of times when I was growing up. How it finally worked was that Bruce did the show Monday, Wednesday and Friday, with Bill taking over Tuesday and Thursday. I learned a great deal from Bruce and Bill, and they both became good friends of mine.

We needed a good way of opening the show, and Ken came up with this great idea: we'd ring a metal triangle, like the kind they used to use on an old-fashioned chuckwagon when it was time to call all the cowhands for dinner.

The only trouble was, we couldn't find one of those triangles, so instead, the guys in the sound effects department came up with a plan: they got a brake drum out of a car, hung it up inside a wooden box, and beat it when it came time to start the show. It worked like a dream!

But I'll tell you, the way I felt after that first broadcast was far from a dream-like state, unless you'd call it a nightmare. Put it this way: I wasn't too sure at that point that there was

154

going to be a second broadcast! There I sat in front of the microphone, shaking from head to toe as one of the crew banged the dinner bell and yelled: "Come and get it!"

"It's the Tommy Hunter Show," Bruce announced for the first time, and we launched into our theme song:

I love those dear hearts and gentle people
Who live in my home town,
Because those dear hearts and gentle people
Will never let you down.

It was lucky that my voice wasn't shaking (that was about the only part of me that didn't shake), and somehow, I got through the half-hour all right. But as for any idea about celebrating after my first show, that was out of the question; I was absolutely drained, and I knew that there was another day right in front of me, and another . . .

Ken, who was the writer as well as the producer, helped me a great deal, especially in my weakest area, which was reading written material. He spent a lot of time going over the script with me after rehearsals in our studio on McGill Street in downtown Toronto, and he was always extremely patient about it.

Ken used to mark every place on the script where I should pause for breath, went through every word with me, and most of all, insisted that I stick to absolutely every letter that I saw on that page. Ken knew that I didn't have the confidence or the ability to ad-lib at that stage of the game (despite having watched Gordie on Hoedown all those times!), so he figured the best thing for me was to learn how to make the prepared material sound as natural as if I was just making it up on the spot. That was very hard for me, and it took a lot of work and practice, but Ken never gave up on me; without ever belittling me in any way, he showed me how to pronounce certain words that I'd been mispronouncing for years without realizing it (like saying "fillum" instead of "film," for example!), taught me how to enunciate properly, and even added some little signs to the script that showed me when I should emphasize a particular word or phrase.

155

Naturally, with all these little pointers to remember, I was fairly nervous even after I'd gotten over the sheer terror of doing that first show. But as long as I stuck to the script the way Ken marked it, I was fine, and to this day, I have always appreciated Ken's help and patience with me. He was really taking a chance on my being able to pick up this very nervewracking on-the-job training; almost putting his own reputation on the line for me, and that has always meant a great deal to me.

There was *one* time, though, that I didn't have any choice but to ad-lib a bit; it actually happened very early in the summer, too. Somehow, we ended up with 20 seconds to spare at the end of the show; I was just getting ready to say goodbye when suddenly I saw the engineer giving me the stretch sign, which meant I had to keep talking.

"Well, that's our show for today . . ." I started, thinking frantically: what do I say next? In a flash, I remembered a scene from the past . . .

It was Sunday in the Christadelphian Church in London, and the speaker was talking about our upcoming Sunday school picnic: "Now, don't forget; the picnic is next Saturday, at the top of the hill at Port Stanley, be the good Lord willing." Sitting next to Mom and Dad, I silently prayed: I sure hope the good Lord's willing, 'cos I really want to go to that picnic . . .

Without hesitating for a second, I continued the sign-off: "We sure hope you've enjoyed our show, and be the good Lord willing, we'll be talking to you tomorrow."

After the show, Ken came over, smiling. "I really liked that phrase, Tommy," he said. "Why don't you try saying it regularly?"

I did incorporate the phrase into the show, but once in awhile, I'd forget to say it, or I'd say goodbye another way; until I saw from the mail that people missed hearing me say it. From then on, I decided I'd always end the show the same way, "be the good Lord willing."

Doing the radio show was also a big challenge to my repertoire of songs; I'd always thought I knew quite a lot of good country songs, but after just a few weeks, it was clear that I was going to run out of material by the end of the summer if I didn't start learning new songs. When you go through 60 songs a month, it doesn't take long!

So I started learning all kinds of new songs from records when I went home at night, and when I went to London on weekends, Shirley would type up all the lyrics for me, at least for a while; there got to be so many of them that I didn't feel it was fair to Shirley to burden her with all this extra work. At that point, I got a secretary, an extremely nice, kind married lady named Wanda March. She was an excellent secretary, and she helped me a great deal by researching various song titles and recordings, then typing them all up for me each week.

With all these demands of doing my first regular radio show, I found that even after the first apprehension began to ease a bit, there really wasn't any time to celebrate being on a network program. When one show was finished, we analyzed it; and then we got ready for the next one, and the one after that. Even the weekends weren't really free time; I'd be reading the script for Monday, trying to learn new songs, and going over them in my mind from Saturday morning till late Sunday night.

It sounds like a real grind, I know; but I was also very enthusiastic about the possibilities, and dedicated enough to see that if I was going to make it on this show, I had to do a lot of work and a lot of preparation to live up to my own expectations and the hopes that people like Ken had for me. Besides, I loved the magic of radio — the way you could create a whole mood just by changing your voice or using all the great sound effects we had at our disposal, like that brake drum we used as a dinner bell; the idea seemed a bit strange, but it really sounded right, and we only really found out how perfect it was one time when we were doing a broadcast from a hospital in Sudbury. We suddenly discovered that we didn't have the contraption with us, and about the only thing we could see that would make a clanging noise was a bedpan; it worked, but somehow it didn't have quite the same ring to it!

All of us felt very comfortable working together on the show that summer, and despite my inexperience and initial nervousness, I guess some of my eager youthfulness must have come across the airwaves along with the more experienced talent of the other regulars, because we got quite a good response from listeners that summer, and we picked up a few new sponsors along the way.

We were all delighted with the support, but it still came as a complete surprise to all us when we found out in the fall that the Happy Gang wasn't coming back and we were being asked to take over their regular time-slot for the next season. We had no idea what was going on behind the scenes as far as the Gang's future went, and I think we were just as shocked as the listeners to hear that the show was being taken off the air after 23 years. I remember talking to my mother about it; she was happy that our show was going to continue, of course, but she was a bit disappointed about the Happy Gang, because she'd been a fan for years.

Looking back on it now, I guess it was probably a part of all the change that radio was going through in those days. Unlike the Gang's heyday, television was now very much a reality, and radio had to keep up with the trends in broadcasting in order to attract more sponsors, who were appearing on various shows much more frequently than in the past. So maybe the various stations and sponsors felt that our show offered a slightly more youthful approach; I don't really know.

Well, if I thought the summer had been busy, that was nothing compared to the hectic schedule I started in the fall, with rehearsals for Country Hoedown as well as the responsibility of a five-day-a-week network radio show. I realized what a great opportunity I'd been given, and I wasn't about to give either show less than a complete effort. I was young, full of energy and enthusiasm, and not at all reluctant to work long hours doing something I enjoyed so much.

At that point, we were into our third season of Country Hoedown, and our enthusiasm for the occasional prank had by no means dimmed with experience!

I don't think any of us will ever forget that one Friday afternoon when we found Ganam asleep in the dressing room he shared with Gordie, Tommy and me. He was all stretched out in this huge makeup chair, which had a headrest and large arms that made it just right for a quick snooze. Well, this little idea started to hatch in our minds; we got some rope and very quietly wound it around him.

As King slept, Gordie turned the clock ahead to 8 p.m. (show time!), and one of the crew members cued the opening musical theme and rigged up a speaker so the voice of Don Sims, the announcer, could be heard clearly in the dressing room.

Then, we turned King's chair toward the window that looked into the rehearsal studio, and made sure he was directly facing the clock.

King finally awoke and blinked uncomprehendingly as he saw the time . . . The music started, and Don announced: "And now, folks, it's time for Country Hoedown! Here he is, the star of our show, King Ganam!"

King lunged forward, only to find himself securely bound to the chair; he struggled wildly, but to no avail: "Get me out of here!" he bellowed.

"Here he is, folks: King Ganam!" Don repeated. "King ?"

The frustrated King struggled even harder than before; finally, we all trooped into the dressing room, hooting with laughter!

We didn't have guests on Hoedown all that often, because with only a half-hour, there wasn't much time for anything except our usual format. But after the first few years, there were a few guest appearances by some of the well-known performers of the day, including Porter Wagoner, Glen Campbell, Johnny Cash and Jim Reeves, who became a good friend of mine after he did Hoedown. (A few years later, when Jim had really made it big, he came to Toronto as a special guest of CHUM Radio, and while he was there, insisted on coming to listen to my radio show; I happened to be doing one of his songs that day, and I suddenly saw him in the audience, grinning like a Cheshire cat!)

Another group we had as guests one time was a trio called Red and Les, composed of Red Shea, his brother, Les Pouliot (Red had changed his surname) and Billy Gibbs. Sometime after their appearance, Les began to get more involved in writing, recording and sound; he learned about orchestration and arrangements, and he did a great deal of research into the history of country music. A few years later, Les returned to Country Hoedown as one of the writers, and I had a gut feeling that our paths would continue to cross in years to come.

There were some other changes in Hoedown during those middle years, and unfortunately, this sometimes meant departures of people we'd grown very fond of: Lorraine Foreman decided to resume her solo career as a vocalist, and Len Casey, whom we'd all very much liked working with, was replaced by a whole series of new producers.

One of the producers who only worked with us once or twice as a replacement also happened to be one of the best: Norman Jewison, a name which many of you may recognize since he's gone to a great success in Hollywood. Norman had a way of getting things done very effectively without making a lot of noise or fuss.

I remember one week, Tommy and I were doing a song called "I Saw Esau Sitting on a See-Saw." Just say the title to yourself a few times, fast, and you'll see how it could be a bit of a problem; well, Tommy and I were having quite a time trying to learn it. We also had to go through the whole routine of sawing a log at the same time as trying to get our tongues around the difficult lyrics. We were just one hour from air time, and the whole thing just wasn't making it. The first run-through was pitiful, and the dress rehearsal was even worse; we just hung our heads and waited for the producer to blow his stack.

But the explosion never came. Norman didn't raise his voice one decibel; to our surprise, he just walked over to us, smiling, and very quietly said: "Sure is starting to get dark out, boys."

Well, he didn't need to say one more word. In that one short sentence, he'd said it all: the rest of the cast and crew

160

had done their jobs and now it was time for us to do ours. Just as simple as that; no pressure, no hollering, just the facts. (Needless to say, Tommy and I stayed on that stage and kept at that song until we finally got it right. As a matter of fact, it was one of the best performances Tommy and I had ever done together.)

Meanwhile, over on McGill Street, our radio show was trying out some new twists, too; but these weren't tongue-twisters, at least not in the usual sense of the word. You see, on a daily radio show, you always have to be thinking of new approaches, or else there's the risk of repeating the same material day after day. One of our ideas was a sort of tribute to various Canadians or their communities: "Now, we'd like to tip our hat . . ." and we'd mention a town that was celebrating its centennial, or a well-known personality who'd just won an award. It was sort of a different way of giving people information, and our listeners seemed to enjoy it as much as we did.

Another idea that proved very successful was our little journeys along the highways and byways of Canadian history; for instance, we'd describe the route between Ottawa and Kingston by talking about how it got its name, who first settled there, how the rivers were navigated and what the battles were. Sort of a history lesson, only instead of rattling off names and dates, we'd relate the events to real landmarks that people would recognize from having travelled those roads themselves.

For even more variety, we'd also focus on special holidays and celebrations, and prepare all our material to fit the occasion. On Memorial Day, there'd be songs about the world wars and Canadians who were involved; then there'd be special shows for Christmas and New Year's, and on St. Patrick's Day, we'd do all the traditional Irish favorites.

Now, all of this was very new for me; suddenly I was confronted with all kinds of names and places I'd never been aware of before, and a whole variety of songs that were completely uncharted territory. I mean, "When Irish Eyes Are Smiling" wasn't exactly at the top of the Country Music Hit

Parade. But we had the kind of show that was expected to acknowledge those occasions, so I learned the songs and material that was appropriate (and ended up enjoying it, too!).

All these new ideas seemed to go over well with our listeners, because the fan mail was growing by leaps and bounds; and I guess some of that response had to do with people coming to associate me with both television and radio. At one point, we were getting 2,000 letters a week; many of these remain treasured memories, but some of them I've kept in my files, like this one:

"I once had a sweetheart who looked like you. Will you please an old lady and send me your picture so I can put it over my bed?" Of course, I promptly signed a photograph and sent it along, with a note of thanks.

Some of the response, though, was not limited to the printed page. Several times, I'd come out of the studio after a Hoedown rehearsal or a radio broadcast and find little messages scrawled in lipstick on the windows of my car: poems, little love notes, even marriage proposals. Now, if you're wondering whether this went to my head, all I can say is that with the amount of ribbing I took from guys like Al Harris and Gordie Tapp, there wasn't much chance of my taking any of it too seriously.

I wouldn't want anyone to get the idea that I considered myself the perfect entertainer at this stage of the game; far from it. I knew I had plenty to learn, especially about doing radio, and when I recall some of the bloopers I pulled, I just shudder. I guess the classic had to be my unique interpretation of "Seventy-Six Trombones," from Meredith Wilson's hit musical, *The Music Man*. Now, that's a great song, but it just wasn't the simple, three-chord style I was used to. There were words and phrases in there that I'd never even heard before! But everyone else was convinced I should do this song, so off I went.

It started out all right, but I could feel as I was singing that I wasn't on solid ground, and somewhere in the middle of the song, I went north and the band went south. I had absolutely no idea where I was or what I was singing, and in this haze that was forming in front of my eyes, I could see Ken come out of his seat in the control room and clap a hand to his forehead in horror. When it was all over, I apologized to Meredith Wilson right on the air for ruining his song that way (after all, he'd been very nice to me when we were on the Godfrey show together, and I figured he more than deserved the apology!).

Another time, when we were doing our show at the Royal Winter Fair, I saw two familiar faces in the crowd; they were both performers I'd worked with during my days with Lloyd Wright and his Radio Rangers. They came over to reminisce about old times, and we had a great chat; as soon as they went back to their seats, I made up my mind to somehow get their names on the air.

Finally, near the middle of the show, I introduced a song called "Old Shep." "But before we get started, I'd like to introduce you to a couple of friends of mine. We all used to work together in my home town of London," and I intro-duced them. The audience applauded warmly, my buddies grinned from ear to ear, and I felt about 10 feet high. I launched into the song with all the enthusiasm in the world and everything was going great until I got to the part where I'm supposed to be aiming a gun at the head of my faithful old dog Shep. Just at that point, I raised my head to glance at my friends very proudly, and when I looked back at the script, dammit, I'd completely lost my place.

I'd gotten the gun aimed at old Shep's faithful head all right, but everybody knows that if you aim, you gotta fire, and if I'd pulled the trigger, that would have meant the end of both the dog and the song. I didn't have much time to think over what to do next, and I really didn't know the song all that well, so I winged it with this classic line: "And I pulled the trigger, but I missed . . ." and, waving my arms toward the orchestra to keep us all in time, I finished singing: ". . . and we'll always be good friends!"

I felt so embarrassed that it took me several minutes to be able to face my two buddies in the audience; they looked just about like I felt. (Strangely enough, we only got one comment, from a woman out in British Columbia who wrote to say how much she'd enjoyed our unusual version of "Old Shep"!)

I've always really enjoyed doing the show in front of an audience, which was lucky, because we were doing more and more of our broadcasts outside the studios. We went to fall fairs, ploughing matches, exhibitions, along with service club functions and other community fund-raisers and all over Ontario. There was something really special about those shows, I guess just knowing that the excitement and energy of the crowd was going out to the listeners at home.

All of us on Country Hoedown were also being invited to perform in shows out of town, and sometimes, keeping a radio and TV schedule straight was a bit of a juggling act. But somehow, I managed to fit all the trips in, although it took a lot of co-ordination at times.

We went *everywhere* on the Hoedown trips; from Newfoundland to British Columbia and everyplace in between, doing service clubs, exhibitions, winter carnivals, trade fairs, rodeos, and all the other terrific local events that are so characteristic of small towns across Canada. (I still take great pleasure in performing at a lot of those functions to this day.)

We were more like a family on the road together than just a bunch of people trying to get from Point A to Point B and back again. After our shows, we'd almost always get together in somebody's motel room and order in a couple of pizzas; then we'd sit around in our pyjamas until all hours, talking about anything and everything under the sun. If there was time, Tommy and Gordie and I might go sightseeing, or Gordie might take me fishing, or maybe the whole bunch of us would just browse along the main street of the town where we were performing.

One time, when we were in Edmonton, Alberta, King Ganam briefly introduced me to a man by the name of Jack Sheckter; I liked him on first meeting, but we didn't have much chance to talk that time. It wasn't too much later that we were back in Edmonton, though, and shortly after I checked into the hotel, the bellman came to the door with an envelope for me. Inside was a set of car keys and a little note:

"Welcome back to Edmonton," it said. "Glad to have you here, and if you have a bit of time, here's my address and phone number. By the way, these keys fit a car that's waiting downstairs for you. I just thought you might like to have it while you're here in town.

Sincerely,

Jack Sheckter."

I went down to the lobby, and there, parked right out front, was a brand-new Lincoln. Well, I headed straight to Jack's house, which wasn't too far away from the hotel, and thanked him profusely for his wonderful gesture. "Listen, that's fine," he said. "It's just a little something I wanted to do."

The whole time I was in Edmonton, Jack took me around to all the places of interest and introduced me to several of his friends, all of whom I found as gracious and hospitable as he was.

Jack and I have been friends ever since, and there's hardly a month goes by when one or the other of us isn't on the phone just to see how things are going with our families. Same goes for many of the other wonderful Edmontonians I've met through Jack, like Don Wheaton, Pat Giannone and Art Ciciarelli, who has a beautiful home near Edson, Alberta, on the McLeod River. Before we move the Hoedown tour out of Edmonton, I'd like to share one little experience of Jack's with you, just to give you an idea of why these particular friends are so special to me.

One of Jack's closest friends is a man named Graham Cocoroch, who owns a little grocery store in Edmonton. One time, when Jack was in there just passing the time of day, a fellow who was more than a little down on his luck came in and asked for Graham. Not wanting his friend bothered by a guy who was obviously just there to ask for money, Jack asked the man to come back another time.

"Just a second, Jack," Graham said, coming out of the back room. "I'd like to talk to him for a second," and he ushered the bedraggled, tattered man toward the door, speaking to him in a low voice and slipping something into his hand as he ushered him gently out the door.

"I saw that," Jack said. "You gave him money. Now, you know he's just going to drink that away, Graham. Why did you give it to him?"

"Yeah, I know that, Jack," Graham said, "but on the other hand, there's just a chance that he might be hungry, too."

Just a chance . . . well, I thought that was a terrific way of looking at it; that statement showed the kind of optimism that allows for hope in even the most hopeless-looking situation. I love to see that kind of spirit in people; and what I most treasure about friends like Jack, Graham and many others is what I've learned from them about principles like kindness and compassion, not just as words, but as ways of living one's life.

Another very memorable individual I met out in Western Canada was George Ross, a cattle rancher who owned something like 285,000 acres out near a small town called Manyberries, Alberta, where he ran about 6,000 head of cattle a year. While the Hoedown cast was doing the Medicine Hat Stampede, George invited Gordie, Tommy and me out to the ranch to have a look around, and we quickly accepted.

I was amazed at George's approach to the cattle breeding business, about which he'd written many articles. We ended up spending the better part of a day out there, looking around and marvelling how all this huge spread was maintained by just George and his six ranch hands, including machines like graders, bulldozers, and George's single-engine airplane.

Toward the end of the afternoon, we went out to the corral and George showed us some wild horses he'd rounded up earlier in the week. Now, these were *wild* horses; never been ridden and never wanted to be ridden.

"Well," said George. "See any in particular that you'd like to ride, Tom?"

"Not today, George."

I spotted this great-looking sorrel-colored horse, with four markings on his feet that looked exactly like white socks. Gordie pointed out one that he liked, too, and before we knew it, George had grabbed a lasso, walked into the corral, picked out the two horses and tied them to a post. "Now, what we'll do is let the foreman ride them for a bit and see how they break, and then we'll ship them down east to you boys. Is that okay?"

"That's great, George," I said, "but what kind of money might we be talking about?"

"Well," said George, leading the way to another part of the ranch, "we'll have to sit down and talk about that at some point." Pretty soon, though, it was time for us to leave, and we still hadn't discussed the price of the horses. But as soon as I brought up the subject, George just said: "Why don't we ship the horses to you and then we can see about it."

Not too long after that, we *did* get the horses; we outfitted them with saddles and bridles, and kept them on Gordie's farm. But, you know, we never did ride them in a parade; until then, we'd been swamped with invitations, but after we got the horses, strangely enough, we were never asked again!

I named my horse Socks (because of the marks on his feet) and I guess he liked me as much as I liked him, because even though he was pretty wild and tried to buck whenever someone else rode him, he was always very gentle with me, right from the first time I rode him around Gordie's corral.

As for the money, I asked George about it again and again; by letter, by phone, and every time I went to Medicine Hat. After literally years of this, George finally allowed as how he'd decided to give us those horses right from Day One. "I just wanted to have a bit of fun with you," he said, chuckling, "that's why I kept it going so long!"

George and I kept in close touch over the years, sending each other cards at Christmas and birthdays, and getting together whenever I went out West. I was extremely sad to hear, a couple of years ago, that George had passed away. I know he is sorely missed by anyone who ever had the pleasure of knowing him, myself included.

You might be wondering why I haven't mentioned the East

Coast yet. I guess we didn't travel there quite as much as out West, but we always enjoyed our trips to places like Halifax, Nova Scotia, Fredericton, New Brunswick, and various towns in Prince Edward Island and Newfoundland. Among the many fine people I got to know down East was Don Messer, the extremely talented and successful old-time Maritime fiddler.

At the time when King Ganam, Gordie and I first went down East, Don had a popular radio show in Prince Edward Island, where he lived at that point; he also had a television show, which was then broadcast only to the eastern provinces, but which would later become a great hit from coast to coast under the name of Don Messer's Jubilee.

One time, when Don happened to be in Toronto doing our radio show, he and I decided to try something just a little bit different in the way of a TV guest appearance. I'd been invited on the Elwood Glover Show, a noontime network program that was broadcast live from the Four Seasons Hotel at noon hour. I was supposed to do two songs, which we'd rehearsed beforehand, and when it came time to do the show, everything started right according to schedule: Elwood introduced me, and I came out and started singing.

Well, all of a sudden, just after I'd done the first verse and chorus, I stopped right in the middle and said: "Let's hang on for just a second," while around me, everyone was going white because they had no idea *what* I had planned. "Now, I've never done anything like this before, Elwood, but there's an individual I know who I feel has great talent, and I feel so strongly about him that I'd like to take time from my performance and introduce him. He's an excellent young fiddler, and if we all give him a big hand, maybe he'll come out and play a tune for us."

I could hear this buzz in the backstage area . . . What's he doing? . . . Doesn't he know we're live? . . . What's going on here? Then, just when I thought they'd go hysterical if another second passed, I motioned to Don, who came out from behind a pillar and walked over, fiddle in hand.

When Elwood and the others saw it was Don Messer, I

thought they were going to collapse. At this point, the Don Messer Jubilee was at the height of its popularity, so of course they were all delighted, but boy, were they surprised! Anyway, Don (who was enjoying the whole escapade immensely) played a terrific upbeat fiddle tune, and then the two of us played our trump card. "Here's a young lady who has a really lovely voice," I said, "and I'm sure if she has a bit of encouragement, she'll come out and sing for us," and out walked Marg Osbourne, Don's star singer!

I've got to say that despite the shock, Elwood handled the unexpected situation extremely professionally, and the audience just loved it; there were calls and letters for weeks afterward. Of course, I don't think Don and Marg would have agreed to it unless they felt comfortable with me, because they were both people who believed in rehearsing their performances thoroughly in advance. I agreed with that approach myself (Ken's lessons in script-reading hadn't fallen on totally deaf ears), but I felt that in this case, a little departure from the routine would be fun, and would only serve to enhance their popularity, which is exactly what happened.

In all this excitement of new shows, trips to New York and tours across Canada, I still tuned in the Grand Ole Opry on a free Saturday night, and my dreams of someday making it to the stage of the Ryman Auditorium were still very much with me.

I'd met Wilma Lee and Stoney Cooper when they were still performing on the WWVA Wheeling Jamboree in Wheeling, West Virginia; and years later, when they'd both become successful members of the Opry, I saw them again one time when we were on tour.

We chatted for a few minutes, and Stoney happened to ask me when I was going to be on the Opry again.

"I've never done the Opry before, Stoney," I said.

"Never done the Opry?" He seemed quite surprised. "Well, let's put an end to that right now. When do you think you'd be available?"

"Tomorrow," I said, quite seriously, and Stoney burst out laughing.

"Well, let's give you a little more time to get ready," he suggested. So we talked awhile longer, and Stoney told me he'd make arrangements for me to be on the Opry.

I still couldn't quite believe it was happening, even when I got a call one night in my hotel room in Red Deer, Alberta, where we were doing a show.

"Hi, this is Louis Buck speaking. Is this Tommy Hunter?"

"Yes, it is." Now, the only Louis Buck I knew was an announcer on the Grand Ole Opry.

Finally, he broke the silence. "I hear you'd like to come and join us on the Opry sometime," he said. "Looking forward to it."

"I'm sure looking forward to it," I said. "You name the date."

Not too long after that conversation, I went to Nashville to do the Opry; Stoney picked me up at the airport, and I appeared on his section of the broadcast.

It's hard to describe how I felt when I stood on that stage for the first time, and looked down at the sign marked: WSM's Grand Ole Opry. It was an awesome feeling; thrilling and at the same time, frightening. There I was, standing on the same spot where some of the greatest country performers of all time had stood; legends, like Hank Williams, Ernest Tubb, Roy Acuff, and so many others that if you wrote their names down, the list would stretch from Toronto to Nashville and back again.

I may have been a 23-year-old performer with his own radio show and a television career, but doing the Opry made a kid's dream come true.

CHAPTER 7

Gaining More Momentum

T hinking back on it now, I'm not quite sure how I managed to squeeze so much activity into just a few years — the early 1960s. Country Hoedown, the Arthur Godfrey Show, our radio show, the Grand Ole Opry, and I haven't even mentioned anything about recordings yet.

About a year before doing the Opry, I made my first record, along with King Ganam, at RCA Victor Studios in Montreal, where we had the good fortune to work with Hugh Joseph, the producer who in earlier years had done some of the most popular Hank Snow and Wilf Carter records. King did a number of fiddle tunes, which were alternated with my two vocal numbers: "I Don't Care If Tomorrow Never Comes" and "Teenage Love Is a Losing Game," for which I co-wrote some of the lyrics and a bit of the melody. I found Hugh Joseph a real pleasure to work with; he's someone who really believed in getting close to his performers, which in my opinion is essential to producing a good recording. (I don't normally like to air my pet peeves, but when I think about Hugh Joseph, it has always bothered me that the Canadian country music associations have never given him the respect and recognition due to one of our recording pioneers.)

After the one recording for RCA, I didn't do any others for awhile, mainly because of my frenetic schedule of radio and

TV work. At one point, I was getting so tired that I finally decided to try something that was a first for me: a vacation! There was a new technique on radio to record shows on tape, and while we still did most of our programs live, there were times when we'd tape a week or so in advance. Well, Bill Bessey and I decided we'd take advantage of this respite so that we could relax for a few days (I couldn't take the full week because I had to be back for Hoedown. Even though we didn't have that much time, we figured there couldn't be anyplace as relaxing as Florida.

Well, the very first day we arrived, there was a phone call for me from Mac Wiseman, at that time the head of the country division of Dot Records, urging me to come to Nashville immediately to sign a record contract and do a recording session at the same time. I mean, he wanted me to get on a plane that same day! Of course, I was flattered by the offer, and I was strongly tempted to agree; but I finally had to say no. Nashville meant too much for me to go there in a state of complete exhaustion and give that recording session anything less than my best.

"I hope you'll keep me in mind later on, Mac," I said, hoping he'd understand that I wasn't trying to be temperamental or anything. "I would like to do a record very much; I just want to make sure that I'd be doing my best."

"Don't worry about it, Tommy," he said. "We'll be in touch."

Not long after Bill and I returned from Florida, I got another call from Mac Wiseman; he was no longer with Dot, and had moved to Capitol Records as a recording artist. He asked me for an audition tape to give to Ken Nelson, the head of Capitol.

I was so delighted by this second opportunity that I made up my mind to do a little more than just send a tape. Instead, I flew down to Nashville, hired a five-piece band and the Anita Kerr Singers, and recorded four songs in Bradley's Barn, using the finished product as my audition tape and paying for the whole thing myself. Now, that would be roughly equivalent to a classical pianist making an audition tape by

172

renting Carnegie Hall and hiring the New York Philharmonic Orchestra! You see, the Anita Kerr Singers are one of the best backup vocal groups in Nashville; they make singing in absolutely perfect four-part harmony sound as easy as saying hello. As for Bradley's Barn, well, it's a legend in country music history — Nashville's first commercial recording studio, which Owen Bradley and his brother Harold built out of an old wartime Quonset hut.

By the time I got to Nashville, in the early 1960s, the whole recording and publishing side of country music had already started to expand, with block after block of booking agencies, publishing houses and recording studios: Decca, Capitol, RCA Victor, Columbia, Southern Publishing, Acuff-Rose Publications, all of them lining 16th Avenue and the surrounding streets.

Pop artists like Tony Bennett, Eddie Fisher and even Jerry Vail (he had a big hit with an old Eddy Arnold song) were enjoying tremendous success with country songs, and there was a lot more interest on the part of pop musicians actually to go and experience country music at its source. The pop Hit Parade and the country Hit Parade were miles apart at the time; "Tennessee Waltz," composed by Redd Stewart and Pee Wee King, hadn't been a pop hit until the version by Patti Page.

So the pop industry started looking, and they liked what they saw. Pretty soon, Perry Como went to Nashville and recorded some songs; his albums turned out to be a winning combination of a relaxed country rhythm and the smooth, lilting sound that Como made famous. After that, just about everybody in the pop music field (even Vera Lynn!) began to realize that the country musicians had great ears and were absolutely flawless in the studio; so they all started going to Nashville to record. The experience gave them a whole new sound.

Accustomed as many pop artists were to studios in New York and Los Angeles, where all their songs were fully orchestrated and arranged before they ever came in for a session, it must have been an amazing change for them to walk into Bradley's Barn and find the musicians and singers all creating the sound right there in front of them, totally suited to their particular style. Never a sheet of music to be seen; those studio musicians could launch into the complete harmony and instrumentation from the first time they heard the song. The recording artist would open his mouth to sing, and everything would be there behind him, almost as if a ventriloquist was making it all happen!

Many of these studio musicians, such as the Anita Kerr Singers, the Jordanaires, Grady Martin, Floyd Cramer, Buddy Harmon and many others, became musical legends in their own right; yet these were the same very talented artists that performers such as myself were fortunate enough to work with, even on our first recording sessions.

The recording studio itself was a fantastic experience for me; just knowing how many of my favorite artists (Red Foley and Ernest Tubb, for example) had recorded right there in Bradley's Barn was enough to make me feel the magic that still lingered in the air after all the legendary performances that had been put on record in that rickety old building. I must not have been alone in that feeling, because I don't think anyone had ever even *cleaned* Bradley's Barn, let alone renovate it in any way. There was dust all over the place, and cobwebs hanging from the walls, and a big crack in the door, through which I could see all the traffic going by while I was recording. They really were afraid that if they moved anything, or repaired or repainted the place, maybe some of that sound would be lost; so they kept it just as it was, which was just fine with me!

The way it works in a recording session is that you have three hours or four songs, whichever comes first. Otherwise, you have to come back for another session. Well, I had only the one session (I couldn't have afforded more!), so I *had* to get my four songs done in that time.

With the help of the great musicians and a producer like Ken Nelson, we managed to get those songs done (two of them, by the way, were written by Les Pouliot, one of the writers on Country Hoedown). Sometime during the evening,

174

one of the singers, or maybe it was the bass player, mentioned to Ken that I'd paid for this session out of my own pocket, and he came over to talk to me.

"You're really taking all this seriously, aren't you?" he asked me.

"Well, yes, I mean, these are the best musicians in the business," I said.

"No, that's not what I meant," he said. "I was talking about this audition tape you're doing. You spent your own money to do this session in the first place."

For a moment, I thought I'd done something wrong; and Ken must have interpreted the look on my face, because he jumped right back in: "That took a lot of initiative on your part," he said. "I don't know many people who'd go to those lengths for an audition tape, and I don't just mean spending the money. Don't think it's going unnoticed, either."

I was a bit embarrassed by the praise, but it also made me feel great, because my whole intent was to do the best possible job I could; and I figured I couldn't do better than working with these particular people in Bradley's Barn.

About two weeks after I got home, a representative from Capitol Records in Los Angeles called and told me they were mailing me a contract!

So back I went to Nashville to do a proper record (they paid for the sessions this time!). We'd already picked out two songs for me to do; one was a kind of bluegrass song called "Poor Little Bullfrog," by Jimmy Martin, and the other was "Penny Wishes," written by the winner of a Capitol songwriting contest in which the winning song is then recorded by one of the Capitol artists.

I had to pick out two or three other songs myself, and the Capitol people had set up a record player, tape recorder, and great, hugh stacks of material right in my hotel room. One afternoon, while we were going through the piles of records and tapes, Ken mentioned that he was going over to Harlan Howard's home that night for dinner. "You're invited too, Tommy," he said.

I couldn't imagine why Harlan Howard, probably the hot-

175

test songwriter in Nashville at the time, would be interested in a young kid from Canada, but I was delighted to go along. Sometime after dinner, Harlan took us down to his rec room, where he had his office set up, and we got to talking. It turned out he'd been to Canada a number of times and had enjoyed watching me on Country Hoedown. "By the way, Tommy," he asked. "Did Ken give you a song I've just written?"

"No, he didn't."

"Well, did he show it to you, or mention it at all?"

"No." (By this time, I was utterly confused.)

"Oh, I know what happened," and Harlan called to Ken, who was over at the other end of the room. "Hey, Ken; too bad we didn't come to terms, because that would've been a hell of a song for Tommy."

(What had happened was that Capitol's publishing company had demanded 50 per cent of the rights on the new song, and Harlan, who owned his own publishing company, refused to agree to those terms.)

Harlan turned back to me. "Well, let me sing you the song, anyway. When I heard you were coming to Nashville, I wrote it especially for you." The song, which began: "Marianne regrets she's unable to see you again," turned out to be a monster hit; for Burl Ives!

I ended up doing just the two records for Capitol, "Penny Wishes" and "Poor Little Bullfrog." It was shortly afterward that Stoney arranged for me to perform on the Grand Ole Opry. At the same time, he got me an audition with Columbia Records, I did the Opry on the Saturday night, and on Monday morning I got a contract with Columbia, which had just taken over the premises of Bradley's Barn. So I was back in the same familiar studio, only under a different label now.

My producer at Columbia was a fellow by the name of Frank Jones, who was originally from Canada; I got to know him and his wife, Gwen, quite well, and we're still friends to this day. Now, Frank was determined to get me a hit record as much as I wanted to make one, and we built up a very constructive direction; but while I was very happy with the work we were doing, that big hit didn't seem to be coming our way, not in the first little while, anyway.

I *was* still concentrating most of my efforts on my work back in Toronto, which was getting more and more demanding by the day; and while I went to Nashville once in awhile for recording sessions, my first priority had to be Country Hoedown and the radio show.

Country Hoedown was going through a lot more changes by this time, and probably the most dramatic event that happened was King Ganam's decision to leave the show. None of us was too clear exactly what the reasons were, but apparently King was not happy with his billing on the show; and although the top CBC network executives sat down with him and tried to work out the dispute, they didn't manage to come to an understanding, and King decided he had to leave.

Because I had an agreement with Ganam to do a lot of his shows with him, I ended up having to miss about a week of Hoedown while the various contractual papers were all sorted out, but in the end, I returned to Country Hoedown and Ganam departed.

(Years later, Ganam and I worked together again under extremely pleasant circumstances which I'll describe later, and I'm happy to say that, for us, at least, there's a lot of truth in that old saying about time being the best healer of whatever disagreements there may once have been between us.)

After Ganam's departure, the show was altered even more, with the addition of a much slicker, modern-looking set and more of a variety show approach, with staging by Bob Van Norman, an extremely nice person and capable professional.

One time, Bob decided to do this big production number to go with a song we were all working on. Now, this was fine for Tommy Common and the Hames Sisters, who all moved very well and had no trouble with the steps Bob arranged. Unfortunately, when it came to Gordie Tapp and me, well, if Gordie had two left feet, I had the two right ones. Getting us to dance was like trying to move two mountains.

On top of that, we were all having trouble learning the

song, which had just been recorded by Stuart Hamblen and was taken from an old Robert Service poem. About the only part we could remember was the first line, which went:

Mush, mush, mush on you malemute, half dog, half wolf, loping through the night . . .

After that, it was just a blank. We pleaded for cue cards, which we finally got, and that helped the singing immensely. But the whole production was still a disaster unless Gordie and I stood in one spot and sang. Finally, Bob coaxed us to march along while we did the song, so off we went, in single file across the studio, looking in the general direction of the camera while the boom operator just went crazy trying to pick up all our voices at once. We were marching at *least* 20 feet apart!

After a few minutes of this, the producer, Dave Thomas, wandered over to see what was going on, and after a short discussion with the audio operators, they decided to try pre-recording the song, a technique that had just been introduced on television. "See, we'll get it all on tape beforehand," said Orm Collier, one of the audio operators, "and then when you're out there doing the show, you just move your lips up and down to the sound."

"Wow," I said. "It sounds great!"

So we recorded "Mush On, You Malemute," with every mush in its proper place, and all the music absolutely perfect.

The dress rehearsal went like a dream, with us marching along and moving our lips to the sounds of the song blaring out of the two big speakers that had been set up behind us.

After that, we started the live show with complete confidence. Just before the first commercial break, Orm Collier suddenly discovered that he'd forgotten to rewind the tape to where our prerecorded song was located. Now, the audio guys on Hoedown used great big Ampex tape machines that held 12 or 14-inch reels. At the end of one of these large reels was a tiny, three-inch reel containing the entire performance of "Mush On, You Malemute"; and that's what Orm was trying to get the machine rewound back to. So he punched the rewind switch, and the tape got going so fast that the little reel just flew right off the machine in a great snarl of tangled tape, hitting the walls and bouncing all over the audio room.

Dave was right outside the room, and when he saw what had happened, he signalled down to the music director that we'd have to go live; the song was lost. Well, the band started playing, but we all thought the sound was coming out of the speakers, so we marched out and began the song very exuberantly with the first line that we all knew:

Mush, mush, mush on you malemute, half dog, half wolf, loping through the night . . .

Then we continued, thinking that the audience was actually hearing the prerecorded version:

. . . and I hate this dumb song, and I'm gonna get real drunk tonight . . .

We said anything that came into our heads, just so we made sure our lips were moving, and those were the mildest words we made up!

Well, the only thing that saved us all was that Orm Collier, knowing us well enough to expect just about anything from us, decided to throw on the echo machine at about 14 times the normal level. Meanwhile, one of the cameramen was trying to shout at us that we were live, but we just went right on, marching along and shouting out words that had very little to do with Mr. Service's original poetic creation.

Finally, the awful truth dawned on us, but by then, the song was over. Dave Thomas was ready to go have a look at how many coupons he'd saved, because he figured his television days were behind him; and I've got to say that the rest of us were in a similar frame of mind.

The head of the network did call us, but instead of handing us the pink slip we were expecting, he said how much he'd enjoyed the show, except for a brief section which he thought had much too much echo on it.

We had a group of terrific singers and dancers on the show, called the Singing Swinging Eight. Now, they weren't so much dancers as they were singers who with some rehearsal could do a bit of square dancing.

Two of them in particular went on to wonderful careers of their own: Billy Van, and another extremely talented young performer who used to come over to ask me about some of the guitar runs I was doing on Hoedown. He also did a bit of songwriting in his spare time; matter of fact, he brought me the very first song he'd composed, called "Remember Me," which I was pleased to introduce on our radio show.

Years later, I was delighted to introduce him once again, this time as a guest on the Tommy Hunter Show: "Ladies and gentlemen, a great singer and songwriter, and still a fine dancer, won't you please welcome Mr. Gordon Lightfoot!"

Getting back to Country Hoedown, I remember that in those days, we used to have a lot of fun outside the studio during our breaks, usually playing pickup baseball. One afternoon, we all got very involved in a game, and Gordie Tapp hit a beautiful line drive toward me. I knew I'd have to do some fast running if I was going to catch it.

With nothing on my mind but getting that ball, I started to run for it, absolutely oblivious to the fact that a station wagon had just parked directly in my path.

SMASH! I drove both knees and my chin straight into that car and collapsed in a heap. As the guys gathered around me, I tried to get up but my knees were completely numb and just buckled under me.

At the hospital, I was told that my left knee, which I guess had taken most of the impact, would have to be operated on if I was ever going to have full use of that leg again. "But I have a television show to do," I protested. "We still have the rest of the season left." After a good deal of arguing back and forth, the doctors agreed to put me in a cast until summer, when I'd go in for the operation. "But you'd better not wait any longer," they warned.

I took their advice; finished off the season on Hoedown and went into the hospital for the operation (the only time I've ever been in the hospital as a patient). It was no accident that my surgeon was none other than Dr. Vince Callaghan, the same doctor who brought me into the world, and came to our house when I was sick with measles or chickenpox. By then, he'd moved on from general practice to become head of surgery at St. Joseph's Hospital in London. What he did for me was to remove a piece of cartilage from my knee. But the operation was only the beginning, as I soon discovered.

After I'd recovered from the surgery, Dr. Callaghan came in to tell me I'd be staying in the hospital a little longer than I'd anticipated.

"It's very important for you to do a lot of exercises and physiotherapy now, so that your leg gets strong again," he said, and I could tell from his tone of voice that he wasn't asking me; he was telling me. "Otherwise, you might develop a limp later on, and there's no reason for that."

I knew that Dr. Callaghan did a lot of work with the football team at the University of Western Ontario, so had a lot of expertise on people with knee injuries. "Okay, Dr. Callaghan," I said. "How long do you think it'll take?"

"Oh, I don't know, Tommy. A month, a month and a half."

Well, I'll tell you, the prospect of being in the hospital for six weeks wasn't exactly wonderful, but it was a heck of a lot more appealing than the idea of walking around with a limp for the rest of my life. So I went through the therapy; and I'm glad I did, because I haven't had a single problem with that knee ever since.

When we started the radio show again in the fall, the whole studio seemed to be talking about a new series that the CBC was planning for the coming summer, a series called Summer Holiday, which would feature a different type of music each night of the week. Our show was supposed to produce one of these broadcasts, which would be called Country Holiday.

Over the season, the details started to evolve. Country Holiday would be broadcast on Friday nights, with Bill Bessey as the announcer and the rest of us regulars and guests providing the music. The real challenge was going to be finding the right locale for the show.

For the first few seasons, we tried doing Country Holiday from a different place each time. Our very first show was

181

broadcast from a Canadian Forces base; then we moved to London, and the following season, shifted to Oshawa.

Around this time, a group of residents from the town of Lindsay, Ontario had written to the CBC about their plans to oppose the proposed demolition of the Lindsay Academy Theatre, which was a local landmark that had come on hard times in recent years. We went up to Lindsay and did a broadcast from the theatre, drawing attention to its plight and the efforts of the local group to turn it into a centre for the arts.

Not too long after this broadcast from Lindsay, Ken Dalziel asked me to stay after rehearsal one day to talk over an idea he had. "I've been talking to Dr. Service, the head of that committee that's trying to save the Academy Theatre," he said, "and I mentioned the possibility of doing Country Holiday from their theatre, regularly. I think it could work; how do you feel about it?"

I was completely convinced, so Ken and I decided to visit Lindsay and see what the community feeling was about having our show there. I didn't think the whole concept would be successful unless there was a lot of enthusiasm about it in the town.

The excitement and support that greeted us when we met with the committee and the local radio station definitely settled the question for us; and for the people in Lindsay, having us there meant a chance to inject some new life into their theatre. That community bent over backwards to help us get set up in the theatre; they even built a special control room in there so that we could create just the balance of sound we needed. Their enthusiasm and excitement made it a pleasure for us to do the show there, right from Day One.

After only a few broadcasts and a good advertising campaign by the committee, people started to become familiar with the name Academy Theatre. They'd come to see our show being broadcast on Friday night, and once they realized that the theatre wasn't the intimidating sort of place they might have imagined, they started to come back to see some of the plays that were put on there from Monday to Thursday. Even when the series was dropped by the CBC (after five seasons), the theatre kept right on going. To this day, it's one of the most successful playhouses around, and I admire the way they've zeroed in on Canadian playwrights and performers, and how they've kept the theatre very much alive.

Doing the show from the Academy Theatre was also a wonderful experience for me personally, because it gave me the chance to put into practice so much of what I'd always enjoyed about radio: the way it exercised my imagination and painted these wonderful pictures through sound alone. When we were broadcasting from the theatre, I'd single out some of the audience members: "I understand there's a group here tonight in the fifth row of the balcony who've come all the way from the Ottawa Valley," I'd say.

I'd mention where we were standing when we did the commercials, or describe the backstage area where all the performers were waiting, and I'd even bring in the weather: "Well, it's a rainy night outside, but it's warm and cozy right here in the Lindsay Academy Theatre."

That way, I hoped that when people came to visit the theatre after hearing our show on the radio, the images would suddenly come alive for them: they'd see the balcony, with all the people cheering and hollering, and . . . Oh, there's that curtain he was talking about.

Once again, in my mind it was all still like going to the Grand Ole Opry at the age of 12 and seeing, for the first time, the performers I'd gotten to know over the years on the WSM radio broadcasts.

We had a number of very fine guest artists on our shows at the Lindsay Academy Theatre, including George Morgan, the talented writer and performer who wrote the hit song "Candy Kisses."

I first met George when he was singing in a bar in Long Beach, California; and later on, I asked him to join us for a show at the Academy Theatre. It was just magic to watch him relate to that audience, with his very low-key approach and his wonderful voice. George was at ease with just about any type of music and I very much enjoyed working with him.

Another great artist we were fortunate to have as a guest on Country Holiday was none other than Tex Ritter, whom I found to be an extremely intelligent and well-read individual, as well as a fantastic performer.

When I think back on it, though, his extensive knowledge of current affairs almost turned into a heap of trouble the time he did our show. Just before we went on the air, Tex was asking me about the political situation in Quebec. In the mid-1960s, the issue of Quebec separatism was just beginning to heat up, so I thought we'd better stay away from that entirely.

"Ummm, Tex," I said, "I think maybe we'd better pass on Quebec."

"Oh, sure, Tommy," he said. "I wouldn't want to talk about anything like that, anyway."

So the show started, and I introduced Tex to the audience, which on that particular evening just happened to include the head of the CBC Radio network. "Thank you Tommy," said Tex, "and now that I'm here in Canada, I ought to tell you folks that there's been a lot of talk down in the States about Quebec seeking its independence."

"Oh no, I thought; and glancing into the audience, I could see the network executive turning a very pale shade of green.

"Now, maybe you folks don't know this," Tex continued, "but Texas once sought its independence too, and now I'm thinking we should seek it once again. Maybe then we could dig a hole in the ground in the middle of Texas, another hole in the middle of Quebec, run a pipeline between the two, and let Texas and Quebec form a new country. Now, Texas would probably want top billing, so we could call the new country Tay-Beck; but then, if Quebec wanted to come first, we'd just have to call it Que-Ass!"

Well, the audience (including the network chief) just burst into uproarious laughter, and the whole incident ended quite happily.

The other characteristic I always enjoyed about Tex was his dramatic and impressive speaking style, which developed more and more as he got older. His voice would become deep and musical, and he would pronounce each word with the greatest care.

Anyway, between rehearsals for one of our radio shows, we were all invited to lunch at the home of some of the folks in Lindsay; and after lunch, Tex and I were just sitting together. I could see this very serious and profound expression come over his face, and I just knew he was preparing himself to say something extremely important. He picked up his pipe, carefully filled it, lit up, took a few thoughtful puffs, and leaned back in his chair with his eyes half-closed in apparent concentration.

What words of wisdom could he be preparing?

Finally, he leaned forward and spoke: "For God's sake, Tommy," he said, dramatically, "don't tell Mother (his wife Dorothy) that I'm smoking my pipe!"

I've always considered myself very fortunate to know Tex Ritter over the years, and I'll be telling you more about him later on. First, though, I'd like to talk about our radio show a bit more.

It wasn't just the summers that were changing on our show in those days. Ken Dalziel decided, after a number of years, that it was time for him to leave our radio show and try his hand at other forms of production, and as a matter of fact, he was promoted within the network. We were all sorry to hear that he was going, because Ken had helped the show, and myself, a great deal during his time there.

After Ken left, the CBC didn't have the budget to pay for a writer, so I ended up writing the whole script myself, which was a great experience for me, although a demanding one: five scripts a week, each of them a half-hour long, and I had to be careful not to repeat myself, because there's nothing more boring than some guy coming on the radio and saying the same thing, day after day. I would sit there for hours with a piece of paper and a pen, just dreaming up new ways of saying hello each morning; one day, I might say, "Hi folks, welcome to our show, from the Atlantic to the Pacific," and the next day, it'd be, "I'm sure glad to say hello to you from coast to coast."

The point of all this wasn't how many ways of saying things I could come up with to impress the listeners; I just wanted to be sure nobody got the feeling that we had one set pattern that we reiterated on every broadcast. We were always looking for new ideas to keep the show fresh, whether it was commemorating a particular holiday, like Valentine's Day, or acknowledging an event going on somewhere; if the International Truckers' Convention was being held in Winnipeg, for instance, then we'd mention that and follow it up by doing a truckers' song.

One time, just to try something *really* different, we broadcast our show from Hawaii, without ever leaving the studio in Toronto! What I did was to collect some Hawaiian recipes, then asked a young lady from Hawaii to come on the show and describe what was going on. In 30 minutes, we walked down to the beach (the sound effects department supplied the crash of surf pounding on the beach), dug a huge pit and lined it with leaves to roast our pig, and held a real luau, complete with Hawaiian songs! We had a great time, and the audience enjoyed the quick trip to Honolulu, judging by the number of letters we got after that show.

What with Hawaiian luaus, and special Valentine's Day presentations, our show wasn't exactly what you might call hard country; and I've got to say that there were times I would have liked to push the program a little more in that direction. Still, I don't think at the time that the CBC would have gone for a live country show five days a week; and we also had a wide audience with a varied range of tastes that we had to reflect.

So we continued to branch out to a greater variety of music. I tried to pick simple songs that had been widely recorded, like "Marie," or "Five Minutes More," giving them my own interpretation. That helped me become more flexible and versatile, and at the same time I was able to maintain the kind of atmosphere I wanted on the show.

Around this time, I happened to run into Wally Traugott, a friend of mine from the Main Street Jamboree days in Hamilton; he'd just been married and was working as an

186

accountant for an auto firm. "Aren't you doing any show now?" I asked, remembering Wally's fine fiddle playing.

"Well, no, Tommy," he said. "I guess the business is just too uncertain, so I've pretty much given it up. You just never know what's going to happen from one day to the next."

I had an idea, but I knew it was going to take some doing to convince Wally, so I invited him to my apartment and asked him about it. "Wally, I was thinking you'd be great as a regular on our show," I said. "It could even lead to a lot of other work."

He balked at first; I guess he couldn't quite believe that this would be steady work, but I'm glad to say I finally changed his mind. Wally was a great asset to our show; his very talented playing and his versatility with just about any style of music provided just the touch we needed.

(The show was good for Wally, too; just as I'd suspected, he made some recordings, was invited on Hoedown, and earned himself a very good reputation among other musicians. Wally is now a producer for Capitol Records in Hollywood, and no one is more pleased about his success than I am.)

Writing the show was also very challenging from the point of view of balance. I really wanted to maintain the intimate feeling that a local show creates, but there were certain approaches a community program could take, like talking about the weather in town, that just wouldn't work for us. If I went on and on about how sunny and beautiful it was in Toronto, the people in Calgary who were in the midst of the worst blizzard in 20 years wouldn't appreciate that very much. But yet, I wanted the show to have a friendly feeling, as if it were coming from a local station in any one of 100 different communities, not one town in particular.

I guess the show I most often thought of as an example of how to achieve that kind of balance was the Arthur Godfrey Show — a very professional, national program coming out of New York, but with the kind of light-hearted laughter and chatter that gave it a community-oriented atmosphere.

Commercials were also very much part of our show, just as they were on the Godfrey show and so many of the programs

I heard as a kid. I never wanted to finish a song and just say: "Now, here is a message from our sponsor." Instead, I talked about our main sponsors, the St. Lawrence Starch Company, as if they were friends of ours. It was almost as if the commercial were another song.

The Rhythm Pals, Al Harris and I would finish a song and I'd say: "Thanks, fellas, that was great. By the way, I was at my folks' place in London this weekend, and Mom was just taking a cake out of the oven when I got there; great cake, Mom. So she told me that instead of her usual solid shortening, she poured in a little of that St. Lawrence Corn Oil. Well, I could taste the difference for myself; I ate half the cake right there."

"Well, that's great, Tommy," Bruce Smith would say, and he'd go into the commercial for St. Lawrence Corn Oil (which, by the way, focussed on the fact that you could "pour your shortening!").

It always seemed so much more personal when we did it that way; and I didn't want to leave the relationship between our show and the sponsor at just doing a commercial a few times a week. I asked to tour the factory, meet the various executives and the fellows who packaged the St. Lawrence Corn Oil or loaded the Beehive Golden Corn Syrup onto the trucks. If they spent $1 on air time, I wanted to give them $5 worth of exposure, including phone calls, visits, and even performing at their office parties. I wanted them to feel they were part of our show, which they were, and that I was part of their company.

What was beginning to emerge, I guess, was that if I'm anything besides a country singer, it's a salesman. If I believed in a product, I figured the world ought to be beating a path to its door, and I wanted to be the one shovelling the path. I thought that was part of my job on the show, and the way for me to do that job was to draw on my natural enthusiasm for the products.

It might sound as if I was handling the whole radio show without blinking an eye: writing the script, doing commercials, and finding plenty of time to stroll over to my Hoedown rehearsals and think about my recordings with Columbia. Well, that wasn't the case at all; the very gruelling schedule did take its toll more than once.

I still shudder to recall one unbelievable 36 hours in which I did the radio show in the morning, drove over to the TV studio to rehearse for Hoedown, jumped into the car with Al and the Pals and the rest of the radio regulars, drove to North Bay to do a show, and returned to Toronto at about 6 the next morning, just in time to set the alarm for a few hours' sleep before getting ready to do the radio show again.

Well, I guess I must have been *real* tired, because I awoke not to the sound of the alarm but the familiar theme music of our show, and the telephone ringing off the hook; they'd been trying to call me from the studio for hours, but I was apparently dead to the world. Luckily, they were able to get Gordie Tapp to fill in for me; but, boy, did I get a tongue-lashing for that one, and richly deserved, too!

Another time, I just managed to get into the CBC building as the show was going on the air; that time, Gordie just did an opening song as I raced breathlessly into the studio.

I guess if I'd tried to laugh these incidents off, I really would have been in serious trouble, but I think the utterly apologetic and guilt-ridden look on my face expressed just how seriously I took the whole situation. (In my own defence, I'll say only that it never happened again.)

There were a few times, though, that fatigue caught up with me in ways that scared me far more than being late. Again, it was after one of those unbelievably long days: a radio show, a TV rehearsal, a program meeting, a few hours in the research department, and a show in Windsor, Ontario that night. On my way back from Windsor, I felt pretty groggy, so I decided to stop in London and have a coffee with my folks. Mom tried to get me to stay the night, but I had to be back for the show in the morning, and off I went.

Somewhere near Woodstock (not too far from London), I must have fallen asleep at the wheel, because I awoke to the sound of stones and gravel hitting the underside of the car, which was completely turned around and sitting on the shoulder of the road. I suddenly realized what had happened: I'd skidded across the highway, spun around, and whipped back into my own lane and onto the shoulder. It began to dawn on me what might have happened on a busy highway like that, with all kinds of curves and bridge abutments along the way. I began to shake so badly that I could hardly start the car again.

Another time, when I was on my way to Hamilton, I turned my car confidently onto the highway only to realize that I was in the oncoming lanes; luckily, I was able to get over to the right side of the road just in time.

I feel extremely lucky that those two incidents were the worst that ever happened to me behind the wheel; given the fact that I kept up that pace for several years, I know very well that it could have been a lot worse. Being young and energetic, I guess I just kept on going without even realizing how much I was trying to pack into an average day. There's no way I could do the same today.

Of course, there was relief from the pressure: comic relief. The guys on our radio show took just as much delight in playing the occasional prank as the cast of Hoedown, and I've got to admit that I was one of the prime instigators. If there was even a spare half-hour when we weren't in the middle of working on something, my mind would conjure up a million ideas . . .

I'd already become very fond of the sound effects room, with all its ingenious contraptions, like a big screened box with a glass plate and a steel ball inside, that you swung when you wanted that unmistakable sound of breaking glass. Here's just one example of how that could be used in a routine:

Tommy: I don't think you should swing that baseball bat near this window, George.
George: Whaddya mean, I shouldn't swing the baseball bat?
Tommy: Well, George, if you happen to swing it the wrong way, it might just. . . (and I'd let the ball go) SMASH! TINKLE-TINKLE! CRASH!

There were machines that would make the sound of a high wind blowing, and gadgets that beat out the rhythm of horses' hooves, and a whole arsenal of other noisemakers that I found in there over a period of months. Anyway, one time we were having an unusually quiet day in the studio; everything was going smoothly. Too smoothly, if you know what I mean. Well, we started the show, and after my first song, the Rhythm Pals were ready to launch into their jingles for the commercials. They were real busy getting set up and waiting for me to do the announcement, so they didn't notice me reach down beside my microphone with the unmistakable look of mischief in my eyes . . .

JINGLE! RATTLE! BING! BANG! SMASH! CRASH! CLANG! CLATTER!

It sounded like half the wall had come crashing down around our ears. What I'd done was get a huge metal pot and fill it with all the chains, balls, metal bells, and anything else I could find in the sound effects room that would make a lot of noise. Then, while everyone's attention was occupied, I'd just thrown the whole potful across the floor.

Well, I wanted to shake things up a bit, and I certainly accomplished that aim by pulling a stunt like that during a live show. (The unfortunate part, and I still feel very sorry about it to this day, was that one of the Pals suffered from a disease of the inner ear that affects the equilibrium, and when he turned quickly to see where all the noise was coming from, his balance went totally off. The other guys had to hold him up during the jingles or he literally would have fallen over.)

Well, things eventually got back to normal, and we went on with our regular week of broadcasting. I usually came into the studio at 10 to run through our music for the day, but one morning, I happened to arrive early. I took my usual route up the fire ecape to Studio G and pounded on the back door until one of the musicians let me in, just like they did every morning.

But this wasn't going to be a regular morning; I could tell from the moment I walked in the door. For one thing, Bert Niosi, our conductor and arranger, was actually shouting at the guys about something they were playing wrong. Now, Bert is a professional who insists on perfection in his arrangements, but he's also a very kind, gentle person who never loses his temper. I mean, Bert's annoyed when he raises his eyebrows and says, "No, I'm afraid you're not playing that quite correctly." Yet here he was, chewing out the band about the instrumental they were playing.

I quietly strolled into the control room where our producer, John Cantelon, was sitting. "Morning, John," I said. "What seems to be the problem out there?"

"Well, it's just ridiculous, Tommy," he said, obviously annoyed. "Here's this very simple, straightforward arrangement Bert's put together, and the band just can't seem to do it; I don't know why."

"Well, what's the point of doing it, then?" I asked. "Let's just do something else."

"No." John sounded quite adamant. "I don't want to do it that way. These guys are being paid as musicians, and they ought to be able to play like musicians."

Out in the studio, it was going from bad to worse as far as that instrumental was concerned. They'd start the number, and suddenly the pianist would be going one way, the bass player would be somewhere else, and the rest of them all trailing off in the background somewhere.

"No, no, no!" Bert shouted, throwing his baton down. "Now what the hell do you think you're doing? How many times do I have to tell you? Now, once again!" So they took it from the top again, and the same thing happened, only even worse than before. This time, the musicians started yelling and throwing their music around, while Bert was just about coming unglued.

I marched back into the control room and told the operator to shut off the sounds of panic coming in from the studio. "Now, lookit," I said to John. "Take that instrumental out of the show. Have them play 'You Are My Sunshine,' or 'Tennessee Waltz,' or get one of them to play the piccolo; anything but this instrumental. We don't need this kind of grief."

192

"No way," John shot back. "It's staying in!"

Now I was really confused. Bert all upset, and now John, who almost always went along when I felt strongly about something; suddenly he was digging in his heels. I tried to stay calm and reason with him.

"Look, John, it's only a minute and a half instrumental, and most of the stations are going to break away from the network while it's playing anyway, for station identification. So why don't you let the band do a simple version of the 'Anniversary Waltz' and I'll introduce it. Please; it's not worth all this aggravation."

"No way."

"Well, I'm going to talk to Bert about it."

"You go right ahead."

Out I went again to try to beg, plead and cajole Bert into giving up this disastrous instrumental, but to no avail. "It's a matter of principle," he said, angrily. "They have to know who's in charge."

At this point, I was getting pretty steamed myself. I mean, it was my name going on the show, and I was going to have to take the flak for anything that went wrong; I made up my mind that we'd all have a serious discussion about this after the broadcast. But for the moment, I had to give in because we were running out of time. I could only hope that by some miracle, they'd get it right when we went live.

So the show started, and I finally had to introduce that awful number. I gritted my teeth, closed my eyes, and prayed . . . but no, they were going off key, just like they'd done all morning, everybody headed 17 ways till Sunday. Then, once again, they threw down their instruments and started yelling and cursing and throwing music at each other. They said things that almost turned the airwaves blue.

The cold slap of reality hit me. My career was finished! Cursing on the air, and fighting . . . I'd never be able to work again. In desperation, I started laughing and telling jokes, trying to pass the whole thing off as a gag. Suddenly, I noticed the tape was running in the control room; I turned around, and Bert and all the band members stopped, and began laughing hysterically, almost rolling around on the floor.

"OK, hold it," John yelled. "Everybody settle down, now."

Well, they finally explained what they'd done. Before I'd even gotten to the studio that morning, they'd prerecorded the instrumental perfectly; and when I arrived, they went through the whole episode to convince me there was going to be a real goof-up on the air. Then, as soon as I'd introduced the number, they switched over onto tape so that the good performance went out on the air, while the pandemonium was heard only in the studio. I didn't know whether to laugh or cry; I was incredibly relieved, but I could almost feel the hairs on my head turning grey one at a time!

Despite all the disruptions that were always going on, we never actually got to the point of having to cancel our radio show. Except for once. That was November 22, 1963, which I'm sure many of you will remember sadly as the date when President Kennedy was assassinated in Dallas, Texas.

As soon as I heard the news, I ran to the phone and called the head of the radio network division to try to convince him to cancel our show. We'd done the programming in advance, and there were two songs planned that would have been terrible to play under the circumstances; one of them was called "Let's Think About Living," and the lyrics included a reference to some fellow getting shot, and the other song, which the Rhythm Pals had done, began: "Are you from Big D?"

I needn't have worried, because the network had already pre-empted our show and everything else scheduled on the radio and TV that day, including Hoedown. We all went home to watch, stunned, as the television news reported the tragic story, which I guess was the same thing half the world was probably doing at the same time. Eventually, we all went back to our everyday lives, but I'll tell you, most people who heard the terrible news that day, myself included, have never forgotten it.

Around the same time, the CBC network began organizing some shows for Canadian servicemen, and we were asked to put together a group of entertainers.

I think we organized a very good group: Gordie Tapp as announcer, Al Harris, Wally Traugott, the Rhythm Pals and myself from the radio show, along with Peter Appleyard on drums and vibraphone, and two popular TV personalities: Juliette and Joyce Hahn. We worked well as a travelling group because we were all flexible enough to do solos as well as instrumentals. That avoided the complications of getting into a 25- or 30-piece orchestra, which would have been close to impossible to take to the remote places we went.

Our first show was in Fort Churchill, Manitoba, and from there we went to Resolute Bay in the Northwest Territories, which was probably the furthest any of us had ever travelled! We met some great people on those trips, and one man I particularly remember was a Royal Canadian Air Force officer by the name of Freddy Carpenter. Some of the guys found him intimidating, with his stern and demanding manner, but beneath the gruff exterior was a kind and gentle man, with a wonderful smile that lit up his whole face.

On our trip back to Fort Churchill, we were flying in an old DC-3. Suddenly, the plane started pitching violently. "Hey, what's the matter with this crate?" demanded Gordie, marching to the cockpit door and poking his head inside. "Who the hell's flying this plane, anyway?"

"I am," Freddy said, turning around in the pilot's seat and fixing Gordie with a piercing gaze.

"Oh, that's fine, sir," Gordie said, backing out of the cabin. "Doing a terrific job too, sir!"

The shows worked out so well that when we returned to Toronto, the network and armed services staff asked us if we'd be interested in entertaining Canadian troops overseas. "You'd start out in Egypt, and go from there to France and Germany," one of the producers told me.

"Egypt?" I was stunned. That sounded like the end of the earth to me.

"That's right, Hunter," he said, laughing at my shocked expression. "You know; deserts, camels; that sort of thing."

Of course, we were all incredibly excited at the prospect, but we also had to do a tremendous amount of advance work and planning. We were going to be out of the country for three weeks, which meant taping 15 shows in advance in addition to our regular broadcasts.

Then there were the shots; 13 different needles, as I recall. Well, I wasn't any better at getting needles than I'd been as a kid; I was absolutely terrified. But I got through it somehow.

We were all working hard getting ready to leave, doing live shows in the morning and taping in the afternoon and evening. It made for a lot of long days, but we got into a pretty good routine; and whenever *anything* starts fitting into a groove like that, I have this uncontrollable urge just to jar it a little . . .

One evening, we had a few minutes to spare between tapings. I couldn't just sit there peacefully, listen to the rehearsal and study my script; I had to go exploring. So I wandered all over the old McGill Street studio, opening doors and poking my nose into all the nooks and crannies that an old place like that is always full of, and finally made my way up to the balcony.

"Hey, guys," I shouted down to the band. "How's it going?"

"Yeah, hi, Tom," one of the musicians said, glancing at the guy next to him as if to say: "There's Hunter, fooling around again."

I stayed quiet for a few more minutes, and as soon as they got into their playing again, I leaned farther over the railing and piped up once again: "Sounding great, guys!"

"Yeah, thanks, Tom." (Won't this guy *ever* stop bugging us?)

I moved even closer to the railing, until I was sitting on the very edge, swinging my feet. "Hey, guys, lookit this!"

"Get off there, Hunter," they shouted. "You're going to kill yourself!"

This time, I waited a good long time and made sure they were completely concentrating on the music again. I inched forward once more and . . .

AAAAAAAAAAAAARHH . . . CRASH!!

They threw down their instruments and went racing to the

back of the theatre. "My God; he's killed himself!"

"I told him not to get so close to the edge!"

Suddenly, they heard sounds coming from the balcony, and they looked up to see me holding my sides and roaring, helpless with laughter. There, below the balcony, lay the object that had made all the noise: an entire row of theatre seats (they weren't nailed down) that I'd tossed off the balcony before ducking down and screaming as if I was falling.

"You're nuts, Hunter," one of them shouted, laughing at the same time. "You oughta be banned from rehearsals unless you're safely onstage."

Amazingly enough, we finally got all those shows taped (despite my interruptions) and started out on our trip. To my surprise, the captain on our military flight looked very familiar; I couldn't think of his name at first, then I suddenly remembered: Bob Fossolde. We'd gone to public school together in London, Ontario. He remembered me, too. We talked over old times for awhile, and that made the long trip very pleasant. (We've kept in touch over the years, and I've got to say that Bob's done well for himself; along with being a jet pilot, he's also a brigadier-general and a doctor specializing in aerospace medicine.)

But any feeling of familiarity ended the moment we landed at the airport in El-Arish and climbed into the military transport that was taking us into the town of Gaza, where the Canadian contingent of the United Nations peacekeeping force was stationed. If the names of these places bring to mind news reports about unrest in the Middle East, that's because we were staying in an area that was at the very centre of the whole crisis: the Gaza Strip.

I don't think any of us, accustomed as we were to the comfort and security of North American life, were quite prepared for what we encountered in Egypt. Our hotel had very small rooms lit by a naked light bulb hanging from the ceiling by a long piece of wire, and the toilet was just a hole in the floor with two footprint-shaped indentations on either side. If we wanted to take a bath, we had to tell the manager days in advance so they could gather enough kindling from the beach to fire up the hot-water heater.

Letter-writing was impossible at night, unless we wanted to train ourselves to write in the dark; at about 8 every night, all the lights were turned down to almost nothing. Jim McPhee, the military liaison officer attached to our group, told us there was a blackout every night in order not to attract bomber fire.

Of course, all this made us extremely nervous, especially since we sometimes had to be out after dark when we were doing our shows for the troops. We'd be going along in our buses on the way back to the hotel, along those darkened roads, and suddenly there would be a barricade in front of us, manned by a group of soldiers with their guns pointed straight at us. They'd climb onto the buses, demanding identification cards and authorization, and we'd be panic-stricken. We understood that they had to check, but that didn't make the experience any less frightening; nor did the fact that we were stopped that way literally every night.

One night, when we were talking about the tenseness of the situation, Jim reiterated to me how important it was for all of us to abide by the rules and stop when a soldier told us to. "A man was shot yesterday because he didn't halt on a soldier's order," he said. "He didn't know the language, and when he was told to halt, he kept on going. The soldier yelled again, and he kept walking, so he was killed on the spot."

Whether that was a true incident or just a way of reminding us of the realities of the situation, it certainly made a great impression on me. A short time later, a group of us went to the hotel dining room, just across the street from the hotel. It was already dark, and we had to pick our way very carefully. Inside, there were candles and lanterns lit; it was hot and smoky, and I was very tired, so right after dinner I excused myself and headed back to the hotel.

Suddenly, in the pitch dark, I heard a sharp commanding voice shout something at me in Arabic. Oh, my God, I thought; it's just like the guy who was told to halt. Up went my hands in the familiar gesture of surrender, and I stood absolutely motionless. Again, I heard the voice, and this time

198

I thought: it's all over; he doesn't care if I've halted or not. I didn't know whether to sing the national anthem or get down on my knees and start praying.

Just then, the door opened and three or four of the other guys came out of the dining room.

"Don't come any closer!" I shouted. "The guy's got a gun!"

They all stood there for a moment, and when the Arabic command came again, Gordie sort of scratched his head and started to move forward. "Gordie, don't move!" I hollered.

"Hang on just a second," he said, and walked into the darkness.

A few moments later, Gordie walked back, chuckling. "Don't worry, Tommy; he's not going to shoot you," he said. "He was only asking if you wanted a taxi!"

After we left Egypt, we flew to Europe and did shows for the troops on every military base in France and Germany; it was a successful tour, but extremely hard on us because of the gruelling schedule. A couple of the guys got sick, and we all lost a lot of weight, what with all the odd hours and box lunches; so the next time we did an overseas tour, the organizers made sure to pencil in some rest days for us, which certainly made a lot of difference.

When we got back to Toronto, all the guys on Hoedown were eager to see photographs of the places we'd been, and we ended up doing a segment about the trip on our show.

Now, one of the servicemen had given me a complete Arabic outfit, with the long, white tunic and a rope to tie at the waist; I'm sure it looked very impressive and imposing on an Arab leader, but on me, it looked more like a long, billowing woman's gown. Anyway, Gordie asked me to wear the outfit on the show, so I obliged, but to tell you the truth, I felt just a little foolish.

Gordie: Now, you were given a little memento of the trip to Egypt, weren't you?

Tommy: Yes, I was, Gordie. (Stands up to display the full outfit to the cameras.) What do you think?

Gordie: Madam, in your condition you shouldn't even be travelling!

199

CHAPTER 8

"Welcome to Our Show"

It took us all a little while to recover from that overseas trip, but we finally got back into our routines: Country Hoedown, the radio show, and our personal appearances, which once again were taking us on frequent tours out of town.

One time, just after we'd finished a tour together, Gordie Tapp and I were doing some shows in Peterborough. By that time, I'd gotten fairly familiar with his routine, especially his opening, which I've got to admit I liked a lot better than my own. Well, I guess it *had* to happen: I walked out on that stage and tried out one of his jokes. It got a terrific response from the audience, so I tried another one; same thing happened. They were just rolling in the aisles. After 15 minutes or so of telling his jokes, I did a song, then told a couple more of his stories, and on it went that way. I ended up interspersing Gordie's entire routine with a few of my own songs, all to the absolute delight of the audience.

What I didn't know was that Gordie's show was scheduled for the very next night, in front of the same audience, and to make matters worse, he didn't have the slightest idea of what I'd pulled the night before. So out he walked and launched into his first joke; there wasn't even a titter. That auditorium might as well have been empty; after all, they'd heard all the jokes just the day before!

Poor Gordie didn't know what was going on until the bandleader shuffled over to him. "Hey, Tapp; I wish you and Hunter would keep your acts straight," he whispered, annoyed. "He went through all of that last night."

Luckily for Gordie, he was able to interject a whole bunch of other jokes, and with his usual ability to ad-lib his way out of just about any situation, he got through the show all right. But Gordie did get even with me for that one, when we were in Lethbridge, Alberta for a couple of shows. This time, Gordie went first, and after singing a verse and chorus of every single one of the songs I'd planned to do (to this day, I still don't know how he found out what I was going to sing!) he very cheerfully introduced me, adding, under his breath: "Have fun out there, Tom!"

Let me tell you, I did a lot of *very* old songs and routines that night, sweating profusely the whole way through; but to be perfectly honest, I've got to say that I did have it coming.

Sometimes, travelling back and forth from doing these shows, or just sitting on the set of Country Hoedown, I found myself thinking more and more about the future, and about the direction I wanted to go, not only in my career, but in my life.

I'd been on television for almost seven years now, and we'd had the radio show for more than four years; I felt my career was much more solid than ever before. Solid enough, I realized, for me to decide that it was finally time to start a life with Shirley.

It's not that I suddenly realized at that particular moment that I wanted to get married. Shirley and I had been seeing each other almost nine years now, and I'd known for a long time that she was the only girl for me; there was no doubt in my mind about who I wanted by my side when I finally made the step. I just wanted to make sure that when we got married, I would be able to offer Shirley more than the guitar and the pair of cowboy boots that were my only worldly possessions when I set out for Toronto at the age of 17.

With several years of network radio and television behind me, I finally felt that I did have that security; and the more I thought about it, the more certain I was about my decision. In the autumn of 1962, I went home to London, Ontario to visit Shirley's dad, and talk the idea over with him. Mr. Brush was very pleased I'd come to see him, and he gave me his complete approval. "Go right ahead and ask her, Tommy," he said. "I hope she says yes."

I realize that going through a nine-year courtship and asking your girl's father for permission to get married may sound old-fashioned today. Many *marriages* don't last nine years, and it's even more rare for parents' opinions to be considered by young people who are getting married nowadays. But I don't think those "old-fashioned" considerations hurt us one bit; as a matter of fact, I think it was of great benefit to us to take the time to make sure we were doing the right thing, instead of jumping into a decision we might regret later.

By the time I went home at Christmas, I was so positive about my decision that I waited until after I'd gone to church with Shirley, her mom, dad and grandparents, and then, when we were all gathered in the living room of the Brush home, having coffee, I turned to Shirley during a lull in the conversation.

"I've got something for you, Shirl."

"Oh, what is it?" Everybody in the room turned toward us, and Mr. Brush smiled knowingly to himself.

"Just put your hand in my coat pocket," I said, as nonchalantly as possible. "It's in there."

Shirley very tentatively reached into my pocket . . . and there was the small velvet jeweller's box. As she opened it, the glow of the lamplight in the cozy room caught a facet of the diamond, which sparkled even more brightly.

Everyone was very happy that evening, and I went home thinking everything was settled except the date. The next day, Shirley and I got together again, and I suddenly noticed she wasn't wearing the ring. "Tommy," she said, handing the little jeweller's box to me, "I'm sorry, but I really need some more time to think it over."

I was stunned. It had never even occurred to me that Shirley might say no; I guess I just assumed that she was as sure about marriage as I was, after all those years we'd gone together and talked about our plans for the future. I just stared at her for a moment, and then (I'm not ashamed to admit it) I started to cry.

Needless to say, it was a pretty miserable Christmas. I went back to Toronto the next day and tried to get back to work, but my mind was on Shirley. I just couldn't believe I'd been wrong about asking her to marry me, and I made up my mind to try again at New Year's. Maybe, after all the time we'd waited, the whole idea had come as a bit of a shock when it finally happened; and maybe Shirley really did need just a bit more time to think about it.

Well, I asked again, and this time, she just smiled when I held out the little velvet box. "Yes, Tommy," she said, and held out her left hand for me to slip the ring on her finger. I'll tell you, there wasn't a happier guy in the world than I was at that moment!

Nine years was a long enough wait, we figured, so Shirley and I decided not to delay our wedding: we set the date for Saturday, March 9, 1963. (I'll bet I'm one of the few husbands who remembers the exact date of his wedding anniversary, although I've got to admit that it's one of the few dates, along with family birthdays, that I *can* remember without looking it up in a book somewhere!)

The day before our wedding, I had a broadcast of Country Hoedown to do, and when we were finished, I got ready to climb into my car for the drive back to London. "See you tomorrow, Tommy," the guys all chorused, smiling at me, and then they all stepped *way* back from the curb as I got ready to start the car. Well, I thought that was a bit strange, but I turned the key anyway, and . . . KA-BOOM!!

Well, my good pals had rigged my car with all kinds of stink bombs and red bombs, and when I hit that ignition, it just about blew the hood right off the car! I might have known those guys would pull some kind of stunt!

The wedding, which was at All Saints Anglican Church in London, was absolutely perfect; both our families were out in full force, and all my friends from Hoedown and the radio show were there to wish us well, with Bill Bessey, our announcer, as my best man, Ted Glover and Al Cherny as ushers, and Tommy Common singing for us. Shirley looked just beautiful in her white gown, and I remember promising myself, as we walked out of the church together, that nothing would ever happen to change the way we felt about each other. I'm happy to say that's a promise we've both kept, through all the years.

We didn't have that much time for a honeymoon, because I had to be back in Toronto to do the radio show and Country Hoedown rehearsals, so we ended up taking just three days for our wedding trip. (Every time we've gone anywhere since then, we've always called it our second honeymoon!)

Since we had such a short time, I wanted our honeymoon to be really special. I couldn't think of anything more romantic than leaving after the church service and the reception, and climbing aboard a train, as everybody waved goodbye from the platform and the cars pulled slowly away into the distance.

We took that same route I'd travelled so often on those train trips I took as a child, from London to Detroit, where we stayed that night at the most elegant hotel in the city, the Book-Cadillac. I'd asked Gordie Tapp to phone ahead for me and book the bridal suite, and order a bottle of champagne to be sent to the room. (I wouldn't have known how to ask for anything as luxurious as champagne, and I wanted to make sure everything was done just right.) When we arrived, the people at the hotel treated us just like royalty; I guess Gordie must have pulled out all the stops!

While Shirley was unpacking, I just flipped on the television set for a moment, because I'd never *seen* such a luxurious-looking TV before. What do you think I saw on the screen? It was my favorite movie of all time: *High Noon*, with Gary Cooper. So that's what we did; we watched the movie. Oh, and answered the telephone about every 15 minutes, as Shirley's dad phoned the hotel just to see how we were doing. He must have phoned three or four times during the evening; I think he even phoned a fifth time, *long* after the movie was over. "Hi, there," he said. "Just wanted to see what you two lovebirds were doing!"

The next day, after visiting my aunt and uncle, we went on to Chicago, where we went to see some of my folks' friends, who'd worked with Dad on the railroad during that brief period he spent in the United States as a young man. We had only a little time for sightseeing before flying back to Toronto, but we both enjoyed Chicago a great deal, and have returned there several times since then.

Even though we only had a few days, Shirley and I both look back on that little honeymoon trip with a great deal of fondness. After all, when you've got each other, even the simplest celebration seems like the most special time in the world.

When we got back to Toronto, we moved right into my apartment on Lakeshore Boulevard, which had a beautiful, romantic view of Lake Ontario from the living room and dining room; just perfect for an intimate candlelit dinner for two. On our very first night in the apartment, we picked out this terrific recipe Shirley had found for a crabmeat dish, with brandy, and cream; about 1,000 calories per mouthful, by the sound of it. We got out this lovely chafing dish that Gordie and Helen had given us as a wedding present, and Shirley put all the crabmeat in there. (The chafing dish was filled to the brim, but we figured we'd eat celery sticks and cottage cheese for the next week or so!)

With the candles casting a warm glow on the table, we sat down to our feast. Shirley spooned the crabmeat onto our plates, and we each took a heaping forkful . . . our first and last, as it turned out. That crabmeat was so rich that we couldn't even force ourselves to take one more bite!

"Oh, look, Tommy," Shirley called from the kitchen; and I went in there to find her giggling over the cookbook, which she'd opened to the page with the crabmeat recipe. "It says here that this stuff is an appetizer, and you're supposed to eat it on toast points. Probably enough for 14 people."

"More like 140 people," I said, laughing, and reached for the peanut butter and jam. "Well, at least now I know how I feel about crabmeat!" (I've never eaten it since!)

For the first few weeks in our apartment in Toronto, we would go back to London on Friday night and spend the weekend with her folks or mine. After the third or fourth Friday that I came home from the Hoedown broadcast to find her packing a suitcase, I finally decided I had to say something about it. "Shirley," I said, "I don't want us going away to London every weekend any more. This is our home now, and I want us to be together here."

In a way, I think that was a lot easier for me to say; after all, I'd been on my own since the age of 17, while Shirley had lived with her folks until she was 25, and I understood that she was going to feel a bit lonely for them at first. But I felt that marriage was a full-time commitment for both of us, and I know that Shirley agreed with me. (I've got to add that both Shirley and I have developed a very good and close relationship with each other's folks, which is still true to this day.)

We both settled into our routines fairly quickly, but one afternoon I came home after a rehearsal and found Shirley in bed, feeling very sick. "What's wrong, honey?" I asked, worried.

"I don't know, Tom," she said. "Maybe a touch of the flu. It's probably just a 24-hour bug." The next day, she was feeling poorly again, and the following morning, she was no better, so we decided she should see a doctor.

That afternoon, at about 2 o'clock, as I recall, I got a phone call. It was Shirley. "So what did the doctor say, Shirl?" I asked. "Was it the flu?"

There was a long pause at the other end of the phone.

"No, Tom," she said finally, sounding extremely happy for someone who was supposed to be sick. "It wasn't the flu."

"Well, what . . . wait a second; don't tell me . . . are you?"

"Yes! I'm pregnant!"

Well, I'll tell you, I was a happy as a lark; I just stood there hanging onto the phone and grinning. Then, the very next thing I did, before calling my folks or anyone, was to look up the telephone number of a real estate agent. That might sound a little unusual, but you see, I was bound and determined that my family was going to grow up in a house, not an apartment.

Again, I realize that many families are very happy and contented with apartment life, but for me, a home represented (and still does) a feeling of roots and a sense of security, which is exactly what I'd been saving for all those years. Even with the relative security of my work on the radio and on television, I was still very much aware that our business was always prone to uncertainty, and I wanted to make sure that my wife and family were well provided for, especially when it came to having a home of our own. I guess that's also why I decided that I wanted to pay off the mortgage in five years, even though I knew that would mean cutting back in other areas for awhile. The sooner that house was really ours, the best I felt I'd be doing for my family. (Somehow, I actually managed to meet that five-year deadline I'd set for myself, and I've always been glad that I did.)

The home we chose was in Clarkson, a small community just west of Toronto. Both Shirley and I preferred to move right out of the city, because we felt that a more rural atmosphere would be far better for us and the family we were just starting. The real estate agent, an extremely nice and friendly gal who later moved onto the same street, had this house right at the top of her list, and as soon as we saw it, we knew it was just the place for us.

It was a long, low, very cozy home ("just perfect for cleaning the eavestroughs without a ladder," as Shirley said) on a ravine lot with plenty of trees and a creek down the back, just perfect for kids. The street was a cul-de-sac, very quiet and private, with the school right around the corner; it was a great neighborhood, and we met some wonderful people there, many of whom we're still friends with to this day.

Strangely enough, we bought our home on the very same day as two of my friends on Country Hoedown: Gordie Tapp and Tommy Common, and what was even more of a conincidence, our closing dates were identical, and we all moved in the same day, too! Now, our wives all thought that was a pretty startling chance of fate; but when we told them we were all leaving on a tour together the very next morning, that coincidence began looking just a little bit planned. Shirley and Helen were certain that we'd gotten together and arranged it all in advance, and I think they're still convinced that's what happened!

Well, the fall rolled around, and with it a new season for Country Hoedown and our radio show. There was an event in store for me, though, that would make the excitement of television and radio pale by comparison, as I was soon to discover.

One afternoon in early October, I went to perform at a ploughing match with Alex Read, another old friend of ours from the Main Street Jamboree days in Hamilton. After the show, I decided to stop off at Alex's house for a beer before making my way home. "Hey, Alex," I said, as we sat down at the kitchen table, "do you mind if I use your phone for a second? I just want to check with Shirley."

So I got on the phone to tell Shirley I'd be home for dinner shortly, and there was a silence on the other end of the line. "Tommy," she said, finally. "I think you'd better come home now. I'm having labor pains."

I went back to the table and sat down. "What was that all about?" Alex asked.

"Oh, Shirley's having labor pains," I said, picking up my beer and sipping at it.

"What?" He started jumping around and shouting. "Hey, you look pretty calm. Aren't you excited? Your wife's having a baby!"

"Yeah . . . having a baby," I said, and suddenly it all hit me. I jumped out of that seat like I'd been shot out of a cannon. "Hey, Alex," I yelled, "I gotta go. My wife's having a baby!"

I raced out of that house, almost breaking my neck as I took the front steps four at a time in an effort to rush to my car.

I guess I must have broken every speed limit on the books getting back to Clarkson; I screeched to a halt, and raced into the house, changing clothes as I ran: one boot landed on the coffee table, the other on the carpet, and my jacket flopped over a lamp. Meanwhile, Shirley sat there quite calmly in the living room with her coat on and her little suitcase all packed and ready to go. "Hang on there, honey; we'll get you there in no time," I yelled from the bedroom, as I rummaged in a dresser drawer for a pair of socks.

At last, we were on our way to St. Joseph's Hospital, right on Lakeshore Boulevard. When we arrived, the nurses took Shirley right to a room. But if I thought it was going to be a short wait, I had another thing coming; an hour dragged by, then another, and I finally got ready to stick it out for the night, if need be. There was no way I was going to leave Shirley alone.

"Now, don't worry, Mr. Hunter," one of the nurses said, coming in and taking one look at my face. "Everything's going to be fine. We're just going to take Mrs. Hunter to the delivery room now, and we'll let you know just as soon as there's any news."

"Bye, honey," Shirley said, with that wonderful smile, as they wheeled her out of the room.

Alex had come down to the hospital to keep me company during the wait, and we both sat awake for hours in that room and talked, until, at about 2 in the morning, Alex finally fell asleep and I was left alone with my thoughts.

I felt so far away from that carefree kid I'd been at 17, racing around the countryside, playing in bars and living in rooming houses. I would always love country music and work to the best of my ability in my chosen career, but I knew then, as I sat in that hospital waiting room in those long hours of the pre-dawn, that my wife and family would always come first in my life. After all, there wouldn't be any pleasure in even the greatest success in the world if there weren't someone to share it all with.

The sky was just starting to get light when I finally dozed off, and then, from very far away, I could hear someone talking to me: "Congratulations, Mr. Hunter," the voice said, "You have a six-pound, 12-ounce baby boy." I awoke with a start and looked around, but there was nobody in the room.

Suddenly, the doctor walked in, smiling. "Congratulations,

Mr. Hunter," he said, pumping my hand. "You have a six-pound, 12-ounce baby boy!"

(I've puzzled it over in my mind ever since, but I still can't figure out how I knew what that doctor was going to say before he ever came into the waiting room . . . Just one of life's little mysteries, I guess.)

October 11, 1963. Our first son, Jeffrey, was born.

I had to do a radio show that morning, so of course I mentioned Jeff's arrival on the air; I was the typical proud father, absolutely thrilled and excited. On Hoedown that evening, I was passing out cigars all over the place, and by the time I went back to the hospital that evening to see Shirley and the baby, I was just about walking on air. I kept staring and staring at my son, so tiny and helpless, his little fingers all curled up, his wee toes kicking gently against the sides of the bassinet. Once again, I quietly promised myself (and Jeff) that I would give him the very best environment I could provide for him in which to grow up.

I'd made a prior commitment to do a show in Calgary on Saturday morning, but I decided that I'd come home first thing Sunday, instead of staying out west over the weekend. Right after the show, I went downtown to Western Outfitters, and told the salesman, Lou Pomeranz, that I wanted to look at a pair of cowboy boots. "About a size 12, Tom?" he asked, glancing at me.

"No, more like a size triple-zero," I said. "You see, they're for my son, and he was just born yesterday morning."

Well, it took some doing, but we finally managed to find this miniature pair of cowboy boots, and I brought them home for Jeff the next day. (He's since outgrown them, but he still keeps them tucked away on top of his dresser as a memento.)

Once the three of us were back home in Clarkson, there was never any question of Shirley going back to work. As a matter of fact, she'd left Bell Telephone about a year before we were married, and quit her job as a receptionist in a motor parts company in London just before the wedding. I'm happy to say that was a decision that was entirely mutual; Shirley had always told me that she wanted to devote all her time to being a wife and mother, and that was very much the way I wanted things, too.

Again, I realize there are many families in which both parents have jobs; and if that works for them, fine. For our family, though, I felt it was tremendously important for a young child to have his mom around all the time; and later on, when he started school, it was essential for him to know that he could come home and call out for her, knowing even before she answered that she was there.

Two years after we brought Jeff home, we had a second son, Gregory, who was born April 16, 1965 (hearing his name all spelled out like that will probably make him laugh, since we all call him Greg!). Our youngest son, Mark, was born September 18, 1967 (our project for Canada's centennial celebrations!).

Let me tell you a little about each of the boys when they were very young; and so there'll be no hurt feelings about whom I describe first, we'll go in chronological order.

Jeff was always an outdoors type of kid, the kind you knew right off wasn't going to be happy later on if he had a nine-to-five office job. As soon as he could walk, he could run; and from the very beginning, he seemed to have absolutely no fear of any kind of outdoor activities. Except for one: swimming. At least, that's what we thought at first.

You see, one of our neighbors was a professional swimmer who suggested, when Jeff was about three years old, that we bring him over to a pool on Lakeshore Boulevard so she could give him lessons. What happened was that Jeff spent the entire time in the water yelling, kicking and screaming so that everybody in the entire pool looked around to see what was wrong. I thought I'd really done it now — made Jeff afraid of the water.

On our way home, I decided we'd stop at a neighbor's house, where they had a pool in the back yard. Maybe he'd feel a little more comfortable if we didn't push him but just let him get used to being around the water for awhile. The next thing we knew, he'd jumped right in, all by himself, and

211

started waving his hands around just the way he'd been shown. "Look, Daddy, I'm swimming!" he shouted. He hadn't been afraid at all; Jeff just made up his mind that he was going to swim when he was good and ready, and not a moment before.

As a youngster, Jeff had quite a bit of trouble with a bronchial condition; at the first sign of a cold, his bronchial tubes would swell so badly that he couldn't breathe, and had to be rushed to the hospital to get oxygen. These attacks used to happen so frequently that we finally had to set up an intercom in his room in case he got sick in the middle of the night after we'd fallen asleep.

Jeff was seeing several doctors at the time, and at one point I became so worried that I demanded to know whether any of them had ever even talked to each other in an attempt to find a solution to Jeff's problem. Finally, one night when we'd rushed him to the hospital absolutely gasping for breath, we met a doctor there, Dr. Leslie Dennis, who recommended a certain medicine; after taking it, Jeff never had to go back to the hospital again. (I'm delighted to add that Dr. Dennis is still our family doctor to this day.)

The other characteristic we noticed with Jeff from a very early age was how easily and how well he got along with other kids; sort of a natural leader. Whenever there was some kind of expedition to go out and climb trees or hop over the creek, you'd be sure to find Jeff right in the middle of it. What's more, most of his friends were a lot older than he was; even when he was just a tyke of seven or eight, most of his pals would be the bigger kids, almost in their teens.

Greg was quite a different kind of kid. While Jeff had been a holy terror as a baby, awake yelling all night, Greg was absolutely quiet and placid; you'd just put him down in his crib, and he'd sleep away, perfectly happy and content.

Where Jeff was a lot like Shirley, comfortable and at ease with just about anybody, Greg took more after me. Very shy, and a bit of a loner, he seemed to be happiest when he was alone in his room, playing with his toys, especially his Leggo set. He was an absolute wizard with that toy; he could build just about anything. I remember one day, after we all watched the first moon rocket being launched on television, Greg disappeared into his room with his Leggo set and re-emerged shortly afterward with a perfect reconstruction of that rocket, complete to the launching pad and all three stages. We were all amazed!

Like me, Greg was late in learning to talk, and when he was very little, Jeff seemed to do all the talking for him. "Mom, Greg wants the ketchup," Jeff would say, as Greg stared silently at his hot dog. Funny thing was, Jeff was almost always right!

At one point, Shirley and I became a little concerned that Greg still wasn't talking, so we started to wonder if he might have a hearing problem; but the tests they did at the Milton School for the Deaf showed that his ears were just fine. "Greg just seems to have more of an affinity for visual contact," one of the doctors told us. "Don't worry; he'll talk when he's ready." Sure enough, just a few months later, Greg started to talk.

An independent type of boy, Greg was also extremely tender-hearted, particularly toward anyone who had problems or was in trouble. He loved animals, especially the underdog type; if you showed Greg ten puppies, he'd pick out the one with an ear missing. Animals responded to him, too; I remember one time Greg came into the house with Shirley, who was absolutely amazed. "You know that dog up the street who's always barking and growling at everyone?" she asked. (I recall crossing the street many a time to avoid that particular canine!) "Well, Greg just walked straight up to him and held out his hand, and that dog started wagging his tail like Greg was his best friend!"

Mark, our youngest boy, was really a fast starter: by the time he was 10 months old, he was already walking, and it became clear very early in his childhood that he was going to be a natural athlete. Whatever the sport, he seemed to take to it: running, baseball, and especially hockey, which he started at about six years of age. All three of the boys were good hockey players, but Mark just seemed to have that little something extra, maybe because he was determined not to take a back seat to his brothers, even though they were older and more experienced.

Hockey was a very serious pursuit for Mark, even when he was just starting out; he'd be in his room getting ready hours before the game, and he always wanted to be at the arena early to practise his skating and shooting. Many of the coaches told us that Mark had the talent to be a professional player, and for awhile, we thought that was the direction he was going to take.

Along with his athletic interests, Mark also showed artistic ability, especially when it came to drawing designs for cars and motors, which really interested him.

Of the three boys, Mark was what you'd call the home-body. He loved being around the house, especially when we'd light the fire in the evenings; and if he did go out to play, I could just about set my watch by his return, only he'd usually be a few minutes early!

Well, if I go on talking about my kids, I'll probably have them right through school and into their own careers without saying another word about my own development as a country performer! That's the thing, though; once I get started talking about our family life, it's hard to stop, simply because our relationship with each other is what I've most treasured in my life. I'll have a great deal more to tell you about Shirley and the boys, and all the memories we've shared; first, though, I think I'd better bring you up to date on what was going on with my career back in Toronto.

In the sixties, the whole feeling of radio seemed to change; it was becoming faster-paced, with many more commercials per hour of radio time. I sensed what the demands would be on us as performers, and I knew we had to alter the format of the show somewhat. But while I understood that we couldn't go back to the Melody Ranch idea and do a Gene Autry type of show, I didn't want to move us into the Top 40, either. Sure, we had to move with the times, but if the show wasn't going to reflect my country music identity, there wouldn't be much point in calling it The Tommy Hunter Show.

What I thought we needed on the show was more depth. I asked the network if we could get a researcher to work with me; someone who could find the kinds of resource material I knew would breathe fresh air and excitement into the show. Audiences were changing, tastes were shifting, and radio stations, especially at the network level across Canada, wanted to respond to these changes. I felt that my idea of creating a show that had the intimacy of a local station, along with the scope and depth that a network could provide, would work very well in this changing climate. All I needed was the material I could use to give this idea substance in our scripts. I needed to know, for example, if there was a blizzard in Calgary, a thunderstorm in Halifax and a hailstorm in Montreal; all at the same time, so that any station, anywhere in the country, would get the feeling from our broadcast that it could be happening locally, even though it was actually coming from Toronto.

The network decided not to give me a researcher, but they did agree that I needed some help to cope with the pressures of having to write all the shows myself. They decided that the show should get a full-time writer. I knew just whom I wanted, too; a man by the name of Chris Bearde, who was fairly new in town and was doing a local television show called Nightcap.

Now, Chris was a fairly offbeat kind of guy, and people used to tune in his show sometimes just to see how bizarre it could get; but I'd met Chris a few times and really liked him. I felt that if he worked on our show, five days a week, I'd be able to establish a really good rapport with him.

I was able to get Chris on the show; and at first, he had a tendency to write scripts that were, well just a little too contrived and artsy for my taste (and, more importantly, the audience's tastes). I finally hit on a strategy that I felt would help. One day, literally five minutes before we were supposed to go on the air, I walked over, grabbed the script, ripped it up into little pieces right in front of him, and asked him to go write me another opening.

"Right now?" he asked, incredulous.

"Yep," I said. "Go to it."

Well, Chris didn't have much choice, so he raced over to his desk and started writing . . . He finished just as I was still singing my first song, and as I concluded the last chorus, he came panting over and handed me the opening. It was absolutely great! Then, while we did the next section of the show, back he went to the typewriter to do the rest of the script, all of which was equally terrific.

Now, that might sound like a pretty drastic method of achieving a goal, but I knew that Chris would come through with the right kind of script if I put him under that kind of pressure. You just can't get cutesy when you're facing a deadline (as any newspaper reporter will tell you!), and I was confident that Chris was a good enough writer that his true talents would emerge if he didn't have the time to dream up something overly clever.

After the show, Chris and I got a couple of cups of coffee and sat down with that script he'd literally done on the run, just so we could analyze what had happened with the writing. We both saw how much more straightforward and sincere it sounded the second way, and from that day on, Chris always wrote good, imaginative yet simple scripts that took us pleasantly from song to song and fit in beautifully with the overall format of our show.

Still, I don't think we ever did fall in line with all the changes that were happening on network radio at the time. It wasn't just that the shows were faster-paced; there were more commercials, and they were being done without the strong connection between the sponsors and the programs, which I felt so positively about.

We continued for about another year and then, in 1965, our radio show came to an end.

Still, I have a lot of very fond memories of our show, and the terrific people I worked with; and I've remained a big fan of radio to this day.

Our radio show wasn't the only casualty of the changes that were transforming the whole environment of broadcasting back in the 1960s; unfortunately, Country Hoedown was also undergoing some drastic alterations.

Unlike the radio show, where at least we'd had a chance to get involved in what was happening to the show, none of us who were performers on Hoedown really had much of a say in what was going on; and I can't say we liked these new developments.

It wasn't just all the dancing and choreography that we'd joked about for the past couple of years; the whole atmosphere and feeling of Hoedown was beginning to change. The producers took away our simple, straightforward backdrop and came up with a very modern-looking set with almost an art-nouveau look to it; and the writers started creating more and more sophisticated skits and sketches for us to do, as if our main job were to be actors instead of country musicians and singers.

As a result, all of us started feeling a lot more awkward; we were totally out of our element, so that the very natural, spontaneous way we related to one another slowly began to disappear. We just weren't having fun the way we did in the early years of the show, and I'm sure the audiences noticed the difference; in all the personal appearances we'd done across the country, the one thing that everyone used to mention was that *they* enjoyed Country Hoedown so much because *we* all seemed to be having such a good time up on the stage.

We all tried talking to the producers about our concern that Hoedown was getting farther and farther away from its country roots (and its fans), but they were convinced that the show needed more variety and sophistication as much as we were sure of our point of view; and ultimately, they were the ones making the decisions.

We went on that way for several months, all of us aware that Country Hoedown was slipping badly. Finally, we got the word that our show was being cancelled, after nine years on network television.

All of us had been through a lot together, and when Hoedown ended, we all felt as if we were losing part of our own family.

For awhile there, I wasn't sure what was going to happen next; it looked like I might just have to start all over again at square one. We'd all been hearing some rumors that the CBC was considering offering me a show of my own, but I wasn't about to get all excited about that until (and unless) it became a reality.

Finally, I got the official word: The Tommy Hunter Show would be starting in the fall of 1964.

After the decision was announced, I was very excited, of course, at the prospect of getting my own show on network television; Shirley was thrilled for me, and so were our parents. After the initial excitement had worn off, though, I realized that I had a lot of very serious work cut out for me.

All the shows I'd seen at the London Arena were very much on my mind, as well as all the fun times we'd had doing Country Hoedown; and from the start of the Hunter show, the CBC and I agreed what direction the show should begin with, and in what direction it was headed.

I was very happy with the people we brought together to perform as regulars on the show. I'd suggested that we bring the Rhythm Pals over to television from the radio show, because I knew the viewers would enjoy Mike, Marc and Jack doing their great Western songs. Along with the Pals, the cast included Al Cherny, the country fiddler whom I knew well also after our fun times during the days of the CKNX Barn Dance in Wingham. Then, we added Maurice Bolyer, who played an excellent four-string banjo and was a talented and versatile musician, and a duo called the Allen Sisters.

As far as a writer, I felt that Chris Bearde was the natural choice, since we'd worked together for almost a year on the radio, and I knew Chris had a clear idea of what would be comfortable for us. But because of his involvements and busy schedule, Chris couldn't do the show; he stayed in Toronto for awhile, doing Nightcap, then moved on to a successful career in Hollywood, where he wrote the Andy Williams Show and the Sonny and Cher Show. The writer who was chosen for us was Bob Arnott, a talented person who had worked on our radio show, first as engineer and then as producer, before becoming a television writer.

Our first producer on the show was Dave Thomas, who had been producing Country Hoedown in its last few years. Now, Dave was an extremely talented professional who helped me a great deal in many ways. He noticed I was still having some trouble with grammar and vocabulary, and Dave thought it would be a good idea for me to take some lessons in enunciation and other speaking techniques; he suggested his brother, an English teacher. I decided to take his advice and went for tutoring; Dave's brother helped me by encouraging me to read different books and find new ways of expressing myself. All that gave me a lot more confidence when I spoke.

One thing I wanted very much for our show as it got started was a different look to the packaging of a country show; I wanted to get away from the stigma of a barnyard, or any other clichés. At the same time that our show started, there were already quite a few programs beginning to make their way across the border as more powerful antennas were developed in the United States; so where the CBC used to be all on its own, it was now up against the U.S. networks.

Big, lavish productions with 23 dancers and dozens of skits were definitely not the answer; I'd certainly found out, during those last few years of Country Hoedown, how poorly that approach worked and how much out of character it was for a country show. On the other hand, I instinctively felt that if we stayed in the barn, we'd never last a month against some of the high-powered U.S. shows that were attracting thousands, even millions, of viewers.

I figured the best setting for us would be one in which we were all comfortable: warmth, coziness, an atmosphere in which all of us would feel very much at home. That way, we wouldn't need production numbers; we could have a show that led from Point A to Point B without any needless clutter. If we had surroundings that encouraged us all to enjoy doing our music, people would enjoy inviting us into their living rooms on a Friday evening, and we hoped the folks who invited us once would enjoy having us enough to ask us back *every* Friday night!

If we showed the folks a well-produced, professional look-ing show with good country music done in an appealing way, I figured we could communicate our music to thousands of people who'd never before watched a country show, but who enjoyed the music of artists like Eddy Arnold, Jim Reeves, the Anita Kerr Singers, and Tennessee Ernie Ford. Now, Jim Reeves is every bit as much a country boy as Grandpa Jones, and Jim and many others have done a lot to break down the barriers that separated country music from a wider listening audience. I felt we could do the same thing on television, with the right setting and the right people.

Dave Thomas and I came up with the idea of a millhouse, with an old winding staircase, large brick fireplace, and win-dows showing the outline of the old mill wheel outside. In-side were comfortable chairs with cozy cushions, and a warm, homey atmosphere. It gave a new look to country shows; a real nice setting for the entertainers, and one that would allow the audience to enjoy the show without it being pigeonholed from the word go.

This approach, we hoped, would bring in a larger audience of country fans as well as many others who just wanted to watch a very entertaining show. As well, we'd be able to get a good, strong start in the midst of all the competition in Cana-dian and American television programming.

Note the airplane. An interest in flying started early
with two of my sons.

A happy outing with my sons.

Mark

Jeff

Greg

Al Cherny has been with the Tommy Hunter Show from the beginning.

Donna and LeRoy Anderson have been regulars since 1975.

CBC Radio's Tommy Hunter Show, with the Rhythm Pals, Al Harris and Bruce Smith.

Above On the set of the Tommy Hunter Show.

Left The Tommy Hunter Show, 1979. Carroll Baker, Tommy Hunter, Donna Anderson.

Hank Snow is a very dear friend. This photo was
taken in the mid-1970s. I recently performed at his
70th birthday party in Nashville.

Above Bill Bessey, Ernest Tubb, Slim Gorden, Tommy Hunter. This photo was taken back stage during the radio show "Country Holiday" I put together with the CBC.

Left With Gordie Tapp. Our "homecoming" in London, Ontario, prior to our show for Prince Philip.

Celebrating twenty years of the Tommy Hunter Show on the CBC.

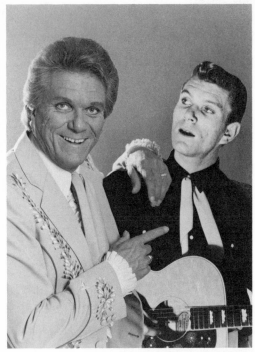

With a blow-up of myself twenty years ago.

I received the Academy of Country Music Entertainers Hall of Honor Award from ACME director Gordon Burnett (left). Charley Pride (right) looks on.

With Kris Kristofferson.

With the Gatlin Brothers.

CHAPTER 9

"The Valley of the Shadow"

T hinking back on our very first show, I'm suddenly reminded of a funny little incident that happened, and I'd like to tell you about it.

Dave Thomas thought it would be a great idea for one of our numbers to involve the Rhythm Pals doing a song called "Stampede," which was a really dramatic western song that lent itself to just the kind of major production which was so popular around the CBC back in those days. Seeing as it was our debut show, everybody really got their teeth into this one.

First the writer got a hold of the song, and he created what had to be the second largest stampede that's ever occurred in the history of the Western world. Then, the set department took over, and by the time they got done, we had a working-size ranch set up in Studio Seven, complete with chuck-wagon, covered wagon, horses, a campfire with all our saddles laid out around it, and even a kettle, pots and pans over the fire. Not to be outdone, the special effects department was standing by with smoke and dust machines; sound effects was ready with a soundtrack that gave the impression of a herd of at least 10,000 head of cattle, and there was even a film clip that showed footage from an actual stampede.

The director was all set to shoot an epic that would make

the best of Cecil B. DeMille pale by comparison. We'd all be around the campfire, singing away, when suddenly in the middle of the song, there's a flash of lightning . . . the cattle are getting restless . . . more lightning . . . the cattle start running . . . and someone cries out: "STAMPEDE!!" One of us douses the fire; the rest of us make a grab for chairs, pots, pans, dishes; we pile into the wagon and get all ready to hightail it out of camp just as the thundering herd bears down on us.

Well, we rehearsed all our movements a couple of times, and everything seemed fine, but we figured it'd be a good idea to try it out with all the special effects too; so we started again from the top.

Three . . . two . . . one . . . Cue the music . . . ACTION! Away we went, and we were about halfway through the song when the yell came: STAMPEDE!! Time for the smoke, and I'll tell you, the operator must have *really* wanted to try out the full potential of that smoke machine, because within five seconds none of us could even see our hands in front of us. Mike desperately tried to pile pots and pans into the wagon, with half of them falling out onto the stage. "There you go, Mike," shouted Jack, tossing one of the saddles in the general direction of the wagon, which was barely visible by then. Well, that huge saddle hit Mike so hard that he tumbled headlong out of the wagon, shrieking with laughter.

"Turn off the smoke!" shouted the floor director. "Turn it off!"

But clouds of dust kept billowing into the studio and all we could see was this great white fog, with the faint outlines of the Rhythm Pals tossing plates, spoons, knives, the kettle; anything they could grab hold of. Meanwhile, there in the corner lay the even more blurred image of a figure (me!) shaking helplessly with laughter.

A lot of the tension we'd all been feeling about that first show went up with all the smoke; it really was a hilarious sight to see.

You know, that little incident gave us the same feeling I remembered so well on Country Hoedown: the sense of being a family. That was just one of the positive elements we began with on the Hunter show.

We began as a 30-minute show, and one of the last CBC shows to be broadcast live, something which I wanted to continue as long as possible. I've always loved live television, and the magical flow of adrenalin we always felt after all the rehearsal and preparations came to life. Sometimes the cameras would break, or the lights would explode right in the middle of the live performance; other times, you might find yourself in the middle of a song with the band going east while you went west; still other times, you might be left with only two seconds at the close of the show, when you'd planned to speak for two minutes. Those were the real tests for us all; to overcome such unexpected incidents somehow and make everything come out right, all within the 30-minute framework.

In the history of live television, there are hundreds of stories like those: stories of how things went wrong, how they were corrected, and how much everyone enjoyed the whole process.

The difference between our live shows and the prerecording that came later was that the urgency of those early days was no longer there. You could always do the show over again if something went wrong; and while the mistake may have been corrected, there wasn't that natural flow of energy you had when you didn't know what was going to happen next; instead, prerecording gave you the feeling that you could always go back and do it over. To this day, many television shows tape entire sections of songs together, right from commercial to commercial, in order to give the performers the feeling of excitement generated on a live show, which builds naturally to communicate to an audience.

I think it's important for a performer to know that if there's a mistake, he or she will appear on the air that way regardless of the presence of machines like VTRs. With this awareness comes a sense of excitement, energy and honesty that is fantastic; and the audience feels it, too.

From the point of view of the writer, producer and set

designer, there's also an urge to take out all the needless clutter and make things very simple, so that they all can be sure it's going to work. The lights are simple, the sets are simple, and the performer does the material he or she is completely comfortable with; there just isn't the time to light and re-light the set, or move the performer around a lot. Now, when everything is made that simple, there's nothing left but for the performer's ability to come shining through.

Some of you may remember the way situation comedies once used canned laughter, until viewers started noticing there was something wrong. The viewers might not have singled out the prerecorded laughter, but the people putting the shows together saw what was being lost in prerecording, so they recaptured the feeling of live television by taping their shows in front of a live studio audience. What developed was a 30-minute televised theatre production; the performers knew they had to deliver their lines to a live audience, and the excitement that had been missing was revived.

Another change we all went through was the move from black-and-white to color. On black-and-white television, everything was accomplished through lights and shadows; there might be a completely flat set, with just a single tree and a fence set diagonally to create depth. You always looked for depth, angles, perspective: the shadows playing across a face, the sense of distance projected by an angle.

Color television changed everything: the clothing, the brighter lights; even the shades of makeup and the kinds of material used for costumes. With black-and-white, the illusion of dimension and perspective could be created, for example, just by placing posts at certain angles along a six-foot fence; as a result, that relatively short fence would seem to stretch for miles. With the advent of color, what emerged was the pure enjoyment of seeing, for the first time, something like Arthur Godfrey's bright red hair (or my blonde hair). You could see skin colors; you could get a real kick out of all the shades of the clothing.

Now, it became even more fun to watch something like a

square dance, seeing all the girls in their bright ginghams, and the guys in co-ordinating plaids. If I wore a blue suit, that could be picked up by using the same shades in the background; and there didn't seem to be the same need for sets, since those co-ordinated blues would create a set in themselves.

At about this time, our show made another giant leap, from 30 to 60 minutes; and we moved from Studio Four to Studio Seven, the big CBC network studio in Toronto, which had much more modern facilities. With the advent of prerecording and color, and with double the time we'd had before, there was a lot more for us to play with. We'd taken our show out of the barn, while still doing country; but, because of our comfortable setting, many different kinds of guests could fit comfortably into our show. I still wanted *country* performers coming into our setting.

The combination of new techniques like color, and an extended time period in which to use them, produced a natural tendency to make a *great* deal of use of these innovations. It was a bit like a kid who's suddenly handed the keys to a huge, brand-new toy store.

Also, we had the kind of flexibility that encourages experimentation. I didn't always have to stand in one spot; we didn't have a large orchestra that was limited to black-tie styles of dress, and there was the kind of overall mobility that allowed for square dancing, and other elements of production, like illustrating a Western song with the beautiful shades of an Alberta sky, the moon in the background, and all of us gathered around a campfire.

Our situation being what it was — a longer show, which had techniques like color and prerecording but didn't have the budget for many guests — we gradually began experimenting with elements of production that slowly built into features. First, it'd be time to salute the West; we'd have a medley, with gorgeous scenery and costumes. Then, we'd portray the Maritimes; then, other Canadian songs; then, pioneer songs, of course with the use of period-style costumes. The logical next step was to try the Broadway style of something like Oklahoma; and this meant a natural flow into more and more production.

Very gradually, things were getting more sophisticated; more emphasis was placed on the sets, and while I agreed with the new approach, I also had this gut feeling of wanting to draw us back to a comfortable setting.

First, there were more suggestions that it would be funny for us to put on different costumes once in awhile; then, it was suggested that we do a little skit from time to time. The Rhythm Pals were occasionally asked to do a Mills Brothers song instead of a Western song, and Al Cherny, a very good natural comedian, was encouraged to do just a little more comedy and a little less fiddling. When we started having guests on our show, it'd maybe be someone like Frankie Laine or Moms Mabley, fine performers in their own right, but who might not exactly reflect the simple, warm atmosphere and country traditions we'd started out with.

As we moved gradually into more productions of that kind, I started to feel a little awkward, because it seemed that the very naturalness we'd had was becoming secondary to the direction we were headed. While I felt we could use such innovations as color and prerecording to enhance the honesty and believability of our show, it seemed we were starting to use these innovations for their own sake. We were doing more highly staged productions, but we were losing the enthusiasm; the sparkle in Al Cherny's eyes when he played the fiddle; and the great sound and feeling the Rhythm Pals created when they did Western songs. For those who know me, I'm not a lot different off the air than on, and this naturalness started to fade. I felt awkward putting on a costume, being choreographed and staged, and portraying someone other than Tommy Hunter.

What I'd gained in my own experience was an understanding of what I felt comfortable with as a performer: the kind of music I'd grown up on, presented in a simple and enjoyable fashion. That's what I wanted to bring to television: an individual believing in his music and surroundings, and conveying that feeling of believability to his audience.

To communicate this feeling in our complex medium of television, however, I knew that everyone on the show had to be in tune and share the same goals. It wasn't a question of one person being right and the other one wrong; all I knew was that if we didn't feel at home on our show, the audience would perceive our discomfort just as surely as if we were walking around in shoes a size too small, with a look of pain clearly written on our faces.

That's exactly the situation in which I found myself in later years; there I was, surrounded by talented individuals who could not relate to my world. It was like being a simple country doctor at a convention of heart surgeons; we could all agree on the basic principles of medicine, but as soon as we turned to heart surgery, we were no longer speaking the same language. All our production team knew what went into making a successful show, and we could all agree that we wanted to create the very best television show going, but when we turned towards more complex productions, we were no longer speaking the same language.

After a few years, I felt the show was becoming more and more unrecognizable; color and production were replacing the honesty and believability we'd started out with. I'd find myself turning to the left and the right, and finding very little understanding of Jim Reeves, Ernest Tubb, Grandpa Jones or Roy Acuff, just as I knew very little about big bands or Broadway-type productions. We were coming at it from totally different backgrounds and perspectives.

I found myself gradually trying to express some of my own concerns about the direction the show was taking; I'd suggest that perhaps I could just pick up the guitar once in awhile. It was fine to do a little sketch occasionally, but let's not lose sight of our honesty, believability and comfortableness by camouflaging them behind too many productions.

The show had my name on it, and I wanted to have a certain influence in the direction it was going, but I guess you might say I was more of a figurehead than anything else, and this was not a role I either liked or wanted.

It was hard for me to express some of these concerns. I'd

had nine years of television experience on Country Hoedown, but at that time, I was part of a closely-knit group of performers who depended on each other for support; for example, if one of us had trouble on a particular song, we always knew that the others were right there to back us up with emotional support. There wasn't the immense feeling of responsibility on my shoulders, which I experienced for the first time when our show started. All of a sudden, I was called on to be the host, the singer, and the announcer; this was an entirely new experience for me, and one which I took extremely seriously. I recall that from the very first days our show was on the air, I felt it was very important for me as a host to make our regulars and guests feel as comfortable as possible. If it came to cutting the show, my part had to go, not theirs.

At the same time, while I was in the midst of all these efforts to become accustomed to my new role, I didn't yet have the confidence to insist on carrying out many of the ideas I had for the direction of our show, in order to create an environment in which all of us on the show would be comfortable.

I think it was my basic stubbornness about the music that I love that enabled me to impart a few (very few, at first) of my own ideas and concepts in those early weeks and months of our show. Most of the time, I didn't so much find acceptance for the approach I wanted; it was more that I sometimes was able to hold off the most glaring aspects of the major productions that seemed to be becoming an obsession on the part of the producers and directors.

One time, when we were rehearsing a group of songs for a show, I got into a discussion with the director and a few of the designers about a set they were planning to illustrate what we were singing. Somehow, I just knew that the choreography experts wouldn't be far behind; I felt I just *had* to convince them all not to go overboard on all the production and dance numbers, before it was too late. These were good songs, and they didn't need all that window dressing.

"I think this music stands up very well on its own, don't

you?" I asked, trying to be diplomatic. "We shouldn't really do anything more complicated than maybe just sitting around the piano and singing, or something like that, wouldn't you agree?"

"Yeah, well, who's going to play the piano?" the director asked. For a moment I was baffled; then the light bulb went on.

"I'll play the piano," I said. "Well, not actually *play* it, but I'll sit there and you can play a tape of an arpeggio in the right key; then I'll move my hands like I'm really playing."

Well, they agreed with that approach, so we went ahead and rehearsed it. Turned out that I did have to hit a few actual notes on the piano, just to give the Allen Sisters the right key before they started; then, as soon as they began singing, the engineer would roll the tape for the rest of the accompaniment. Anyway, they told me the notes I had to play, and I got some black tape to stick on the keys so I would be able to see where they were on the piano. So we got ready for the show that night, and I walked over to the piano with all the confidence in the world. "What would you like to sing for us tonight, girls?" I asked.

"Well, Tom," they said, "we'd like to do 'Your Cheating Heart'."

"That sounds great, girls," I said enthusiastically. "Now, just before we start, let me just give you the key," and I struck the notes I'd marked with the tape.

The only trouble was that some of the guys in the crew had shifted the pieces of tape! Well, nobody was more startled than I was to hear the out-of-tune chord come out of the piano, but we got back into the right key as soon as the recorded accompaniment came on, and everything went fine after that.

It wasn't so much the songs or the piano that were important; it was more the feeling of camaraderie and enjoyment that we hoped to convey to the audience, and that little mistake turned out to be something funny that the audience could enjoy.

A lot of the time, though, I'd be gaining an inch with suggestions like using the piano accompaniment, only to find myself losing a yard. You see, in those days, the producer was the one in control of the creative end of the show, so it was perfectly natural for him to revert back to the kind of atmosphere he was comfortable with. I guess he hoped I'd eventually get used to choreography and sets, but I didn't; if anything, I became more uncomfortable, and more convinced that somewhere beyond the sets and routines, there was somebody named Tommy Hunter, struggling to get out.

In the meantime, the discussions became more intense. The writers would present me with a very elaborate script, and I'd just shake my head. "I don't understand this at all."

"Well, see, Tommy," and they'd start explaining all the subtleties. We'd rehearse it again, and it still wouldn't make that much sense to me.

"Look," I'd say, "I've been standing here for an hour, and I still don't get it. Do you really think the audience is going to understand it? Why don't we just try something simpler?"

"Oh, well, you don't want to be talking down to your audience, Tommy," they'd say.

I'd stand there and try to imagine Mom or the neighbors attempting to figure out what the hell I was talking about, and I'd just draw a complete blank. Talking down to the audience? I couldn't see how it was insulting to make your show easy for people to understand. I mean, this was supposed to be a relaxing and entertaining program for folks to watch on a Friday night, after a hard week's work; I wasn't under the impression that we were supposed to be presenting a university course in higher philosophy. Well, sometimes I'd get my way and we'd be able to rewrite the script so that someone with less than a PhD degree could understand it; but it was always a fight for every little phrase in that script that I wanted just faintly to resemble my own identity as a performer and the tastes of our audience.

Musically, I found myself beginning to run into the same sorts of conflicts. As time went on, our band steadily expanded into a bigger orchestra. Once again, I'm not detracting from the talent that existed in the orchestra; these were some of the finest musicians around, the cream of the crop. The only problem was that the crop was being harvested from an entirely different field than the one I'd grown up in. When I was singing a country song, I'd hear this jazzed-up sound, and it fit my music just about as well as a pair of patent leather shoes fits a country boy heading into town for the Saturday night dance.

Well, I'd just ask the arranger if he could take out the brass and give me a steel guitar, fiddle, bass and drums, which I felt better suited me and the music. But they heard it one way, and I heard it completely differently. They were raised on "Starlight Serenade" and I was raised on "Wabash Cannonball."

Now, I had learned, by this point in my career, that a performer isn't always the best judge of what works well for him; I'm sure many of you have heard singers being interviewed about their latest hit records, and they've often said that they didn't even think the songs were all that great when they first heard them. Well, very often the performer works with that song and sticks with it because of a producer's confidence in him and the song; later on, it turns out to be a big hit and it's primarily because of the trust and rapport that developed between the performer and producer.

So when I talk about going against some of a producer's ideas, I didn't do that in order to stay within the confines of a narrow little world. I had lots of ideas about our show that I wanted to share and express; how we could take country music out of the barn and present it to television viewers in an entirely new way which would be relaxed and entertaining without getting away from the basic roots of our music.

The trouble was that I couldn't even get to square one in explaining my concepts, because the two of us were coming at the whole show from two different approaches. Only it was my name coming up on the screen every Friday night, and I felt a great deal of responsibility for what we were presenting. The longer we went on, the more nervous and worried I became about meeting my responsibility in the environment that was being pushed on our show. I started to feel that with the host playing all kinds of parts, the audience wouldn't really know just who I was any more, and I knew they wouldn't like that feeling any more than I did.

One idea that I'd been trying to get away from for months was the suggestion that I should sing a song called "Trouble in River City" on the show.

Every couple of weeks, the idea would come up at a program meeting, and I'd try to fight it, but I knew that, eventually, I'd walk in and find "Trouble in River City" staring me right in the face. That's exactly what finally happened.

Once again, there I was, faced with doing a song that was all wrong for me, but absolutely perfect as far as the producer was concerned. Well, we discussed it endlessly, and this time, he insisted that I do the song. So I buckled down and tried to learn it, and let me tell you, it was quite a struggle.

Anyway, I finally learned the song and memorized all the lyrics, only to find out in rehearsal that there was more in store for me: all kinds of staging, and then, to add insult to injury, they said it had to be prerecorded and lip-synched.,

I felt our audience and I had been done a disservice; I think that Dave Thomas' sincere belief in my ability to do this performance was very flattering. "Once you get over this hurdle, you can do anything," as Dave said. The point was, I sincerely and honestly felt it was wrong for me, and I felt (and still feel) that the audience sees me singing "Don't Let the Stars Get in Your Eyes," not "Trouble in River City."

After the show was over, Dave and I discussed my triumphant leap over the hurdle, and I said that the only thing I felt I'd accomplished was memorizing the lyrics of a difficult song. Other than that, I thought the whole exercise was a waste of time.

Ned Powers, a columnist in Saskatoon, wrote some interesting comments in his column the next day; he said that he just couldn't understand why Tommy Hunter was being given material that was so unsuited to him, like "Trouble in River City."

Ned Powers now visits Toronto each year to attend the CBC's fall launching party, and each year, I saunter by, laughing and singing a few bars of "Trouble in River City." I've always appreciated the honest observations Ned made in that article, and I've thanked him many a time for making them.

The only thing I figured I could do was to keep pushing for the kind of show I knew was right for me. Little by little, I began to get more confidence in expressing my point of view, almost as if all these negative experiences were just serving to strengthen my convictions about the kind of show I wanted. Even "Trouble in River City" turned out to be an experience I could learn from, if only to show me very clearly a path I wanted to avoid.

So what I wanted to do was to try to get more involved in the day-to-day decisions of the show. I met with the writers in the planning stages, where the creative ideas begin.

It's not that I was off on some giant ego trip about getting my way as the star of the show; I just wanted a show where we could all work together as a team dedicated to creating the best country music program and the most welcoming atmosphere for our guest artists. I felt that all of us — myself, Al, the Rhythm Pals and all our regulars, along with the producer, the crew and everybody behind the scenes — had to be on the same wavelength for this to happen.

I knew this wasn't all going to come together overnight. Again, it was a constant battle to gain even a few inches of ground, and I intensely disliked the feeling of having to struggle so hard to achieve something that was very natural to me. I didn't want to be in the position of telling the producer, "I'm right and you're wrong." It wasn't a question of right and wrong; it was a matter of feeling comfortable.

For example, I wanted very much to close our show with a song of inspiration, or a reading, because that was something I'd grown up with; a totally normal and natural extension of my identity. On the other hand, the feeling around me was that it would be better to end with a peppy, upbeat song.

The songs of inspiration and readings I have done in recent years on our television show have been among the most important parts of our show to our viewers, and extremely meaningful to me personally. I believe that the reason for their success is the total conviction I have in these songs and readings. All I've ever been after in those songs and readings is a simple, clear little story that, for example, communicates to a young couple just starting out in a marriage, or parents whose children are moving away from home for the first time: something all our viewers can relate to, and something that is a sincere expression of my own experience.

Another time, I attended a writers' meeting to find they'd come up with a really interesting idea that had gone off track somewhere down the line. I thought it was such a good idea that it was worth taking some time trying to rework some parts of it, and the writers finally agreed. "Okay, give it a try," they said.

I called Shirley to say I'd be fairly late that night, rushed back to our office, sat down, and started in on that script, never stopping once until it was done. Must be getting late, I thought to myself, glancing at my watch; it was 5:30 in the morning! I decided to go home and have a shower, maybe grab a few minutes of sleep; but in spite of the fact that I carefully set the alarm, I woke up behind schedule and got into the studio about 20 minutes late.

Everyone was gathered in a tight little group, and there was an air of tension you could cut with a knife. I went over, holding the script, and began to explain what had happened, but before I could even finish my first sentence, the producer started up one side of me and down the other, and right in front of everybody.

I just stood there, feeling just about as small as I'd ever felt in my life, and waited for him to finish.

"What's more, Hunter," he concluded, topping off his tirade, "I'm filing a report with ACTRA (the Association of Canadian Television and Radio Artists) about your lateness!"

I honestly didn't think he was serious; but a few nights later, I received a notice from ACTRA advising me that I was being fined $50 for being late.

I can't tell you how angry I was; I mean, I'd been working 12-hour days and nights to do my very best for our show, and here I was being fined for coming in 20 minutes late after staying up all night to work on a script that I never should have had to rewrite in the first place! Well, I paced the house all night long, and at about 8 in the morning I finally got an official from the union on the phone.

"I don't think I should have to pay this fine," I said, explaining the circumstances of my being late.

"I'm sorry, Mr. Hunter," he said, "but you *are* being charged and you *will* pay the fine."

"Well, I'm not paying it."

"Tommy, I'm afraid that if the fine is not paid by the end of the week, we may have to consider cancelling the show."

"Okay," I said, my anger and frustration now at its height. "Just so you'll understand: for $50, I'm going to throw my entire career down the tubes."

"For $50 you'll throw your entire career down the tubes?" he repeated, bewildered.

"That's right," I said, "and I'll tell you, for *five cents* I'll throw my career down the tubes, because in this instance, I am right and you are wrong."

"Just remember," he added, "at the end of this week your career may come to an end. Is that what you really want?"

"Well, just you remember," I retorted, "there'll be musicians, directors, choreographers, all going down the tubes with me. Is that what you really want?"

To this day I have no idea what happened to that $50 fine, because there was never a peep about it from that day to this.

Not long after we'd all gotten over that little incident, a new little project was unloaded on us, and this time, try as I might, there was no persuading anybody to give up on this skit. "Rusty Rails" was going to be on our fall schedule, like it or not.

They had cast Paul Soles as the station master, one of the Allen Sisters as his wife and the other one as his young daughter, and then added Al Cherny as the hotblooded young bachelor and, unfortunately, myself as the dimwitted son. There you have a pretty clear idea of what we were dealing with.

I'll never forget the sinking feeling I got as the announcer proclaimed the start of that brand-new series: "And now, it's time for another episode of 'Rusty Rails'!"

If they'd set out to gather up every scrap of information about the type of television programming that I most detested, and rolled it all into 9-1/2 minutes, they couldn't have done more to horrify and devastate me than coming up with "Rusty Rails."

It seemed the viewing public was just as appalled as we were, because the negative mail started pouring in by the carload after that very first episode. Things got so heated that at one point, a Member of Parliament from northern Ontario finally made a protest in Ottawa because so many of his constituents had been complaining about "Rusty Rails."

One day, after about the second "Rusty Rail" sequence had been shown, I got a call from one of the network executives, Tom Benson. "How many episodes of that bloody "Rusty Rails" thing have you people taped?" he asked.

"I'm really not sure," I said. "I think we've done six."

"Well, we've got to put a stop to it," he said. "It's absolutely dreadful."

"Please, please," I begged, "put a stop to it!"

Tom then called our producer, and told him that "Rusty Rails" would have to be derailed; but the producer refused. Shortly afterward, we were told that there was going to be a staff change on our show.

Our new producer was a man by the name of Bill Lynn, who was doing his first stint as a producer at the CBC. Now, Bill was a very talented writer, but after working with him for a short time, it seemed to me that he wasn't the kind of person who could visualize what he wanted, which, in my opinion, is the main task of a producer.

Bill's attitude was to tell the wardrobe people or the set designers that they should make the decisions about what we should wear or how our sets should look on the show. "They're the experts," he would say. "How should I know what kind of suit Hunter should be wearing?"

Well, that kind of talk frightened me, because if the producer is not taking an interest in the details, then none of us were ever going to know just what we'd end up with as an overall show. With Dave, he always got involved in the specifics of the show, and if I didn't always agree with him, at least I knew where he was coming from on his decisions; so I'd have some sense of consistency on his part which we could then discuss and, hopefully, resolve to some extent.

Now I just didn't know where Bill was coming from, or where he was going; there was just one shock right on top of the next.

One time, I remember Bill rushing into my dressing room all excited about something: "Hey, Tommy, have you seen the set?"

"Not yet," I said, shuddering inwardly.

"Wow! I can't believe it! It's absolutely amazing!"

"How come you're so surprised?" I asked. "Isn't it the set you asked for in the first place?"

"No, of course not," he said, as if it was the most obvious thing in the world. "I just asked them to build a set, and they came up with it."

At this point, I knew I had to redouble my efforts to be on my guard: the sets, the writing, even the painting and carpentry had to be watched; otherwise, I might not know just what was going to turn up next.

So I went looking for this fabulous set Bill had been talking about, and I tracked it down just as the painters were getting started on it. Well, I got as far as the door of the paint department, anyway; and there I stood, speechless with shock. What I saw before me were some very modern-looking shapes painted in the wildest, brightest, most far-out colors I could imagine in my life.

I knew they were supposed to be Newfoundland fishing huts, but I just couldn't recognize them at all, and, I'll tell you, if the viewers from Newfoundland had seen that set on the air, they'd have been marching on Toronto the very next morning to string me up on the nearest telephone pole; and I wouldn't have blamed them, either!

"You can stop painting right now," I told the painter in

charge. "That isn't going on the show."

As it turned out, the set was redone, luckily for everyone.

One morning, the elevator door opened and out walked a man (let's call him Frank) who seemed to be suffering from the worst case of asthma in medical science; he was gasping for breath and turning beet-red with the effort of lifting these two gigantic steamer trunks that had to weigh at least a ton apiece.

"Oh, how do you do, Mr. Hunter," he said. "I've got an appointment to do an audition for your show, and I'm so thrilled to have this opportunity."

"What kind of act do you do, Frank?" I asked, as we helped him haul those trunks into the studio.

"I do rope tricks," he said, "and I juggle."

In my mind, I was already trying to picture what kinds of songs we could do around his act; maybe Al could play the fiddle or something while Frank juggled. I felt very sympathetic toward him, and I wanted to find him a place on the show without getting *too* far into the Ed Sullivan approach, where next we might be bringing out the dancing elephants!

Seemingly exhausted by the walk from the elevator to the studio, Frank sat down to rest for a few moments, wheezing and puffing. Finally, he reached into one of the trunks and pulled out two bowling alley tenpins. "I'll just warm up with these, if you don't mind, Mr. Hunter."

"Sure thing," I said, and stepped back to give him room.

Up went the two tenpins in the air, and with a wild grab, he managed to catch them, turning to me with an awkward smile.

"Don't worry, Frank," I said. "You're just a bit nervous. Take your time, now."

So he tried again, throwing one of the pins up in the air and catching it; then the other. He just couldn't manage to get both of them going at the same time, though, and finally he gave up and turned to me again.

"Hey, that's great," I said, trying to be as encouraging as possible while wondering at the same time where we were going next. Well, he reached into the trunk again and came up with two more tenpins. In my mind, I could just hear the roll of the drums . . . the moment of anticipation approaching . . . He got all four pins in place and now he was looking up to judge the distance . . . crouching down and getting ready to throw them . . . the tension was mounting . . .

Suddenly, he threw them, and down they came. One hit him on the head, another one bounced off his foot, the third clubbed him on the ear, and the fourth, by some fluke, landed in his outstretched hand before bouncing off his chest and onto the floor with a great clatter.

At this point, I wasn't sure whether Frank was trying to be funny. I didn't want to laugh for fear of embarrassing him, so I sort of sneaked a peek over in his direction. He was just standing there, wheezing helplessly, and his face was as red as a prize tomato. I felt like crying and laughing at the same time, and I just couldn't imagine what was going to come next.

"Mr. Hunter," he said, and I braced myself, "I'm going to do it blindfolded now."

Now I was totally baffled. He couldn't juggle two tenpins, he'd almost killed himself with four, and now he was going to try it blindfolded?

Over he walked with the blindfold, holding it out to me, and I had no choice but to tie the thing over his eyes.

Up went the pins again. Three of them scattered across the floor and by some miracle, he caught the fourth, turning around with a wide grin to show me he'd cut a hole in the blindfold (I shudder to think what might have happened if he'd *really* been blindfolded!).

Then came the rope — about 9,000 yards, by the looks of it. Frank pulled out a lasso and got it going around his feet, jumping in and out of the circle one foot at a time, to the accompaniment of wheezing, huffing and puffing. The faster he spun the rope, the harder he gasped for breath, until his face was so red that he could have gotten a job in a lighthouse as a beacon for incoming ships!

Finally, he launched into his last act by pulling out this gigantic rope which he proudly proclaimed as the world's largest lariat. "I'm the only person in the world who can do this trick," and at this stage of the game, none of us were inclined to disagree with him!

We all moved back against the wall of the studio to give him space; I mean, our studio on Sumach Street was fairly good-sized, but it would have taken an auditorium twice the size of Maple Leaf Gardens to accommodate *this* rope. Anyway, he got the lariat going, and it started to spread like a giant fan. We moved right up against the wall. Faster and faster it spun, and Frank's face was now turning such a shade of purple that I became fearful for his life. Now the lariat was spinning dangerously close to the giant pillars at either end of the studio . . .

Suddenly, the rope went completely off kilter and started winding itself with a vicious twist around Frank's neck; and in a few seconds, he was completely entwined in it.

We all rushed to his side, and under the layers of rope we could hear a muffled sound: "Uhhhh . . . uhhhh . . . uhhhh . . ." as Frank gasped for air. As quickly as we could, we got him all untangled and sat him down to have a rest.

"I'll let you know what the producer says," I told him as I escorted him to the elevator. "Thanks a lot for coming, Frank."

So far as I know, Frank was totally serious, but I'll tell you, it had to be one of the funniest acts I ever saw in my life, and I certainly hope he had the chance to present it somewhere.

Now that I think about it, Bill Lynn was a pretty funny guy himself; always doing some kind of pratfall in the studio, like falling off his chair over and over, until we were all laughing so hard that we practically couldn't go on with the rehearsal. One time, though, he went on with it so long that the floor director finally told him to leave the studio; can you imagine being thrown out of your own television studio?

Bill was always telling me that his claim to fame was once writing for the Ed Sullivan Show, and on one particular occasion when he was describing that experience, I couldn't resist putting in my own little comment.

"I wouldn't be too quick to tell people you wrote for Ed

Sullivan if I were you, Bill," I said, poker-faced. "I mean, they might wonder why anyone should earn good money to write: 'Wunnerful, just wunnerful' over and over again!"

"Hunter," he said, "do you want to hear this story or not?" He cast me a meaningful glance.

"Sure," I said, pretending not to notice the look. "That'd be just wunnerful!"

Well, it seemed that in later years, Sullivan never used to show up at rehearsals; he'd just arrive for the show and make like he was ad-libbing everything, even though the show had lots of writers and used cue cards. Anyway, one time the show was being broadcast out of Memphis and being transmitted back to New York. "Right here on our stage in Memphis, Tennessee," announced Sullivan, "we have for you the flying trapeze and helicopter artists . . ." and all of this was delivered in his usual deadpan style that so many viewers came to know and love over the years.

Then, the act began.

A helicopter came roaring over the ballpark where the show was being filmed, and the noise caught Sullivan's attention, so he looked up to see the cameras focus on a man emerging from the door, lowering a trapeze bar, and very slowly descending to the bar. All of a sudden, he's out on this bar, 900 feet in the air, doing twists and somersaults and hanging from his big toe! I mean, you have to understand that there were no nets for this act, so one false move and it was all over.

Sullivan gazed at this spectacle with his mouth hanging open from sheer amazement, as the helicopter descended to just above ground level and, with a thundering drum roll from the orchestra, the trapeze artist stepped onto the grass and bowed.

Now the camera moved slowly back to Sullivan's awe-struck face, and for a moment, it seemed he was totally at a loss for words. Finally, he turned toward the camera.

"That's the damndest act I've ever seen!"

I just thought that was a great story, especially since it was so different from the Ed Sullivan character most people were

249

used to. I'll never forget the time he appeared on the CBC during their fall launch; that time, his actions were a great deal more familiar.

Every autumn the CBC would do a week of previews as part of the presentation of that year's upcoming programs; each night, there'd be highlights of the various shows. On Friday night, we had our turn, so we showed some special clips from our show and then I came out to greet the station owners and representatives in the audience who'd come from all over Canada. "Thank you, ladies and gentlemen," I said, "We're happy to welcome you to Toronto and we're looking forward to a great new season on our show," and that was it.

Well, come Sunday night, the announcer walked out. "Well, everyone knows that Sunday night means The Toast of the Town, and ladies and gentlemen, here he is, the toast of television, Mr. Ed Sullivan!" Nobody had expected Sullivan to be part of the fall launch, so when he walked out like that, the entire audience broke into tumultuous applause.

Thank you, thank you," he said, staring out into the audience. Just then, he noticed a group of musicians sitting in the front row. "I bring you greetings from Local 149 in New York," he continued, looking at them.

Well, that seemed like an odd thing to say, considering that the audience was full of the most important people in the entire Canadian television industry and Sullivan chose to talk about the New York local of the musician's union! Still, those kinds of remarks were very much in his style, and viewers came to appreciate them over the years.

It was at functions like these that I had the opportunity to meet some of the panel members of the public affairs show, Front Page Challenge, which was (and still is) one of the most popular programs on television. Up until then, I'd never really met many people who worked at the network outside our own show, because most of the departments, like news, variety and drama, were kept separate from each other except on such occasions as fall launchings and press parties.

I was scheduled to appear on Front Page Challenge to

publicize the brand-new Polaroid Land Camera. It was close to Christmas, and the Polaroid company had bought time on our show and Front Page Challenge; and what they wanted Fred Davis and myself to do on each of our shows was to go through the commercial right in the middle of our programs. What we planned to do was finish a song, introduce the sponsor, and then ask someone in our studio audience to come up while I demonstrated how the camera worked.

We were all ready to get started with the commercials, when suddenly Fred Davis found out he couldn't go through with it because he was already committed to another company. Well, the network couldn't back out at this stage because the contracts were already signed, so they asked me if I wouldn't mind going on Front Page Challenge to do the six commercials Fred was to have done, as well as the ones on our show.

I don't know how many of you remember those very first Polaroid Land Cameras, but they sure seemed like magic to us at the time; you shot your photo, out came the print covered with a thin strip of film, you waited for the little beep from the camera, and then peeled off the strip to reveal a perfectly developed print. They're commonplace today, but at that point, they seemed just amazing.

Well, Front Page Challenge was broadcast live, so I made sure I knew every step of the procedure for that first commercial: introducing the sponsor, photographing the model who was posing for us, and finally, displaying the finished photo: "There, isn't that a great picture?"

When it came time for the broadcast, we got all set up as the Polaroid executives and advertising people watched expectantly from the audience. Everything went perfectly: the model came out, she posed, I shot the picture, said everything I was supposed to say, waited for the beep, and peeled off the film as the camera zoomed in for a closeup of the finished photograph. "There," I said, displaying the print, "isn't that a great picture.?"

Well, there was nothing to look at. That print was completely blank!

251

What could we do? We were live . . . Finally, they just faded to black and came back up on Fred, who was standing there looking utterly bewildered.

During the course of doing those commercials (the rest of which resulted in superbly developed photographic prints!), I got to know some of the panelists on the show, including Pierre Berton and Betty Kennedy, and especially Gordon Sinclair. Despite his reputation as a pretty tough and crusty individual, I found him to be an extremely kind and gentle man, as well as very intelligent and thoughtful. Canada lost a very special human being, as well as a memorable television personality, when Mr. Sinclair passed away.

Another time I was on the set of Front Page Challenge, I had occasion to meet another memorable Canadian who was making an appearance as one of the surprise guests on the show. I was walking down the hall toward the room where the guests were kept hidden before the show so none of the panelists would see them, when who should walk out of the Green Room but the guest himself: John Diefenbaker, the former Prime Minister of Canada!

I was stunned, and just stood there staring at him, but he came right up to me. "How do you do, young man," he said.

Can you believe that? I thought to myself. He actually knows who I am! At this point, I'd been on television almost 15 years, five years with a show of my own, so I figured it was possible that he'd seen me on TV sometime. But I was just being a bit too optimistic, because he went on: "And what line of work are you in?" fixing me with the characteristic Diefenbaker glare.

"Ummm . . ." I didn't want to tell him how long I'd been on television, for fear of embarrassing him . . . "I'm in communications, Mr. Diefenbaker."

"Well, I hope you'll be very successful at it," he said, shaking his head in that familiar way of his and walking down the corridor.

Not five minutes later, we bumped into each other again: "Hello there, young fellow," he said. "What line of work are you in?"

"Oh, I'm still in communications, Mr. Diefenbaker."

"Well, I hope you'll be very successful at it," he said once again.

"I hope so too," I answered, and this time it was my turn to shake my head. At that point, to my great relief, one of Mr. Diefenbaker's aides came long to usher him back into his private room.

That may not have been the ideal way to meet a famous statesman, but I'll always be glad that I did have even a brief opportunity to talk with Mr. Diefenbaker. To me, he and other men of his ilk were always a breed unto themselves; brilliant orators who always spoke out so eloquently about their vision of Canada.

Tommy Douglas, the former leader of the New Democratic Party, was another politician I met when we were in Western Canada to open a shopping mall and do a few shows. At one of these functions, various representatives of all the political parties were giving speeches, and one particular speaker was taking a *very* long time with what he had to say. Just as he started to wind down, a dump truck full of junk began to back out of the parking lot after loading up.

"Well," said Douglas, taking his turn on the platform, "I'm certainly gratified to see that someone was well prepared for my honorable friend's conclusion!"

On the flight back to Toronto, I met another memorable individual who happened to be sitting next to me on the plane. We struck up a conversation, and after a few minutes, I realized I hadn't introduced myself.

"Glad to meet you, Mr. Hunter," he said. "My name's Walter Bick."

"Oh . . . You wouldn't happen to be the same Mr. Bick whose company makes the pickles, would you?"

"Yes, that's right," he said.

"I'm very pleased to meet you," I said, enthusiastically. "Our family really enjoys your products."

Now, many executives would have just smiled and left it at that, but Mr. Bick was not an ordinary executive. "Really?" he asked. "Which brands do you particularly enjoy."

"Well, we like Yum-Yums," I said, and mentioned a few of his other varieties.

He still wasn't finished. "Tell me," he asked, "where do you buy your pickles?" I told him the name of the supermarket where Shirley did her shopping, and even gave him the name of the street where it was located.

"That's great," he said.

Just before the plane landed, he asked for my name again, and my address; then we said our goodbyes. I'd almost forgotten about it by the next morning, but just before I left for the studio, there was a knock on the door and there stood a delivery man with a gigantic crate packed full of every kind of Bick's Pickles you could imagine!

There was also a note:

"I really enjoy talking with a man who knows his products, and I thank you for using ours. Secondly, I really admire a man who knows where his wife shops. Enjoyed flying with you,

Sincerely yours,
Walter Bick."

Well, I thought that was just terrific, and you know, we still use your products, Mr. Bick!

At about this same period, I was still trying to devote some time to my recordings with Columbia. Both myself and Frank Jones, the producer, were trying to find new ways of putting together a hit record.

About the closest we came was a song called "Mary in the Morning," which did very well on the charts, getting right into the top 30 songs at one point. A lot of radio stations in Canada and the United States were starting to play it fairly frequently; so I started writing letters to some of the station managers and doing interviews on a lot of radio programs.

One of the times I went to Nashville, Shirley came along with me because she'd never been there before. One afternoon, Frank, Shirley and I were in the elevator on our way out of the building when a striking-looking woman got on. In the lobby, as we were walking toward the door, Frank held me back for a moment: "Do you know who that is?" he asked, pointing toward the woman. "That's Billie Jean Horton."

Over coffee, Frank told us an absolutely enthralling story about Billie Jean and Hank Williams, who were married shortly before Hank's death in 1952. It seems that the night Hank left for that date in Canton, Ohio, just before New Year's, Billie Jean was in the bedroom brushing her hair when he came in to say goodbye. After he left, she sat in front of the mirror for a few more moments, and just as she was about to put the brush down, she suddenly felt as if there were a presence in the room. She glanced in the mirror, and it was Hank, standing there looking at her. "I just wanted to say goodbye one last time," he said.

Later that night, she got the news that Hank was dead.

"Hey, wait a second, Frank," I said. "Did that really happen?"

"Well, that's how I heard it," he said. "There's more, too."

Some time later, Billie Jean married the singer, Johnny Horton, and after they'd been married for some years, Johnny recorded a song for the soundtrack of a movie called *North to Alaska*, starring John Wayne. At the premiere of the movie, Johnny was supposed to sing that theme song at a big gala in New York, but at the last moment, he decided he didn't want to go. Now, Billie Jean was really upset because she'd been looking forward to the trip, and when he came into the bedroom to tell her he was going out hunting, she just ignored him and went on brushing her hair. After he left, she was sitting there in front of the mirror when once again, she felt a presence in the room. It was Johnny: "I just wanted to say goodbye one last time," he said.

Later that night, she found out that Johnny had been killed in a car accident.

"That's frightening," I said. "I remember the night Johnny Horton was killed, because I was here in Nashville at a disc jockey convention, and someone called me to tell me about the accident. Still, who knows for sure if all that happened?"

"Right," said Frank. "Who knows for sure?"

Not too long after that trip to Nashville, I went in to see my manager, Saul Holiff, who also managed the Johnny Cash Show. He'd just gotten the latest reports from the recording trade magazines, and it seemed that "Mary in the Morning" had reached Number 28 on the charts.

Saul decided he'd put in a call to Clive Davis, then the head of Columbia Records. "Have you seen the latest charts on 'Mary in the Morning,' Clive?" he asked.

"Yeah, it seems to be doing very well."

I shouted across to Saul: "Ask Clive if he thinks we should maybe give this record a bit of a push," I said, full of enthusiasm. "It's really going great!"

On the other end of the phone, I could hear Clive. "Tell Tommy to relax," he said rather dryly. "When it gets to Number 10, we'll really put a push on it."

Jokingly, I hollered back: "When it gets to Number 10, we won't need any push on it!"

Well, Saul finished the conversation and I thought that was that; but I guess Clive Davis didn't really take my banter in the spirit in which it was intended. Shortly after that phone call, Columbia told me they wouldn't be renewing my contract.

After I left Columbia, RCA Canada offered me a recording contract; that was good news, because I figured I'd have a lot more time to work closely with the producer in trying to develop a really good rapport.

Well, I didn't have to worry about having enough time; as it turned out, it was over a year before I ever made a single recording with RCA! The first word I ever heard from anyone at the company was when Robert Cook, the vice-president, called to ask why he hadn't yet heard any recordings from me.

"Are you not happy with your contract, Tommy?" he asked. "Or are you just trying not to make records with us?"

"Well, you see, Mr. Cook," I said. "I haven't heard from anyone at RCA since the day I signed my contract."

Mr. Cook was very understanding, and shortly after our chat, I started to do some recording sessions. I always found Mr. Cook to be a fine gentleman and capable individual whom I liked very much.

CHAPTER 10

A New Beginning

Back on our show, there seemed to be no inclination on the part of the producer to move towards
more of the country music atmosphere I felt we should have.

Once again, I think it was a question of Bill Lynn's and my
coming from completely different worlds as far as our concept of doing a television show. I liked Bill's sense of humor
and appreciated the fact that he was a talented writer; at the
same time, I could see that he understood very little about
country music and the kind of country show I wanted. Time
after time, the big productions and comedy skits would keep
cropping up in the script like so many recurring nightmares.

Any feeling of satisfaction I may have derived from steering a particular show toward the atmosphere I wanted to
create just evaporated as the script for the next show
appeared, with all the same emphasis on elaborate sets,
period costumes and pop-style arrangements of even the
most straightforward country songs.

One time, we were planning a show where we'd do a few
songs around a campfire, and I figured there was no way
anybody could complicate that one. Well, I walked into
Studio Seven to find a set depicting the entire scenery of northern Ontario; why, they'd even built a river! The Rhythm
Pals got into a rowboat and paddled their way downstream to
the heart of the pines!

There had to be $5,000 worth of evergreens, rocks and
tents; and that set couldn't have cost less than $30,000 or
$40,000, when all I'd wanted was a simple little campfire and

a few small bushes in the background, just to give people the idea of what we were doing. The music would have taken care of the rest.

Once again, this extravaganza was the result of one of Bill Lynn's pet theories: "Let producers produce, let directors direct, and let set designers design." So when he asked for a camp, well, he really got one; so much so that if you'd switched on our show in the middle, you'd have sworn you got the wrong channel and had accidentally tuned into the Mutual of Omaha wildlife series!

By this point, almost 10 years into our show, you might be wondering why I didn't just pick up and leave, if all my efforts to create the kind of atmosphere I wanted didn't seem to be meeting with any success. Well, I'd thought of it more than once, after weeks and months of fighting for every camera angle, set, costume and song on that show, only to come into the studio the following day to face the same problems all over again.

Sure, there were even times I *wanted* to quit; times I thought I just couldn't face any more of the complete lack of understanding for my point of view on the show. But somehow, I just couldn't pack it in.

What I just couldn't give up were those fleeting moments when all of us very naturally started performing on the same wavelength. I'd be strumming my guitar, Al would suddenly break into a fiddle run, and we'd all be caught up in the pure enjoyment and fun of the song. Everything would come together, almost like magic: the cameramen honed right in on what we were doing because they were enjoying themselves as much as we were; the lighting crew adapted a very simple, warm light, and the whole scene was focussed on the essence of the music we were playing.

These were the moments we lived for; and I wanted it to be like that for us *all* the time on our show. If we could somehow get down to the essentials, we wouldn't have any more need for the elaborate sets and complicated techniques that just put up barriers between us and our audience, and between us and our music.

The producer just didn't see it that way, however; and that was the problem. To him, the elaborate productions *were* the essentials, and he couldn't understand our spontaneity any more than we could understand his onstage rivers, pine groves and campgrounds.

Once again, I became involved in the direction the show was taking: scripts, sets, musical arrangements and even the signing of contracts each year. I felt that without our regulars, there would be absolutely nothing between me and a full-tilt variety show. With Al Cherny, Maurice Bolyer, the Rhythm Pals, the Allen Sisters and me doing *some* country songs in comfortable surroundings, I felt we had at least a chance to build slowly toward a show that allowed for a lot of honesty and believability.

One time, despite my continued efforts to watch out for the other regulars, one of the producers informed me Al Cherny was being taken off the show.

"Al Cherny is back on this show," I said, firmly, "and this is not a matter I'm prepared to discuss. He is back on the show, and he *stays* on."

It's not my nature to be that forceful or adamant, but when I was confronted with the possibility of losing what is one of the strongest elements of our show, Al and his music, I dug in both heels.

When it concerns my loyalty to a member of the cast or crew, I have no choice. I felt (and still feel) that all the regulars and crew members are a family structure that I've struggled hard to build, and when one of the members of my TV family is threatened, I can't stand idly by.

I would have much preferred a comfortable structure that allowed the performers on the show to project a naturalness and honesty so that their talents would be conveyed to the audience without needless distractions. Even the simplest presentation must be produced, directed, staged and orchestrated, but the setting should allow the performer to feel comfortable and not distract from the very honesty of his or her performance.

While I felt comfortable with that philosophy, I'm sure that many of the people with whom I was working did not share a confidence in me, or more particularly, country music. It was almost as if they were trying to justify some hick music by making it look Hollywood.

Once again, I don't mean to imply at all that these people were in any way less than the very best in their fields. I had the privilege of working with some of the most talented arrangers, writers and directors in Canadian television. It's just that the producer and I had different views; mine was of a very simple, straightforward approach, and his was of a more highly produced presentation.

I can understand, looking back on it now, what the Pals and the Allens were going through at the time; they were in a very difficult position. On the one hand, they had a guy whose name was written on the show and who was very insistent on a simple approach to country music (still is, by the way). On the other hand, they had a producer who wanted a variety show and who also happened to be the guy with the power to pick up or take away the option on their contracts each season.

So I think what happened was that the Pals and the Allen Sisters got to the point where they became caught between the highly staged approach of the producer and my insistence on simplicity. I'm sure that in their minds, it was just a question of trying to survive.

What this boiled down to was that in the midst of all this confusion, their talent was just not coming through the way I knew it could.

We were getting so turned around on the show that I didn't know just where we were any more. We had the Rhythm Pals doing some Mills Brothers songs, Debbie Lori Kaye doing show tunes, the Allen Sisters doing a highly staged club act, and even Al Cherny putting away his fiddle and performing comedy routines, something which I knew he intensely disliked doing.

Time after time, I'd tried to tell them how much confidence I had in all of us doing good country; or, in the case of Debbie and the Allen Sisters, the nice, soft middle-of-the-road country songs, like "Rose Garden" or "Gentle on My Mind." Maybe they thought I was fighting just for the sake of fighting; it must have been very hard for them to understand that I was just trying for the kind of show we'd all be comfortable with.

Whatever the reasons, it got so that there just didn't seem to be very much camaraderie among us. I was sure the audiences wanted them to be doing the country songs as only they could do them, and not the pop-type songs the producers or writers had convinced them to concentrate on.

What we were left with was a show in total disarray. The fact that Al Cherny was no longer playing fiddle now seemed totally appropriate to the situation. All the music was starting to sound like a supper club act; the guests were completely outside any context of country music; and the elaborate sets were looming even larger than before. I kept trying to get things back into some semblance of order — rewriting a script here, having a set repainted there — but I couldn't block all ends. Something had to give eventually.

Anyway, it came about that the Allen Sisters and the Rhythm Pals were offered a shorter contract at the beginning of one particular season; how it worked was that they'd be on the show one week, off the next, and so on. Usually, if the question of shortening the contracts of our regulars came up, I'd be dead set against it; but this time, I decided not to put up an argument.

That was a tough decision, one of the hardest I've ever faced. I guess I came to the conclusion that there wasn't much point in continuing the fight. Maybe I was just running out of steam. I felt that a shortened schedule would still give them plenty of opportunity to seek work outside our show, especially since they'd still be getting network exposure. At the same time, it would open up a couple of spots on the show that I wanted to fill with guests like Porter Wagoner, Hank Snow, Wilf Carter and many others.

The Allen Sisters decided to go along with the arrangement for another season, but the Pals said they wanted either the full contract or none at all. I tried to change their minds, but they wouldn't budge, so they ended up leaving the show. I learned a great deal from Mike, Marc and Jack, and there's still no other group around who can perform those Western songs with that special charm, the way they do.

Not too long after the Pals left our show, and while I was at a meeting, the writers played me a song by Aretha Franklin they had planned for Debbie to perform on the show. After listening to it I thought it was all wrong for our show, our audience, and, most important, for Debbie.

I suggested to the writers something a little lighter and more in the context of the show. "How about 'Knock Three Times'? It's light, it's bouncy, and I have all the confidence that Debbie will perform it very comfortably." I can't remember whether she sang the song I'd suggested or not, but at the end of the night, she marched straight over to Bill Lynn and told him she was leaving the show.

I was sorry to see Debbie leave, because she'd done some great things on the show; at the same time, though, I think her decision to move on to other opportunities was probably best in terms of the direction she saw for her career.

At about the same time as Debbie left our show, Bill Lynn was asked to do a new comedy show the CBC was producing, and we got a new producer, David Koyle.

Now, Dave was different from Bill in that he placed much more emphasis on organization, and he assumed a lot more responsibility for the approaches being taken by the writers, set designers, and other departments of our show. It didn't take long, however, for me to realize that Dave's priorities and mine were just as far apart as with the producers who'd come before him.

Once again, I didn't set out to fight against his decisions; just as with the others, I hoped we would be able to achieve a good working rapport, and I felt very disappointed that there we were, on opposite sides of the fence again.

One time, when Tom T. Hall came up to do the show (one of the few occasions on which we had a real country artist as a guest), we'd put together a fast-moving group of songs we could all take turns singing.

The way I saw it was very simple; we'd sit around and do some country songs for the audience. But Dave had this idea that we should start off the whole medley with a closeup shot of a pig in the typical barnyard image I'd been trying to escape for years. I kept writing the shot out of the script, and he kept putting it back; finally, he got a hold of a pig somewhere and brought it into the rehearsal.

Well, I decided we'd see how things went, so we started the rehearsal, and all of a sudden, I could hear the pig squealing. That's funny, I thought; it wasn't making any noise before. Anyway, we had to try the whole sequence over again because the sound wasn't great, and this time, I kept my eye on that pig the whole time that Tom T. Hall and I were waiting to go onto the set. Just then, I noticed Dave prodding that pig to make it squeal.

I was so angry that I just about saw red. "Hang on a second, Tom," I said to Tom T. Hall, "we're not going to do this until I get something settled right here and now."

I walked over to Dave. "Why are you hurting that animal?"

"Because it'll make a great opening shot to hear him squeal, that's why," he said.

"Opening shot or no opening shot, that part is not going on the air," I said. "When you get rid of the pig, we'll start the production."

Tom T. Hall never said a word, but I could tell by the look he gave me that he understood *exactly* what I was going through. Luckily, we got the matter settled, and the pig was returned to the farm, where it belonged.

What irritated me, though, is that we had to go through any of that conflict at all; if we'd just taken a very simple, straightforward approach to those songs in the first place, none of these problems would have arisen. All that complication succeeded in doing was to demean our music, upset and embarrass the performers, myself included, and needlessly harm an innocent animal. What was the point?

Unfortunately, that was a question I found myself asking with increased regularity as time went on. After the incident with the pig, I tried to keep close watch on all aspects of the show even more than before, but even so, there'd always be some little surprise cropping up. It wasn't as if Dave and the others were deliberately setting out to do things that would upset me; they just didn't seem to understand my viewpoint at all. To them, the elements they were introducing were just perfect for the show; to me, they were devastating.

Dave never seemed to trust the music to stand on its own; if he got hold of a song that said: "Darling, I'm dying of a broken heart," he'd want to put you in a rundown old hotel room with a bottle in your hand and have you sort of lying there as if you were literally dying of a broken heart!

Our judgement was at odds on just about everything. After the Rhythm Pals left our show, followed by the Allen Sisters about a year later, there was a short period when neither of them was replaced. Then, Dave brought in a group called the OK Chorale.

Now, this particular group sang, and danced, and set up their different numbers in a choreographic way, especially those highly staged numbers that Dave and the writers were coming up with, much to my dismay. There was nothing actually wrong with the OK Chorale, except I think that style was more suited to a variety show than a country show. It bothered me that some of the routines they did almost forced me into the choreography; all of a sudden, in the middle of a song, two of the girls would come sweeping in and pull me from one side of the set to the other, as if I were Dean Martin or something.

At about this same time, we had a young couple on the show as guests; two talented performers by the name of Donna and Leroy Anderson. I thought they were excellent, and after the show, I went over to chat with them about their plans for the future. After we'd talked for only about five minutes, I knew they'd be perfect for our show; they loved country music, shared many of the same perceptions I did, and, most of all, they seemed like a couple of really enthusiastic, hard-working young artists.

"What would you think of the idea of coming to Toronto and doing the show with us?" I asked. "Full-time, I mean."

Donna and Leroy looked at each other; a little tentatively, I thought. "Well, you see, we're just trying to see if we can make a solo career right now," Leroy said. "It sounds fantastic, but right now I just don't know what our plans are."

It seemed to me that Donna and Leroy just weren't ready yet to commit themselves to a television show, so I decided not to push things. I knew the idea would work out eventually, so I just thanked them for doing the show and told them I'd keep in touch.

About a year later, I heard they were performing at a hotel in Calgary, so I decided to call and see how they'd feel at this point about the possibility of doing our show.

"I can't promise anything," I told Leroy over the phone, "but I think you and Donna would be really good for the show, and I'm sure the show would be good for you."

By this time, Donna and Leroy had grown a lot as performers, and it was clear to me from talking to them that they were now prepared to give all their time and energy to the demands of a television show. We chatted a few more minutes, and by the time I hung up the phone, I was determined somehow to get them at least a trial run as regulars on our show.

Now came the tough part: convincing David Koyle that Donna and Leroy were perfect for us. He agreed to fly out to Calgary to interview them, and that evening, I got a frantic call from Leroy.

"Tommy," he said, obviously very upset, "Mr. Koyle told us he wanted us to do rock music. 'What? Rock music on the Tommy Hunter Show?' I said, and he said, 'That's right.' I mean, we don't even do rock, Tommy!"

"Don't worry, Leroy," I said, fuming on the inside. "I can tell you for a fact that you and Donna will not be doing rock music on our show, because we don't *do* rock music on this show."

Next morning, Dave came over to talk to me. "Donna and Leroy seem to have some possibilities," he said. "I'll consider them."

"No," I said, no longer concerned that I was treading on

the hiring powers of a producer, "you will not *consider* using them," and totally ignoring his shocked look, I continued. "I want them on the show, and what's more, they will be doing country music. Country, not rock, folk or pop music. They're country singers, and this happens to be a country show."

I even surprised myself with how strongly I spoke, but by that stage of the game I felt I just couldn't tread softly any more. This was my chance to start building a strong base of country music on the show, and to give two talented young country artists a chance. There was no way I was going to back down on this one.

What I ended up doing was going to one of the network executives and asking him to give Donna and Leroy the opportunity I knew they deserved.

"Well, I suppose we could try them out for a week or so," he said.

"I don't really think you could tell after just one week whether they'd work out or not," I said.

"Well, supposing we give them a four-week contract," he suggested.

At this point, I figured I might as well go for broke; I'd gotten this far without incident, after all. "I still don't think that'll really give them the chance to show what they can do," I said. "How about a 10-week contract, and then if they work out, they could get the other 10 weeks of the season."

"I don't know, Hunter," he said doubtfully.

"They're excellent performers, and we really need good country music on the show. Couldn't we give them the chance?"

Well, I guess he understood that I wouldn't be pushing that hard unless I really believed in Donna and Leroy, so he finally agreed; they'd get a 10-week contract.

As it turned out, this particular executive kept a close eye on Donna and Leroy during the first few weeks they appeared on the show, and after just a short time, he called to tell me he'd really enjoyed their performances.

"I'm very pleased to hear that," I said, crossing my fingers and wishing, "and since that's the case, why don't we just tell

266

them they're on for the rest of the season, so they don't have to go around on pins and needles for the next two months."

"I've got to hand it to you, Hunter," he said, chuckling. "You really drive a hard bargain. Okay, they're on for the season."

Shortly after Donna and Leroy got the good news, they started looking for a new apartment in town; they'd been living out in northwest Toronto temporarily. One day, Donna and her mom, who was visiting from her home in Sault Ste. Marie, Ontario, were out seeing some places and decided to drop into the studio to say hello. "I've just seen a great condominium, Tommy," Donna told me, all excited.

"Oh, really?" I asked what it looked like and where it was located. "Really great, Donna. How much does it cost; do you mind my asking?"

"Oh no; it's about $1,200 a month," she said.

That stopped me. "Come here a second, sweetheart," I told her. "I want to whisper something in your ear." When she approached, I continued: "If you rent that condo at $1,200 a month, I will personally kick your behind right back up to Sault Ste. Marie!"

Donna's mom overheard me, and nodded approvingly. "I'm glad you could talk some sense into her; that's exactly what I was saying."

I could see Donna was a bit disappointed, so I tried to explain that I felt she and Leroy should consider the practical side. I understood that they were excited over becoming part of the show; on the other hand, I also knew from personal experience how important it was to build up some security.

"Donna, I feel our show is good for a number of years, and I certainly hope that's the case," I said, "but I still think it's very important to save your money, because there are no absolutes in our business. We can never say for sure what might be in store for us somewhere down the road."

Well, Donna and Leroy decided against the condominium, and at about that time, I found out that a friend of mine who owned a beautiful townhouse was planning to move to Chicago and was looking for a buyer. "I think I know a couple who might be interested," I said, and I promptly called another friend, who worked in real estate and whose husband had built our home, to show the townhouse to Donna and Leroy. They fell in love with it immediately, and they lived there until just recently. They just purchased a new home, which isn't that far from where we live.

Right from Day One, I always felt that Donna and Leroy were two super-duper kids; we've always had a great relationship based on mutual respect and admiration for each other's abilities. They completely understood that my advice about the condominium was based on the experiences I'd learned from when I was just starting out in television; and they were equally responsive to the demands of doing a good country show under some pretty adverse conditions we had to deal with in those days.

Over the years, Donna and Leroy have consistently carried their weight on the show, and I'll tell you, when performers give of themselves 100 per cent, instead of waiting for someone else to pick up the slack, that makes the difference between a top-notch performer and an adequate one.

Donna and Leroy were also very much aware of the difficulties that existed on the show when they first started; they knew what I was going through in my constant efforts to try to get us turned around to where we belonged. You know, just having them on the show made a difference in how I felt about the whole atmosphere.

Oh, there wasn't any lack of lavish productions, skits, sketches, and the rest of it; and my efforts to get us going in more of a country direction were still as frustrating and nerve-wracking as ever. Still, for at least a few brief, wonderful moments each week, I could relax in the knowledge that I was working with two performers who knew what country music was and what I was trying to achieve on our show. I didn't have to stop after every bar and explain where the song was going. I'd just start to play and sing, while Donna and Leroy instantly picked up the harmony without hesitation; just like in those terrific recording sessions in Nashville.

Along with Al Cherney and Maurice Bolyer, I felt that for

the first time, we had a group of regulars who really fit well together. Maurice wasn't a country player, strictly speaking; he played four-string banjo rather than the five-string style of performers like Earl Scruggs. What Maurice did was play his style of banjo better than anyone in the world, and he was an important asset to our show; in addition to being a great banjo player, he also played a wonderful honky-tonk piano and very good rhythm guitar.

With Al Cherny, if you named a style of fiddle music you wanted to hear, Al could play it: traditional Ukrainian music, Southern style hoedown, bluegrass, traditional down-east fiddling, even French-Canadian fiddle music. What Al and Maurice both shared, which made their talent shine even more brightly, was that they had fun performing; and this was the same quality that made me so enthusiastic about getting Donna and Leroy on our show the first time I heard them.

I knew that with these four performers giving our audience the kind of music they wanted, we could eventually overcome the variety-show syndrome that had been plaguing us for years.

The trouble was that the producers, writers and directors didn't really see the direction we all wanted to go, even now that we had regulars who were as strongly committed to country music as I was. They still preferred the pop-music guest artists, the Broadway production numbers, and all the skits and sketches. (I've got to say that I came to detest the word sketch, and the images it conjured of us all jumping around like fools and telling bad, tasteless jokes.)

From all the ratings, it seemed that our show was continuing to be quite popular, and those statistics were usually quoted triumphantly by the producer whenever we objected to a sketch or an extra-lavish production number.

The thing about statistics, though is that they can be used in a number of different ways, and I always wondered: what if there had been some kind of rating system that showed *why* people watched our show? Maybe they'd say that they tuned us in for the country music, the readings, and the simple hymns; not the elaborate production numbers that they could have gotten just as easily on the Dean Martin Show, if that's what they really wanted.

I had a pretty good reason for thinking that way, too. Wherever we'd gone to do our various personal appearances, the message we were getting from people who watched our show was that they wanted good country music, in a straightforward and simple setting. The aspects of the show they *always* found fault with was the latest attempt to bring Times Square onto the Hunter Show; and they told us that they kept on watching the show in the hope that next time, there'd be a little more Nashville and a little less New York (or maybe we should say a little less downtown Toronto and a little more rural Canada!).

So that's why I kept on pushing; not just for myself and the kind of approach to television that I happened to prefer, but for our country audiences, and what *they* wanted.

Now, I've probably said all this many times before; and you know, when I think back on that period of time, I can recall actually repeating it to myself again and again: *our audience wants good country music*, I'd say it every time a producer tried to bring in a $40,000 set depicting some abstract, psychedelic concept of a Newfoundland fishing hut; every time we had a guest like Roger Whittaker, Frankie Laine or Moms Mabley (all wonderful performers in their own right, but totally wrong for our show); and every time a director asked me who Grandpa Jones was, or Junior Samples, or Ernest Tubb.

Then I'd get to thinking about country music, and the way it had fared on network television.

There was Country Hoedown, which started out as a bright, bouncy, fun show that performers and viewers enjoyed. It ended up being pushed into the mould of a highly choreographed, elaborately staged variety show.

The people in charge of production on Hoedown decided to move the show into a more uptown production, and in the many directions that Hoedown went, they lost sight of the enthusiasm and the family feeling we had. We were just struggling to survive, because we no longer had a comfortable base from which to work. Eventually, the show fell in the ratings and was cancelled, in 1965.

Then, there was the Don Messer Jubilee. Don's show didn't budge from its identity as a good, simply produced show that made old-time, down-east fiddling popular all across Canada. Yet it too was cancelled, in 1967, despite the fact that thousands of people demonstrated in front of the Parliament buildings in Ottawa to protest the decision.

Over on the other side of the 49th Parallel, a lot of similar decisions were being made. The Johnny Cash Show, which hadn't even been on television that long, started being pushed more and more in the direction that NBC executives in New York wanted. As a result, viewers were seeing more of the Bob Hopes than the Minnie Pearls (those network executives had probably never even heard of Minnie!), and the next thing you knew, the show was cancelled in 1971.

The very same year, the CBS network pulled the plug on one of the most popular shows in their history: Hee-Haw. Unlike the other shows, however, Hee-Haw survived by turning to syndication, and is seen to this day by millions of television viewers.

All these decisions seemed to add up to one thing: a complete lack of faith in the very large and loyal audience for country music among television viewers, and an extremely narrow view of the art form itself.

Because there wasn't the confidence in country music, the acceptance of it as an art form, or the awareness that it would draw large ratings, the decision was to go with the Al Martinos instead of the Roy Acuffs. The result was that the performers felt awkward, and the audiences felt cheated and deprived of the country artists they knew and wanted.

This was exactly the kind of situation we were facing on our show. I wanted country performers and a country show for our audience, and I wanted *our* music, with no apologies for that music.

I remember one time when I almost got into a fistfight with one of our writers, Jerry O'Flanagan, over a script I knew

271

would be offensive to our viewers; we got so heated up that at one point, we threw off our jackets and really got ready to wallop each other. Suddenly, we both burst out laughing. "Okay, Jerry," I said, "just to prove a point, we'll put the script on the show as it is, but you'll have to sit down and personally answer every single negative letter we receive, and I know we'll get thousands of them."

"That's fine," he said.

I went away and thought it over for a moment, then came back and found Jerry again. "No," I said, "it's no good. I don't want to prove my point by insulting the audience. They come first. So I'll tell you right now that the script isn't going on the air as it is now." He refused to change it, so I took that script home and literally rewrote every word.

Just a few years later, after Jerry had moved to Los Angeles as a writer involved in television production, he called me one day to tell me that he now understood why I'd rewritten that script. "Now that I've been out here for awhile," he said, "I know what you were fighting for."

Even when we were able to introduce certain elements to the show that more reflected a country audience, there seemed to be very little awareness on the part of the producers and directors of what we were trying to accomplish. I remember a producer saying to me one time: "We've got to get you to be a little controversial. You've got to make some sort of social comment."

"Well, I don't know where you've been recently," I answered, "but yesterday I spent five minutes on our show criticizing the established church."

"What do you mean?" he asked, totally confused.

"I mean that reading I did called 'Trouble in the Amen Corner'," I said. "I talked all about this very sophisticated church with the most wealthy parishioners in town and the greatest, most artistic choir. I described how the choir members decided they were too good to allow this elderly man to remain in their ranks, because age had touched his vocal chords and his voice was cracked. I told you how they formed a committee and climbed into their big, fancy cars so they could go tell this man, Ira, that he couldn't sing in the choir any more; and how Ira died shortly after they returned to their fancy, elegant church."

After a long silence, the producer finally spoke. "I guess the point is he should have been allowed to sing in the choir, but the church considered it more important to maintain their social status."

"Well, then how can you say I never talk about anything controversial?" (I wasn't going to let him off *that* easily!)

"I don't know," he said. "I guess at the time I just thought it was another one of those hokey readings."

Well, there was my dilemma in a nutshell. How was I ever going to communicate that simple, beautiful message when I worked with people who weren't even willing to *listen*?

I'd like to be able to say that after that particular incident, the producer finally saw what he'd missed up till then, and began to understand and support what I was trying to accomplish. Unfortunately, that was not the case.

What happened instead was that year after year, I'd talk till I was blue in the face, spending hours at a time with producers, writers, directors, musical arrangers, set designers; everyone who worked on the show. I'd tell them about some of the country music legends like Hank Williams; I'd describe some of their life experiences; and I'd try to explain that people loved their songs because they talked about what is most important: real feelings, and real lives. "I never wrote a note, except in my heart," as Hank once said. Then, I'd try my very best to convey to them all the excitement, joy and sadness I'd experienced growing up on that kind of music, hoping against hope that they'd understand how much I wanted to communicate those feelings to our audience.

"Oh, that's a great story," they'd say, and off they'd go to build an even bigger set and design another $40,000 production. It was as if they'd been in another room the whole time I was pouring out my heart to them; they hadn't heard a single word of it. This happened time after time, no matter how often I repeated it all, no matter how many great country artists I told them about. It just went in one ear and out the other.

273

Just imagine what it feels like to sit in a boardroom for maybe the 1,000th time and reach down into the depths of your soul to explain why the hair on the back of your neck starts tingling when you hear the sound of a guitar ring out, or a singer reach for that one absolutely perfect note, or a fiddle burst into a lightning-fast run. You talk and talk, gazing intently at the faces of all these writers, producers, directors and designers who are supposed to be part of your team, and finally, when you're completely hoarse and exhausted from the effort, you sit back, praying they'll understand.

"Yeah, yeah, I can relate to that," one of them says, all excited. "Let's get a whole orchestra on it, and we'll do a real dynamite arrangement, and, oh, let's have some dancers and build a railway station with a real train so we can illustrate it. That's going to be a real blockbuster!"

In other words, nobody has the slightest idea what you're talking about, once again; and I'll tell you, there are few situations more frustrating and frightening than that. I mean, this is your future on the line, and the future of all the performers you work with!

I'd come home most nights dead tired, feeling battered and beat, wondering how much longer I could go on, and wishing there was some way out of this nightmare when I'd gain an inch only to lose a yard.

I'd sit and talk with Shirley for awhile, and then I'd go downstairs to my little office, pour myself a couple of good stiff drinks, and turn on the country music good and loud.

I had to hear the music, just to know it was still there; and I just hoped all this bedlam would go away. As the music played, I could see the Smoky Mountains, and hear just a simple old fiddle playing in the background . . . the tranquillity of watching a farmer going over a little hill, ploughing a little bit of land . . . some humble work, some humble pay, some humble food, and two or three down-home happy kids.

I was so sick of this complex world of white suits and Moon Rivers; big orchestrations and bigger productions. All I kept hearing in the background was this simple music, and I could just about see the gentle haze of a sunny afternoon over the

Tennessee hills.

So I'd just sit there, basking in the sounds, until finally I'd go to sleep with the music still ringing in my ears.

Looking back on it now, I realize that when I went down to that office, mixed a few drinks, and listened to my kind of music, it was like an escape valve for me. The liquor calmed me down, and being able to listen to country music reassured me that I hadn't been struggling for nothing all those years.

At the same time, I felt I was drinking too much for my own good; I'd have one or two to relax when I came home, and maybe another couple after supper. This really concerned me, because I was aware of the long-term effects; and sometimes, I can recall purposely driving through the most run-down areas of Toronto on my way to rehearsal and telling myself that I'd better watch it if I wanted to avoid ending up like some of those guys I saw reeling down the street.

It's not that I really felt I would end up on the skids like that; I think the great sense of responsibility I felt for my family and for our show helped me to keep my drinking within the strict confines of a relaxant that I felt I needed at the time. Still, I've got to say that I wish I'd been able to find another form of release, because I don't think alcohol was a good habit by any means. (I'll tell you just a little later on how I gave it up completely.)

Right in the midst of all my struggles to keep our show off the Broadway production line, I got a call from the network asking me to participate in a special presentation to pay tribute to all the shows being carried on the CBC. Fred Davis was the host, as I recall, and I was supposed to be the only entertainer on the show, which was going to be held in a major hotel with all kinds of elaborate displays of the various CBC programs.

"We really hope you can be part of the show, Mr. Hunter," the network representative said. "I mean, we at the network are so proud of you and your show, and we really feel your presence there would add to our presentation."

Well, that was very heady praise, and I said I'd be honored to represent our show. Anyway, I got down to the hotel and found a huge ballroom with aisles set up so people could walk up and down looking at various photographs depicting all the CBC shows. I decided to have a look.

I must have walked those aisles for two hours, looking at those displays; and I'll tell you, I never realized, until then, how much programming there was on the CBC: Canadian shows, British and American shows, programs that had been cancelled because of poor ratings, old shows . . . Everything except our show.

Totally confused, I checked through the publicity kit and found the Friday night listings of CBC programs; our time slot was *totally* blank.

Now, I wasn't after a great big glossy photograph of myself stuck up there in the centre; I didn't care about that at all. But what about a picture of Maurice, or Al, or Donna and Leroy, or even the guy who swept up after the show? What about these listings? I mean, one minute we all get a nice vote of confidence from the network, and the next minute there's not one scrap of evidence in this entire ballroom that there's even such a thing on the air as the Tommy Hunter Show.

Well, I drew this little oversight to someone's attention; their response was to rush out and get an eight-by-ten glossy picture to put on display. "Thanks very much, and I don't wish to seem rude," I said, "but putting up a photo at this stage of the game is simply not the point. What I'd like to know is how all this happened in the first place."

After a lot of checking around, I finally got in touch with the man in charge of publicity for the event (I won't embarrass him by mentioning his name) and asked him bluntly what had happened.

"Um, well, Mr. Hunter . . ."

"I'd certainly appreciate a straight answer," I said, "for once."

"Okay, well, when we were making up the schedule for the presentation and to send to the magazines . . ." and he hesitated again.

"Yes?" I asked.

"Well, we forgot about you . . ."

Isn't that a great line? They forgot about me; they forgot about our show; they just plain *forgot*.

When I heard that, something snapped inside me; it was as if that one incident capped all the frustrations I'd been experiencing for so many years. In a strange way, I feel almost grateful to that unfortunate publicity man for providing me with a very valuable lesson. What that experience taught me was that from now on, I was going to grab hold of the reins on our show and never let go for a single instant.

As of that moment, absolutely *nothing* on the show would be done unless I checked it first.

If a writer told me he had the greatest script in the world, I wanted to see it *before* rehearsals started; if a set designer said I could look at the set when it was finished, I quickly told him that I would look at it right then and there; if a musical arranger chatted excitedly about the great songs he had planned, I demanded to see the music. No stone was left unturned; I checked press releases, photographs, lists of guest artists, costumes, makeup; *everything*.

Even the producer was no longer the very powerful figure with all our futures in his control; he was just a guy who stood in my way, in my fellow-performers' way, and in our audience's way. As of now, I was the individual in control; it had to be that way. I had no other choice if our show was going to survive.

Most Monday morning meetings became a nightmare, as I'd walk in to find whole chunks of material I'd taken out of the script the week before. "I'm sorry," I'd tell the producer, "this is not going on the air," and I'd yank those pages right out again.

One time, they started talking about doing a sketch again, despite my having said endless numbers of times that I thought those sketches needlessly turned country performers into actors and comedians.

By this time, I was getting pretty tired of saying the same thing over and over; still, I felt I'd better try to explain once again, so I sat down with them at the program meeting and reiterated my concerns for the umpteenth time.

"If we're going to do anything," I said, "why don't we do a medley of railroad songs showing how the railways have linked this continent together." Well, they didn't seem too impressed with the idea, but I kept hammering away at it until they gave in, probably more to shut me up than out of any great enthusiasm for what I was proposing.

For that particular show, we had invited Orval Prophet, a really fine Canadian country singer who grew up on a farm in the Ottawa area; and I figured that Orval, having recorded several railroad songs, would really enjoy doing this kind of show. So I eagerly awaited the completion of the script, and when the writer arrived at our next program meeting, I asked him how things were coming along.

"Oh, we're going to do that railroad medley on this week's show," he said, sliding a sheaf of papers across the table to me. "Here's the script; I think you'll be impressed."

Impressed was not exactly the word to describe my feelings after reading just the first paragraph of that script; devastated would be a far better description.

I literally started to shake when I saw what they'd done. They had a set built depicting an old-time railway station, with Al Cherny as the stationmaster, myself as the conductor, and Orval as one of the passengers. I don't think there was *one* song for Orval in this entire script, but he had at least 900 pieces of dialogue and maybe one or two choruses that added up to about 90 seconds of music in the entire 15 minutes we were supposed to be devoting to this so-called medley (which was really just another one of those awful sketches).

I simply could not believe that they were so cruel as to take a talented country singer and force him into a situation where he was going to sing perhaps three notes, and spend the rest of his time reciting dialogue and telling bad jokes. Yes, that's right; it was cruel, very cruel, and I still bore the scars from "Rusty Rails" to prove it. There was no way I was going to allow that to happen again; I liked Orval a great deal, and I knew that such an experience would leave him feeling completely humiliated and probably set his career back 15 years.

I put down the script and looked around the room. There were maybe 10 or 11 other people in there: directors, writers, designers, and arrangers. "Why don't you all have a look at this?" I asked, tossing the pages over.

One after the other, they read through the script, pausing now and then to nod their approval: "Hey, this is great, eh, Tommy?" one of the writers asked. "Wish I'd written it."

Okay, I thought; that's it. I've finally cracked. All these people must be right, because I'm the only one who thinks this script is a disaster. Somewhere down the road, I guess I totally lost my perspective of what's right and what's wrong, and I guess this is the end of the line.

I stepped out in the hall just to get away from all of it for a second, and who should I see walking towards me but Les Pouliot, the country singer and writer I'd enjoyed working with so much back on Country Hoedown. He'd just come back from the States, where he'd been working on the Johnny Cash Show and several other network programs.

"Les," I said, holding out the script, "I wonder if you'd mind having a look at this and just telling me what you think."

"Oh, no, Tommy, I don't really want to do that," he said.

"Please, Les," I said, looking straight at him. "I really need you to tell me what you think of it." If I was wrong, I thought to myself, I wanted him to be the one to tell me.

I guess Les sensed how important this was to me, because he finally agreed, and held out his hand for the script. After just a moment or two, he handed it back; I don't even think he'd gotten through the first paragraph.

"Well?" I asked. "What do you think?"

"Tommy," he said, "this isn't even a good high-school play."

"It's pretty bad, isn't it?" I said.

"It isn't just bad, Tommy," he said. "It's absolutely atrocious. I feel sorry for you putting up with this kind of nonsense."

You know, when Les said that, I felt all my confidence come back to me. The people who'd come up with this script were from a completely different world than mine, just as I'd always thought; and I just needed someone from *my* world to confirm just how many light-years away they were.

"I'm not going to put up with it any more, Les," I said, "and I want to thank you. You have no idea how much you've helped me."

"Any time," he said, starting to walk away.

"Well, I may hold you to that, Les," I called after him. Then I headed back into the meeting.

Looking around the room, it suddenly occurred to me that I'd just proved to myself how true that old expression really is: To those who understand, no explanation is necessary; to those who do not, no explanation is possible. I decided just to end this nightmare as quickly and simply as I could.

"Okay, I'd like everyone to go home," I said. "This meeting is over, and you'll be called when you're needed." Without even waiting for any comments, I went down to the editing room and found the producer. I threw the script down in front of him and asked if he'd read it.

"Sure, I've read it," Dave said.

"Well, have you approved it? Is it going in the show?"

"Yes, it is."

"No, it is not," I said. "This script will never appear on our show." I didn't give him time to argue; just asked him to endorse that sheaf of paper, which he did. Then, I mailed a copy to my lawyer, got on the phone to Jim Guthro, the acting head of CBC Variety at the time, and asked for his opinion.

The result of all this was that the sketch never appeared on our show, and the relationship between me and the producer became more and more tense as the year went on. But at least there weren't any more sketches proposed.

That summer of 1978, most of us regulars were doing quite a few personal appearances at events like fairs and rodeos. As it happened, Gordie Tapp and Maurice Bolyer were scheduled to work a personal appearance one Saturday night in August. On Sunday evening, the phone rang and it was Joanne Bolyer, Maurice's wife, telling me that Maurice wasn't feeling well. Apparently, he'd started feeling ill after doing the show the night before, but he decided it was just something he'd eaten. Next morning, he wasn't feeling any better, so the doctor was called in.

. "The doctor didn't know what was wrong, but I knew it had to be something serious, because he didn't even take his banjo out of the car," Joanne said. "He just left it in the trunk, and he *never* does that. You know, Tommy."

"Yes," I said, getting that awful sinking feeling, "I know, Joanne."

Later that day, Maurice started feeling so bad that his wife insisted he go to the hospital, where they admitted him immediately and started running tests to determine what the problem was.

On Monday, Maurice seemed to be getting weaker, and the hospital still didn't know exactly what was wrong; then, the next day, he slipped into a coma. We were all shocked, but we tried to hope for the best; and I'll tell you, there had to be a good many prayers being said for Maurice during that time.

Gordie was going to be out of town until Thursday, so I called his wife, Helen, just to let her know I'd checked with the hospital. "Maurice is still in a coma, Helen, and I'm not sure, but it doesn't look good," I said, "Would you have Gordie call me as soon as he gets back?"

Friday morning, I called the hospital again, and this time, the news seemed more promising; Maurice was still in the coma, but they told me he was holding his own. That afternoon, I got a call from Gordie. "Hi, Gord," I said. "Boy, am I glad you're back in town."

"Yeah, I just got in," he said. "Do you have any idea what time the funeral will be?"

Funeral . . . I just dropped the phone. Somewhere in the distance, I could hear Gordie's voice calling: "Hello? Hello, Tommy?"

Through a mist of tears, I saw Shirley rushing to pick up the phone. It turned out Gordie had assumed that I'd been told that Maurice had passed away that afternoon, and there I was, thinking all the time that he was getting better. It was a shock to find out that way, but it would have been a shock no matter how I'd been told. Maurice was a dear friend, and there's no easy way to lose a friend.

It was hard, too, accepting the fact that Maurice was gone just at the point of starting to gain the worldwide acclaim his talent so richly deserved. He was becoming known in the States; and his records were receiving widespread attention. It was painful to realize that Maurice would no longer be there, making those magical sounds only he could create, reaching out with his very soul to touch anyone who heard him.

When our season started in the fall, David and I felt it would be a good idea to do a tribute to Maurice on the show, and I'll tell you, that was one of the most difficult things I've ever done on television. I chose a reading that talked about seeing a good friend pass in the street; how you think to yourself that you should really give your friend a call one of these days; and how you finally do call him, only to find that your friend is no longer there.

It was something I knew had to be done, had to be said; and I knew it was going to be painful. It was all I could do to get through it without starting to cry, and when it was finished, I was in tears and headed straight for the dressing room.

Even years later, when we did a tribute to Maurice on our 20th anniversary show, it was still very hard for me to read the words without breaking down completely. Why don't I share them with you, in case you couldn't be there for that particular show.

While I read, we had a little tape of Maurice playing "The Green, Green Grass of Home," as only he could play it:

"One of the finest gentlemen I ever worked with over the past 20 years was not only a great musician. He was a truly good human being and a friend.

"Before his passing, he was hailed the world over as the King of the Banjo, but to us, he will always remain just one of the gang, and if he were here tonight, I know that I'd be introducing him again as I did for so many of our past shows: the King of the Banjo, Maurice Bolyer. . ."

There's a comforting thought at the end of the day, when I'm feeling weary and low; and it sort of grips this crusty old heart like nothing else I know. It gets in the soul, and it lingers there, in that strange way that some memories do; and from time to time, I think to myself that I'm glad I rubbed shoulders with you.

You knew your song, and you knew it well, with a voice and hand so true; and from time to time, I think to myself that I'm glad I rubbed shoulders with you. . .

You know, when I think back on it, I'm glad we never tried to replace Maurice on the show, because that would have been impossible. No one — not then and not now — could ever take the place of Maurice Bolyer.

At the beginning of our first season without Maurice, which was 1978, David Koyle came to me one day and said he'd decided to hire eight professional dancers and a choreographer for our show. Well, I was still very upset about losing Maurice, and I really wasn't in the mood to go through another one of these endless arguments.

"Dave," I said, "if you want dancers, go out and hire some *authentic* square dancers," and I walked away.

A few moments later, he came over and started to insist that the show needed dancers every week. With a choreographer, he said, they could even be trained to do a few square-dancing routines.

"Look," I said, feeling I would just explode if I discussed this any further right then, "why don't you come over to the house this evening, and we'll talk about it at that time."

I guess Dave thought that meant I was bending towards his viewpoint, because he was bursting with enthusiasm when he arrived at our home: how we'd always be able to stage the various songs we did if we got these dancers; how they could provide such a wonderful framework for my solos, and so on, and so on . . .

I let him go on for awhile, and when he paused, I said, quite simply: "No." I knew better than to try to explain to him, after all this time, that professional dancers who'd be right at home in the National Ballet were just not appropriate for a country show.

"But the show needs variety," he said.

"Well, David, I think you and I have a different concept of variety." I mean, I wanted variety, too; within the confines of a country show. It's not as if those confines are so narrow, either; we could have down-east fiddlers, Western fiddlers, country bands, trios, Southern fiddlers, banjo-pickers, duos, trios, French-Canadian fiddlers, female vocalists, male vocalists, country comedians, singing comedians like Grandpa Jones, gospel singers, legitimate step-dancers, bona fide square dancers . . . What we did not need was modern jazz dancers, any more than we needed a couple of elephant or giraffe acts. I mean no offence to jazz dancers; it's just that they're from an entirely different environment and would probably feel as awkward as we would.

"Look, Tommy," Dave said, breaking in on my thoughts, "I really feel this is a good idea. The show needs it."

"No," I said, "the show does not need it."

At this point, Shirley came in with a pot of coffee for us; she put it down, gave us the mugs, and paused for a moment. Now, Shirley hardly ever has anything to say when I'm in the middle of a business discussion; and that's the way we both want it. On this particular occasion, however, her remarks couldn't have been better timed:

"Let me fill you in on one point, Dave," she said, "when Tommy makes up his mind about something, you'll never budge him; so whatever it is you're talking about, you might as well try to bend his way, because he's never going to do the bending."

Well, Dave showed no inclination to take Shirley's advice, so we batted it back and forth a few more times, until I'd finally had enough, once and for all.

"Look," I said, "I don't really feel I can go on this way, Dave. I think we're going to have to get our situations clarified by the network."

"That's an excellent idea," he said.

"Well, you know what this means, don't you?" I asked. "I don't see any other solution; either you're going to leave, or I'm going to leave. I mean, do you really want to push this?"

He did.

Before I called the network, I had a long talk with Shirley and then got on the phone to my lawyer, Sam Lerner, who has been doing my legal work since I was 16 years old. There was no way I would face even the possibility of having to leave the show unless I felt absolutely confident that the futures of my wife and children were secure.

At this point, I've got to make a very strong statement about the CBC network, and that is that the CBC has had more needless criticism than any other organization I can think of. The network has gained recognition around the world for shows like Man Alive, The Nature of Things, the great dramas and documentaries, and the insightful public affairs shows. I'd like to add that many, many favorable comments I've received about our show from American viewers have included the CBC; people might say something like, "I knew from seeing the good quality of the show that it had to be part of that terrific CBC network."

We have people working at the CBC who are absolute geniuses in every field; the very cream of the crop. But television is like everything else: there are going to be gaps, and I happened to fall into one of them at the outset of our show.

Now, when the so-called higher-ups at the network decided on the overall concept of the show right at the start, they turned it over to the appropriate department, and the department heads chose the people they felt were most appropriate to make a team for the performer.

So the network was not aware of any problems; the ratings were good, and they just assumed the direction we were taking was our choice. They didn't see the slow, gradual changes that were taking place on our show to the point that the whole original concept they first supported was disappearing. From my point of view, I had never wanted to start complaining to the higher-ups. I felt it was appropriate for me to deal with the producer, which is exactly what I did, *until* it became clear to me that what was at stake was the very idea of the show that the network wanted in the first place. At this point, I felt I *had* to talk to the network.

Once I'd thought it all through, I called Jim Guthro, the acting head of TV variety at the network. By then, it was almost 2 in the morning, but I couldn't leave it another day.

"I'm sorry to bother you so late, but I really feel we must discuss the future of the show. Could we meet in the morning?"

Mr. Guthro agreed, and we arranged to get together at 10 the next day. Before we went into that meeting, though, I tried to talk to Dave again; perhaps we could avoid this whole mess if only he'd reconsider his views.

"Dave, please change your mind about the dancers and choreographers," I said. "I don't want to see your career end this way, I don't want to see the show end this way, and I don't think any of it's necessary."

"No way," he said.

I asked him once more just as we were heading into the meeting: "Dave, I don't think you can come out a winner on this one, so I'm giving you this opportunity to change your mind."

He still refused.

"All right, Dave," I said, "but don't you ever say somewhere down the line that I didn't give you fair warning or that I tried to stab you in the back because of this."

"Fine," he said.

So we went into the conference room with Mr. Guthro, and Dave spoke first; he'd brought all sorts of paraphernalia with him on the ratings, which supposedly showed how much the show had improved since he took over as producer. Then he made another argument for the dancers.

When he'd finished, Mr. Guthro turned to me: "Tommy?"

"I'd like to ask a question," I said. "What is your interpretation of variety as it pertains to the Tommy Hunter Show?"

"Well, what the network wants is the best country show it can have," he said. "As for variety, as long as it's within the boundaries of country music, that's fine."

"Okay, then" I said. "I don't think professionally choreographed routines are within the boundaries of country music."

286

Jim Guthro agreed, and Dave announced his resignation shortly afterward.

Of course, we now needed a new producer, and I knew just who would be perfect: Les Pouliot. He'd never been a producer before, which made the network a bit hesitant at first; but when I pointed out that we hadn't really done all that well with producers who had briefcases full of credentials, they finally changed their minds.

So I gave Les a ring.

"Hi, Les," I said. "Remember reading that script for me?"

"Uh-huh?"

"Remember how I thanked you, and you said, 'Any time'?"

"Uh, yeah . . ."

"Then remember how I said I might hold you to that?"

"Right . . . Hey, Tommy, what's this all about?"

"There's one more thing I'd like you to do," I said.

"What's that?"

"I'd like you to produce our show."

Long silence. "I don't know, Tommy . . ."

Well, we talked it out, and Les finally agreed to give it a try. He may have had his doubts right then, but I knew that he'd turn out to be ideal for our show, and I was right.

From his very first day, Les exemplified to me what a producer should be: extremely well-organized; able to visualize what he wants to create; and most important of all, very knowledgeable about our country audience and the kind of show he wants.

His entire attitude, right from the start, was so completely different from producers we'd had in the past that I wondered if we were even on the same show as before. I remember one of the network people asking Les what he thought his first job should be. "To make Hunter comfortable on his own show," Les said.

That is precisely what I'd been fighting for all those years — for someone who would let me feel comfortable on the show, so that I could then communicate my own enthusiasm and the enjoyment of my music to the audience.

That was a lesson I'd learned 20 years before on Country

Hoedown: if you're having fun in what you do, the audience will have fun. Simple as that.

For the first time in years, I started practising my guitar again; for the first time in years, I started loosening up on the reins around the studio. I'd come into rehearsal and find a simple, perfect set; no artificial rivers or psychedelic fishing huts. I'd pick up a list of proposed guest artists and it was music to my ears: Mel Tillis, Roy Clark, Tammy Wynette, Ray Price . . . on and on, every single one of them genuine country artists. I'd listen to the sound mix and hear Nashville instead of Broadway. *Everything* was different!

This change was no small feat, either; sets had been designed and scripts had been written way in advance. Well, Les cancelled sets, and rewrote the show so that for the first time, the performers were being highlighted instead of the staging and sets. Like me, Les knew there wasn't any point building a huge production that would just swallow up and overwhelm the performers; what he wanted was an atmosphere that would allow the talent of these artists to shine forth without any needless encumbrance.

Of course, Les and I also had to make some tough decisions about some of the people working on the show. Some of them were under contracts, so we couldn't alter all the departments overnight; but even during that first year, quite a number of people working behind the scenes ended up moving to other parts of the network, because we just didn't feel they were right for our show. Sure, it was tough letting these people go, but we felt that if we did otherwise, it would be a compromise.

The change was dramatic: very quickly; almost overnight, it seemed, we had a team dedicated to creating the very best country show on television: cameramen, musical arrangers, makeup artists, musicians, set designers, directors — absolutely everyone shared the same goal.

Instead of having the cast sit around the set for two or three hours, like in the old days, Les instituted a very tight, efficient schedule that we still use to this day. No one can give less than 100 per cent, and knowing our cast and crew, no one ever will. We've never regretted that decision, because that system really works for us. Grace under pressure, I think Hemingway called it.

I can still recall the decision Les made that settled the question of what kind of professional future we'd have together. As I mentioned, we still had a number of people under contract to appear on our show that season, and one of them was a group; I can't remember its name. Les decided to pay them what they'd been contracted for, then told them they would not be doing the show.

That night, I noticed that the group's name had been taken off the schedule. "What happened to that band, Les?" I asked.

"I paid them off and asked them to leave," he said.

"Well, couldn't we have gotten one song out of them?"

"Sure," Les said, "but if you'd heard that hard rock sound, you would have started second-guessing me, and one thing I don't need is someone like you looking over my shoulder all the time."

When I heard that, I knew I could let go of the reins completely. Finally, I could start to concentrate all my time and energy on my job as a performer and host of a show that I feel mighty comfortable doing.

CHAPTER 11

Having it Your Way

A bout three weeks after Les took over as producer of my show, I was sitting in the living room with a cup of coffee when Shirley came in and joined me. "Hi, Boo (that's my pet name for Shirley). What's up?"

"Tom, what made you decide to stop drinking?"

"Stop drinking? I haven't stopped drinking."

"Well, when was the last time you had a drink?"

"Jeez, I don't know." I started thinking about it, and suddenly I realized I hadn't had a drink ever since Les took over on the show.

I walked over and started to pour one, and then I thought: Hey, wait a second. I've worked all these years to get the show the way I want it, and wouldn't it be stupid to do anything that would prevent me from enjoying it now. So I went and poured that drink down the sink, and you know, I haven't had another one to this day.

Even more important than the show was what could have happened to my family if I'd gone on drinking. I don't think I had what could be described as a serious drinking problem; nevertheless, there was going to be no gambling with what comes first in my life, before television, before country music, before *anything*, and that is my wife and three sons.

When I think back on those difficult years on our television show before Les came along, I realize that more than anything else, it was the sanctuary of our home that helped me to survive even the roughest and most depressing times. It was like a shot of adrenalin to me each time I headed west out of Toronto, knowing that in just a short time, I'd be in the peace of our home and surrounded with the warmth and security of my wife and boys. This was my world I was coming back to; and in the midst of all the chaos and confusion that surrounded me for so long on our TV show, just knowing who was waiting for me at home made all the difference.

None of those feelings about home and family changed even after we got the show turned around. As much as I love doing our show and working with all the fine professionals we have around us, Shirley and the boys come first, and always will. When I cross the Humber River on my way home to Mississauga, that television studio is forgotten.

I know that going down the road is a way of life for many people in our business, and I understand how they feel: maybe they've got 10 hit records, but they feel they have to go for the 11th, or the 12th; they have to keep getting up on that stage; they feed on the applause and the lights. For some performers, that's just the way it is, and I've even had some of them tell me they go almost stir-crazy if they're home for more than a couple of days in a row.

For me, what's important is going for a walk on the beach with the girl I love, watching the sunrise, knowing that my boys are all right and on their way to fulfilling lives of their own. As long as I'm secure in these fundamentals of life, then I can go out and do the show with all the enthusiasm and feeling in the world. I don't need to have people watch me climb out of a Rolls-Royce or a private jet in order to feel successful, because to me, success means having a family to share your life with, good times and hard times alike.

I've got to say that in many ways, I've been lucky in a business that crushes a hundred young dreams for every one that comes true. I've had a television show that's enabled me to stay away from the life on the road that many performers are obliged to live, simply because they don't have the luxury of something like a weekly TV show. So I'm not saying that their lifestyle is wrong; I understand the necessity of doing as many performances as possible when you don't have any kind of regularity in your career. Besides, there are no absolutes in our business (as I've probably said more than once by now!) and I have no way of guaranteeing, even after all these years on television, that there'll always be a contract waiting for me at the start of each season. There's always the chance that I might also have to consider doing a lot of those kinds of road trips myself.

For the moment, though, the situation I'm in is absolutely ideal as far as allowing me to concentrate on my priorities: Shirley, Jeff, Greg and Mark Hunter. I feel I'm a very fortunate man in being able to say that I have the time to devote to my wife and sons, and the resources to be able to enjoy fully the pleasures we appreciate as a family.

I guess what we most enjoy is being together at special times like birthdays, Christmases and anniversaries. Sitting back in the coziness of our home and sharing one another's company and a few simple gifts that come from the heart: that's my idea of a celebration. We've been lucky enough to enjoy a comfortable lifestyle, but there's a level of comfort beyond which I don't need or want to go. All of us Hunters would feel completely awkward and ill at ease in a home glittering with crystal chandeliers and mahogany furniture that looks so luxurious you wouldn't want to stretch out and put your feet up for fear of breaking something.

On the other hand, while the boys were growing up, I did feel it was important to introduce them to some elements of formal living; I remembered all too well how I felt those times we visited my uncle's home and I was confronted with so many different pieces of silverware that I didn't know which one to pick up first. I wanted my boys to know how to tell the difference between a fish fork and an appetizer fork, not that they were going to have a whole set of them at home (which they don't), but just so they wouldn't feel out of place at a formal affair, even if they only went to one or two of them in their lives.

So what we'd do is every Sunday, we'd get out the good china and the silverware and have our Sunday dinner at the big dining room table; even with candles and flowers, sometimes. Just on Sunday, though; the rest of the week, we'd be back to our more casual suppers around the kitchen table, which I must say we've always liked a lot better as our regular routine!

Our home is our haven; if you were to ask either Shirley or me where we'd sooner spend an evening, it would be right here by the fire, talking quietly together or maybe not even saying anything at all; just basking in the glow of the fire and knowing everything we need or want is right here.

Even on occasions like New Year's Eve, we've never felt the slighest desire to go out to a fancy hotel where we'd spend an evening with people we don't even know. The standard New Year's Eve at our house has always been Shirley coaxing me into a few dances (I only step on her feet once or twice, as a rule!) and then, at midnight, a glass of champagne for Shirley and coffee or orange juice for me. Of course, now that the boys are grown up, they aren't always here on New Year's Eve, but at midnight, in very quick succession, there'll always be three phone calls to wish us Happy New Year and say, "I love you." I don't ever have to wonder if those calls will come; being as close a family as we are gives me just about as secure a feeling as knowing the sun will come up in the morning.

Shirley and I have always been in total agreement about the kinds of activities we prefer. We don't always do exactly the same things; for instance, Shirley really enjoys playing tennis and is very good at the game, while I like tennis but maybe prefer going fishing just a little bit more. When I say we're in total agreement, I'm talking more about the basics: we'd both rather spend a casual, relaxed evening alone at home or with friends or some neighbors.

We occasionally attend formal affairs, and at those times, I will put on my tuxedo (I have a couple of them, both Western-style), and I know I can always count on Shirley to rise to the occasion with all the style and class she brings to everything she does.

That's the thing about Shirley; everything she puts her mind to, she does well, whether it's the hobbies she enjoys, like tennis or knitting, or getting ready for one of those elegant evenings even when she might very well prefer to be curled up at home with a good book. Like me, when Shirley decides she's going to do something, she goes after it with all the energy and enthusiasm in the world, which is one of the many qualities that make us so compatible.

Shirley's a people person; she likes just about everyone and feels at ease in just about any situation. Guests in our home have often remarked to me how welcome she always makes them feel, a compliment which I'm very proud to pass on to her.

Throughout our marriage, Shirley has also always shown a great ability to keep her composure in situations where many other people (myself included!) might lose their cool; and that capacity of hers is something I've greatly valued over the years. Shirley has put up with a lot of my frustrations and anxieties over the direction our show was going in the past; and many's the time I remember her sitting patiently and letting me blow off steam when I've been upset, rather than fighting me on it.

One time, when we were in Europe on one of our overseas tours to entertain the Canadian Forces, Shirley came along with me; she'd never been to Europe, and I thought it would be a great opportunity for her to enjoy some of the sights. Well, I'll tell you, Shirley and I have enjoyed many wonderful trips together; but most of the sights my wife saw on this particular occasion was the spectacle of her husband absolutely beside himself over one little calamity after another!

It all started back in Canada, when the whole gang of us performers got split up onto two different flights because of weather problems. Shirley and I ended up on a flight that was due to arrive at our destination in West Germany just 20 minutes after the others.

Somehow, we managed to reach Frankfurt all in one piece; I checked my watch, and it looked like we could just about make the 8 p.m. show if we were lucky enough to find a good driver to get us to Lahr, where the military base was located. "How much will the fare be?" I asked the driver; he said it'd be the equivalent of $50 Canadian. "Here's $100," I said. "Just get on that Autobahn and put your foot down." Well, he took me quite seriously, and floored that Mercedes so hard I thought his foot would go straight through the floorboard. We were absolutely terrified for our lives, but luckily, nothing happened except that we reached the military base in what had to be world-record time.

I knew I was going to be late, but I thought I could probably make it in time for the second half . . . Suddenly, I remembered the time change between England and Germany, and we approached the theatre to find everything was black.

I'm sure we've all had days when nothing seems to go right, and throughout it all, Shirley was like a brick.

The very first day we got back to Toronto, I headed downtown to do a bit of shopping, and by the end of the day, I'd found exactly the item I was looking for, had it wrapped up in a great big box, and headed home to Mississauga. "Here, Boo," I said, handing her the box, "this is to make up for Germany."

"What is it, Tom?"

"Well, why don't you open it up and see?"

She very carefully peeled back the layers of tissue paper and then let out a shriek of delight as she saw the folds of shimmering fur. "Oh, Tommy!" she gasped. "A mink coat! It's absolutely beautiful!"

When it comes to Christmas and birthdays, and special occasions like the one I was just telling you about, I like to make sure Shirley always gets something very special to let her know how much I appreciate what a terrific wife and mother she is.

One of the nicest things about our relationship is that we enjoy each other's company so much. I know that sounds like a pretty basic reason to embark on a marriage; but believe me, there are many, many couples who prefer to cultivate their separate interests to the point where they hardly spend any time together. If that approach works for them, that's fine; for us, togetherness is a way of life. If I'm going for a long walk to watch the leaves turn in the fall, Shirley'll be right at my side; and if she wants to go on an outing, I'll be right there with her.

There are some activities we pursue separately; for example, if I'm out fishing, Shirley might prefer to go shopping, play tennis, or chat with some of her girlfriends. Nine times out of ten, though, if you see one of us, the other one won't be far behind.

That's the way it's always been in terms of family decisions, too; Shirley and I have always talked together about our plans, whether it's something like buying a piece of furniture, or a more serious matter pertaining to one of the boys. I feel there has to be one boss in a household, so most of the time (not all), I'm the one who makes the final decisions; but Shirley and I *always* talk about it first.

Back when the boys were still young, we enjoyed spending time in Florida and hoped someday to live there part of the year. We were both entirely in agreement about the kind of place we wanted: a comfortable, relaxed spot in a very quiet, easy-going community; and when we discovered Hutchinson Island, we knew it was for us. Hutchinson Island is on the Atlantic between West Palm Beach and Ft. Pierce, and the island itself is connected to the mainland by three causeways, so it has all the secluded feeling of an island while still accessible to various amenities.

Not too long ago, a friend of ours came over to me and said: "You know, you're very lucky to have a wife like Shirley."

Quick as a flash, I came right back: "Luck has absolutely nothing to do with it. I knew what I was getting the very first time I saw Shirley, and the intervening years have only proved just how right I was!"

It was always important for both Shirley and me to raise our boys without any influence at all from television. Shirley has never been interested in being a stage wife; she might go into the studio once a year, if that, and her attitude to the business is that while she appreciates the work I do, she doesn't feel comfortable getting involved in the day-to-day aspects of it. As for me, I've always felt that I want to keep my family life entirely separate from the business, so between the two of us, we've gone to some lengths to make sure that the boys have never been overwhelmed by show business.

What we wanted for the boys was a completely secure environment in which to grow up, without anything around them to make them feel that they were any different or any better than someone else just because their dad happened to earn his living by performing on TV. If you walked into our home while the kids were growing up, or today, for that matter, you wouldn't find a single clue as to my profession. There are no guitars standing in the corner of the living room, or pictures of myself playing in a show (there *is* a photo Shirley and I treasure, which shows the two of us together). I mean, you wouldn't expect to walk into a doctor's house and find his diplomas and certificates hanging all over the walls, and there's no reason why I should parade my career throughout my home, either.

Even when they were very young, I know that the boys appreciated the distinction between who I was at work and who I was at home; and there was never any doubt which one was Daddy. I still remember, one time, sitting them down in front of the TV on a Friday night and asking: "Who's that?"

"IT'S TOMMY HUNTER!!" they'd all chorus, imitating the announcer's voice and shrieking with laughter.

"Okay, then who am I?" I'd ask.

"Daddy!"

That was probably the only time I ever asked my boys to watch the show, and even then it was only so that I could see how they'd react to the difference. Other than that, it was pretty much up to the boys what kinds of programs they watched (of course, there were *some* guidelines). I wanted the boys to make up their own minds when it came to their interests, and it didn't really bother me on a Friday night than to see them switching to all kinds of different programs *except* mine (which was very often the case!).

What Shirley and I couldn't always control was how the world outside our front door would react to our boys; when you're doing your job on the television screen and everyone's watching, that tends to expose you, and to some extent your family, in a public way that isn't always comfortable. That's part of the territory, and I've gotten used to it over the years (although I'm still basically a shy person). On the other hand, that kind of exposure can sometimes be hard on young children.

I remember one summer afternoon when Jeff decided to wander over to the day camp that was being set up for kids on the school ground; there were various sports, crafts, and all kinds of activities. Anyway, one of the supervisors came over to talk to Jeff about joining the camp. "Do you like running, son?"

"Oh, yes," Jeff said.

"Do you want to get involved in lots of different sports?"

"Yes, very much."

"Okay, now what's your name and address?" he asked, taking out a notebook to write down the information.

"Jeff Hunter," he said, and then gave his address.

"Oh," the supervisor said, and stopped writing to peer down at Jeff, "you must be Tommy Hunter's son."

When he heard that, Jeff turned around and went straight home; he never returned to the camp. That supervisor hadn't really done anything wrong; after all, it was a natural enough question. But even at such a young age, Jeff and all our kids wanted to achieve things on their own, and not as the son of a television performer. Of course, they were proud of my work, but it was the kind of pride any son takes in a father who works hard to earn a living, and it certainly did not mean that they wanted to go through life being known as so-and-so's son. What a tragic disadvantage that would be to the development of *any* young person's sense of individuality!

From my end of things, it was very important to become

involved in all the activities and interests of my boys. There was always a telephone number where either they or Shirley could reach me, either at the studio or in a hotel if I was performing out of town.

I still remember when the boys were actively involved in hockey that I rushed from the studio to go and watch them play; or between takes, I'd go to the phone and find out, in *considerable* detail, how the various games were going.

Here's a story that any father would treasure for the rest of his life, and I hope you won't mind if I share it with you. It was during a hockey game in the finals for the city championships, and I was sitting in the arena next to a man whose son was apparently playing for the other team, because he kept pointing toward Mark's bench and shouting: "No talent on that team!"

Right at that very moment, Mark moved in toward the goal and lined up a shot: "HE SCORES!"

"That's number one," I said, turning to the guy next to me.

"Awww, lucky goal," he said. "No talent on that team."

A few minutes later, Mark came swooping in again: "HE SCORES!"

"That's number two," I remarked to the guy.

"Lucky goal, lucky goal," he said again.

Well, would you believe it? Two minutes later, Mark got the hat-trick!

"Well, that's number three," I said, "all scored by my son, who's wearing the big Number Five."

"Come on, come on!" he shouted in the direction of his son's team. "We can still beat them . . . No talent on that team," and then he hesitated, "with the exception of Number Five!"

Mark ended up scoring five goals as his team went on to win the championships, and I think he got most of the assists, too. I'll tell you, even Wayne Gretzky's dad couldn't have been prouder.

For awhile, Mark talked about going into hockey as a career, but when he was 15, he quit because his team at the time was going through coaches at an unbelievable rate, and there was a state of complete disorganization among the ranks.

Mark was also extremely interested in car racing, and he became so familiar with the various drivers and statistics that it got to the point where he could just about predict the outcome of any race, from the European Grand Prix to Mosport. I enjoyed racing myself and had a friend who was a stock car driver, so Mark and I often went to watch him together.

One of the nice things about our business is that you get invited to enjoyable events such as fishing shows, golf tournaments, and fund-raising events. One of the most interesting invitations I can remember was to a promotional auto race at a track in Atlanta, Georgia, organized by a Toronto promoter by the name of John Graham. I very quickly accepted John's invitation (although Shirley thought I'd surely gone crazy!).

Of course, with all his interest in race cars, Mark naturally wanted to go along; but I had to say no, because I just didn't want to be encouraging him to make racing his career, with all the dangers and uncertainties that I knew existed in the sport. It was a tough decision, but in retrospect, I think I made the right call.

As it happened, one of the first people I spoke to out there was Darrell Waltrip, who lent me his racing uniform for our little race. We got to talking, and I mentioned how I was trying to discourage Mark's interest in a racing career. "Well, just have him call me," Darrell said, "and I'll give him 100,000 reasons why he shouldn't do it!"

Well, they explained all the rules and showed us the brand-new cars we would drive; then we strapped ourselves in, checked all the equipment, and started our practice laps.

I let everyone get out ahead of me so I'd have the whole track to myself, then put my foot to the floor and shot down the back straightaway just going for broke; kept my foot there as long as I could and then backed off very slightly going into the corner. What a thrill that was to feel the car stick that curve!

From watching a lot of races, I knew the best way to come

out of the corner was to brush as close to the wall as possible and then dive for the inside of the track again; it worked just like a charm.

After a couple of practice laps, we started the race, and everything was going fine until I happened to come up on one of the other celebrities and decided to pass him on the outside. Now, this guy had driven a race car before, and one of the organizers had warned me not to try to pass him on the outside because he was very keen on winning the race. I wasn't trying to prove a point or anything by passing him, but I had the opportunity so I decided to go for it, though in retrospect I wish I hadn't.

He must have sensed I was coming up on him, because he suddenly stepped on the gas and started to slide out of control; then ploughed straight into the concrete wall. A photographer who was standing there just managed to jump out of the way in the nick of time, and very luckily the driver walked away without a scratch, even though the car took the brunt of it and a good 12 feet of concrete was gouged out of that wall. Needless to say, a very nervous track owner called it quits!

I've got to say that all three of the boys were very good athletes when they were growing up, and I've always urged them to give 100 per cent to whatever they were doing, whether it was hockey, or track, or swimming. I'm just as glad, though, that none of them decided on a sports career, because it's one of those professions (even worse than entertainment!) where there's a thousand guys sweating it out in the minor leagues for every one that makes the big time. That's why I'm glad I've always encouraged the boys to explore all the avenues and options open to them, so they could have the chance to make up their own minds about what they wanted.

I wouldn't want anyone to get the idea, though, that my sons spent their entire childhood doing exactly what they wanted; that's certainly not what I mean by independence and exploring your options! As important as it is for youngsters to have the freedom to choose the kinds of activities they enjoy, I personally believe that it's even more crucial to have rules and guidelines that must be followed.

The way Shirley and I see it, you're not doing children any favors by letting them have their way. They have to learn early in the game that there are good reasons to learn discipline and responsible behavior.

There were strict curfews for all three of them, whether on a school night or the weekend, and you'd better believe that if they were late, they were very promptly grounded; no amount of pleading and cajoling would get me to change my mind once they'd broken the rules. Those were the consequences they had to face, just as when they got into a scrape like breaking a window while playing baseball, or going across the creek when I'd told them not to (don't worry, guys, I'm not naming names!), they knew they had to take responsibility for what they'd done. If something was broken, the boys were very well aware of who was going to pay for it, and that someone was not me.

Jeff, Greg and Mark are good kids, so it's not as if we had these discussions every night of the week. At the same time, they're not angels; they're average, normal boys who shinnied up the neighbor's apple tree just like I did. That's part of being a kid, just as it's perfectly normal for them to be a little reluctant to call it quits when they're having a good time. I understand how my kids felt, but on the other hand, that didn't mean I was willing just to let things ride and hope they'd grow out of it. If a kid doesn't learn discipline when he's growing up, in my opinion it becomes close to impossible to achieve it as an adult, when it's essential to getting anywhere in life.

To me, it was also just as important to sit down and talk with my boys about why we had these rules and what consequences they could expect if they were broken. I'd explain to them how much they would benefit in years to come from learning these basic priorities, and how they would enjoy having fun all the more after first putting in the complete effort it takes to get a job done well.

There was never a time when I put my foot down unless I

talked to the boys about my reasons; I don't think there's any point in behaving like a tyrant with kids (or with adults) because the resentment and hostility they'd build up as a result would be just as detrimental to them as no rules at all.

You know, they're only with you a short time, and there's going to be a tough world waiting for them out there; so you want to give them your very best to help them along the way.

For Shirley and me, rules were just one aspect of providing the best environment for our boys while they were growing up. To us, it was just as important for them to feel that home was a place they would enjoy being and bringing their friends.

We've always been delighted when all the neighbors' kids were over here either for an evening or overnight; it almost became a regular Saturday morning feature of the Hunter household for me to pick my way through all the boys stretched out on the living room floor as I made my way to the kitchen to cook their favorite breakfast of pancakes and bacon. I'll tell you, there were plenty of mornings when I'd go through 10 or 12 pounds of bacon for those feeds we used to call cowboy breakfasts!

I also felt it was very important for us to have a bar in the house, definitely *not* under lock and key, because never did I want the boys to get the message that alcohol was something very secretive and unattainable that they had to sneak out to some bar to indulge in. I would always explain to them when they were young why the liquor cabinet was kept open, and that I didn't want them going into it at this stage of the game. When they were old enough, I would offer them a drink; and I can remember a few times, if we had friends over and the opportunity was right, that I'd ask one of the boys to join us for a drink.

Another aspect of our home life that's always been very important to Shirley and me has been to provide an atmosphere of mutual respect and affection for the boys. It goes without saying that we love Jeff, Greg and Mark more than anything in the world; at the same time, we've always felt that it's essential to be open about showing those feelings.

Ever since they were babies, there was never a night went by without Shirley and me kissing the boys goodnight and saying, "I love you, honey."

"I love you too," they'd always say right back.

To this day, all grown up as they are, the boys will never end a phone conversation without saying, "I love you," and if they're home at Christmas or on a vacation, they still kiss us goodnight when they go to bed.

Shirley and I have also been very comfortable about showing our affection for each other in front of the boys; if one of them happened to come into the kitchen while I was hugging Shirley or giving her a great big kiss, we wouldn't instantly jump apart and stand there looking embarrassed, because we never felt that our love for each other was something to hide from the kids.

As a family, we've always been extremely close in many different ways, and one of the most enjoyable elements of our closeness has been some of the wonderful trips we've taken together.

During the time when I was doing a lot of travelling with our shows, Shirley came up with the great idea that we should get a motor home which I could take on the shows and then use for the whole family on vacations. We started out exploring Canada, because I wanted the boys to appreciate their own country first; and I guess we've been across the country and back three times, along with some trips to the United States as well. Those sure were fun times for us, and there's a lot of wonderful memories to go with them.

I don't think any of us will ever forget the time we were in Alberta, just near Athabasca Falls. We were ready to stop for the night, except that every campground was full. It was getting pretty late, and I was tired, so we decided to stop for awhile and have a look at the falls before driving on. The view was spectacular; the river narrows to such a sharp point that the water just rushes over and plunges into a deep, deep gorge.

By the time we'd had a really good look, it was completely dark and we decided the best thing to do was camp right there, despite the sign clearly marked: NO CAMPING. I figured we'd just explain our situation to the parks people in the morning.

It was a bit chilly to start the barbecue outside, so I just sat back and relaxed with a coffee while Shirley started dinner. I was just getting really comfortable when suddenly I got this feeling someone was watching me. I turned towards the window and looked straight into the face of an enormous black bear; just a thin screen separated us.

Well, he took one look at me and opened his mouth: *"Roarrr*!!"

The boys started screaming at the top of their lungs; the hamburger Shirley was flipping ended up on the floor; and I went racing into the kitchen to get the window closed before our uninvited guess could try out that route. Got there just in time, too; he was coming around the corner as I slammed it shut.

Needless to say, none of us got much sleep that night. I mean, this was not Smokey the Bear we were dealing with; this was a wild animal, and if he'd made up his mind he was coming in, those windows wouldn't have stopped him. Luckily, it turned out he'd had enough of camping life for one night; and as for us, I'll tell you, we never stopped overnight again at a place with a NO CAMPING sign on it!

Another time, we pulled into a motor park in South Carolina and no sooner had we climbed out of the camper when Jeff started yelling: "Dad, look!" and pointing to a nearby pond. "Dad, there's fish in there!" Before I'd even looked over at the pond, he had the pole out and some bait on the line; he was already over there by the time I was getting out of the camper. Just as I looked over, he threw out his line and at that very instant, a seagull dived straight at the bait and promptly hooked itself very firmly on Jeff's line!

Well, poor Jeff didn't know what to do; he just started running and screaming: "Dad, I caught a bird! I caught a bird, Dad!" and I went running to look for someone who *did* know what to do, because I was just as baffled as Jeff. Fortunately, we found a couple of guys who'd apparently seen this happen many times before.

"Don't worry, son," one of them said, gently freeing the gull and setting it loose. "He'll be just fine; see?" and Jeff looked up to see the bird take off, obviously none the worse for its unusual fishing expedition.

Those were real fun trips we took, just meandering across the country without any kind of fixed schedule. If we stopped in a park where the boys met other kids their own age, we'd just stay an extra day or two, and that was a wonderful feeling for all of us, being able to come and go as we pleased.

One time, we happened to stop in a little town and I found a store that sold all kinds of tapes of the old radio shows, like Amos and Andy, Inner Sanctum, and a whole bunch of ghost stories narrated by Alfred Hitchcock. I recalled the wonderful memories of listening to the radio as a kid, so I thought I'd buy some of the tapes and give the boys a real treat that night.

All three of them were especially good about the usual after-supper routine that night; they had their showers, got into their pyjamas, gave Shirley and me a kiss goodnight, and crawled into bed in record time. "Is it time for the ghost stories yet, Dad?"

"Not quite yet, Greg," I said. "Not dark enough yet."

Thirty seconds later: "Now, Dad?"

"Pretty soon, pretty soon," I said, setting up the speakers in the back where the kids' beds were (Shirley and I were up front because we were going to be driving that night).

As soon as it was completely dark, I turned on a tape . . . Well, we heard more shrieks and squeals and noises from those kids, and I could just imagine the pictures that were in their minds as they visualized those horrific stories. So the nightly ghost story or radio show got to be a regular routine on our camping trips, and the kids got to know all the same shows I'd grown up with.

Of course, not all our trips were equally enjoyable; there's one in particular that doesn't exactly stir pleasant memories.

It all started on a trip down to Florida, when Greg got sick in the motor home and it turned out he had tonsillitis. We'd no sooner got him recuperating down there when I got a phone call asking me to return to Toronto to do a special Easter show. Anyway, I did fly home and just before I was ready to come back, I phoned Shirley just to let her know when to expect me.

"Oh, Tom, I'm so glad you called," she said, sounding distraught. "Jeff has cut his foot on an open clam shell and we had to take him to the hospital . . . He needed 12 stitches!"

"Oh, my God," I said. "Look, will you be okay for a couple of days?"

"Other than that, we're all fine," Shirley said, "and I'll pick you up at the airport."

So I arrived at the airport, and the three boys were waiting for me, along with one of our neighbors from the campsite, who told me that Shirley had been feeling really ill and they'd taken her to a hospital. We rushed over there immediately, and one of the doctors told me he didn't know exactly what was wrong. "I think she may have had a bit too much sun."

None of the other doctors could shed any more light on the situation, so Shirley came back to the motor home with us and I started trying to find another doctor for her. After the fourth doctor told me I could get an appointment in about two months' time, I started to panic, because Shirley was feeling much worse and her temperature was really high.

Finally, I went into a pharmacy and explained the situation to the man behind the counter. "I know you're not supposed to recommend doctors," I said, "but we're from out of town, and my wife is really sick. Could you suggest anybody who could see my wife now?"

The pharmacist kindly gave me the name of a doctor, who agreed to see Shirley immediately. It turned out she had a very serious case of bronchitis, and the hospital just hadn't run the right tests to find this out. The doctor gave her a shot of penicillin and also recommended acupuncture, which was the first time either of us had ever even heard the word. As soon as he'd used the procedure on her hand, Shirley looked up, amazed.

"It feels like somebody just took a lead weight off my head!" she said.

Between the acupuncture and the penicillin, Shirley was feeling 100 per cent better in a couple of days, and from then on, that vacation improved immeasurably.

One of the few times we didn't take the motor home on a trip was after we'd done a show in New Brunswick; we met a lawyer down there who invited us to stay in his cottage on the Miramachi River. "I'm not going to be there for a while yet," he said, "and I think you and your family would enjoy it."

We decided to take him up on his kind offer and we all trooped down there. Two of his employees took us across the river, and there we saw an absolutely beautiful, spacious 1920s style summer home, with screened-in porches and huge living and dining rooms. There waiting for us were three other people; the cook, the maintenance man and the guide, all smiling warmly and welcoming us. The only difficulty was that we didn't understand exactly what they were saying, because they were speaking French, which none of us knew, any more than they knew how to speak English. So we had a little trouble communicating, but we managed to overcome the language barrier by nodding and smiling a lot, on both sides.

Maybe they all thought we hadn't seen solid food in a month, because when a little dinner bell rang and we came into the dining room, we just didn't know what we were going to do with all this food: appetizers, fish, steak, vegetables, salad, at least six different desserts. It was delicious, but when we were finished, we absolutely *had* to go out for a walk or they'd have had to wheel us to bed.

Believe it or not, when we got back we heard the bell rung again, and came in to find piles of sandwiches, coffee and hot chocolate; as if we hadn't just finished a lavish feast less than a half-hour before.

Next morning, we found giant platters heaped with eggs, bacon, pastries, jams, cereals, and loaves of bread, as if a party of 50 were expected instead of a family of five. The thing was, the food was so good and the people so kind that we didn't want to hurt them by refusing, so we ate such quantities that we ended up on diets for the next four months (Shirley and I did, anyway; kids tend to burn it off much faster!).

Later on, we tried to recover from lunch by taking another walk down by the river, which came to a fork just at the end of the path. There was a little island right at that fork, and the instant the boys saw it, they were off and running, making their way along a fallen tree with me following behind at a much more leisurely pace. Suddenly, I stopped to watch Jeff, who was right up to his knees in the water and gazing down at something very intently.

Then he started lifting his feet up and down very carefully, trying not to disturb the riverbed, and suddenly . . .SPLASH! He'd reached down into the water as fast as lightning and pulled out a salmon with his bare hands. I'd never seen anything like it; he looked just like a bear! Amazingly enough, he held onto that fish long enough to toss it straight onto the island; it landed right in front of Mark, who jumped into the air as if he'd been shot out of a cannon.

At this point, Shirley was back on the shore, doubled over with laughter at this whole picture; I was also finding it hard to keep a straight face, especially when Jeff raced over and threw the salmon back in the water. Turned out he'd been so upset about scaring Mark that he decided to get rid of what had caused the fright!

That evening, the lawyer and his family arrived; even though his two boys spoke no English, there was absolutely no barrier between them and my kids, who got along just great. We all enjoyed ourselves a great deal during that visit, and it's a pleasant memory we still have to this day.

Of course, every vacation must come to an end when school starts again, which leads me to a subject on which I've developed some fairly strong opinions after my years of experience with the education system and the effect it had on my three boys.

My kids happened to enter the public school system at a

time when they were changing to a more permissive, open concept of education; and some of you parents may recall phrases like: "Allow the children to develop at their own rate," and the one I always shuddered at: "Open classroom." Jeff and Greg, being slightly older, were thrust right into the middle of this system when it started in the 1970s, and I've got to say that they were perfect examples of why it just didn't work.

Just for openers, this whole free and open system went totally in the face of everything I'd been trying to convey to the boys about the importance of discipline, responsibility and motivation. I remember going in to the school one time with Jeff and finding one of his notebooks with all kinds of gold stars sprinkled all over it.

"Oh, that's nice," I said to the teacher. "Jeff's been doing well in his subjects."

"That's right, Mr. Hunter, and he's gotten all these stars for playing the tape recorder and the movie projector so well."

Instead of learning to spell, or add two plus two, he's getting gold stars for playing with a tape recorder. "I'm sorry," I said, "but I have an entire audio room downstairs in our home that I can teach Jeff to play. But while he's in school, I'd much prefer him to learn history, or math, or geography."

From then on, I became a little more involved in what was happening to the boys in school. The gold stars were just one example; as time went on, it became clear to me that this entire open pod concept was not doing Jeff and Greg any good. It was frightening to me that they weren't being taught what I considered (and still do) the basic components of a good education, like math and spelling.

Whenever I'd discuss the matter with a principal or a teacher, they'd always say the same thing: "The board of education feels this method will benefit the majority of students." After awhile, that statement became very frustrating. To me, if 80 per cent of the children did well in the open system, that left another 20 per cent who suffered because of it, and if my two kids were in that 20 per cent, the system was a complete and total failure as far as I was concerned.

I realize that certain children can work in an environment that's full of noise and constant activity without much organization; but other kids freeze up or become easily distracted and find it impossible to concentrate.

I kept asking the school board what they intended to do about those youngsters who couldn't work in the open setting. What was going to happen to kids who went through Grade 8, 9 and 10 in this system before the school board realized the whole concept wasn't working out as they'd hoped? Who was going to go back and erase the damage that had already been done?

The report cards had just been given out, and I was asked to go and see a particular teacher whom Jeff had always disliked intensely. I thought his feelings probably stemmed from the natural resentment a kid has when a teacher puts a bit of pressure on him. Our appointment was scheduled for 4 o'clock that afternoon, so Shirley and I arrived a few minutes early, just out of courtesy.

At 25 minutes to four, we were ushered into the classroom. What I saw when we walked in the door did nothing to improve my mood.

Let me just say at this point that Jeff kept his room just as neat as a pin; that was the way he liked it. Well, the first thing I noticed when I walked into this classroom was an entire wall full of books, not one of them placed in any semblance of order; just shoved into the shelves backwards, forwards and upside down so it looked like someone had stood back 20 feet and just flung those books at the bookcase.

The whole classroom was very disorderly, and dark because all the shades were pulled down; and then, the teacher walked toward us, hands shoved into the pocket of her jeans and a pack of Export A cigarettes sticking out of her shirt pocket. She introduced herself as Jeff's teacher, then walked back behind the desk, sat down, put her feet up, pulled out a cigarette and lit it up.

"Well, Mr. Hunter," she said, the cigarette dangling out of the corner of her mouth, "we're having a few problems with Jeff."

Looking at this teacher and her classroom, I quickly arrived at the answer to why Jeff was having problems.

That happened to be an unfortunate event, and doesn't represent the whole school system, which has many fine, dedicated teachers. Nevertheless, I still feel that there are some kids who work best in a more structured setting.

I was still very concerned about the problems Greg was having in the open classroom system. I only learned just how unsatisfactory this system was the year that Greg was lucky enough to get a teacher from the "old school," a wonderful lady by the name of Jessie Finlayson. She believed in concepts like discipline, motivation and basic learning, which were ideas that were completely foreign to the open classroom concept at the time.

Within just the first few weeks of school, Jessie realized that Greg was having speech problems, so after a discussion, we brought in another teacher to give him help with that difficulty.

I'll tell you, that year was the best one Greg had ever experienced in school. Along with the speech therapy Jessie recommended, she also gave him the encouragement he needed by bringing him right up to the front of the classroom, making sure he understood everything that was being taught, and providing the kind of strict supervision that had been totally lacking until then.

It was after seeing the great performance Greg was capable of turning in that I realized how much he needed a structured situation at school, so we decided to send him to a private school, Ridley College, to see how he would do in that kind of setting.

Well, Greg made such a tremendous amount of progress there that we decided to give him another try in public school for Grade 8. Shirley and I had missed Greg a great deal during his year and a half at Ridley, and we thought it would be good for him to be back home with the family; we also figured that taking Grade 8 in public school would be a good preparation for high school, and that with all his achievements at Ridley, he'd be able to handle it just fine.

By the time he was about halfway through Grade 8, we began to see how wrong we'd been. Greg's grades were slipping, and to make matters worse, he'd fallen in with a couple of kids who proved to be the worst possible influence on him.

To me, these were kids who had absolutely no idea who they were or where they were going, and the only feeling of confidence they ever achieved was when they were together. His marks continued to slip, and by the time the first report cards came out in Grade 9, it was obvious to me that we were losing ground quickly.

So I discussed the whole situation with Shirley and Greg, and we told Greg we thought he'd do a lot better if we tried a private school again.

Shirley didn't like the idea at first because it meant losing Greg at home, and Greg couldn't have been more opposed if I'd suggested sending him to prison. He absolutely hated the idea, and much as I tried to explain that this was an opportunity for him, not a punishment, he couldn't get it out of his head that I was doing something terrible to him.

"Besides," he said defiantly, "it's too late in the school year to get me into a private school."

Well, all I needed was that kind of challenge. I immediately went to work looking into every private school I could find, and finally spoke to a man who recommended a school called Grenville Christian College, in Brockville, Ontario.

I called Grenville and spoke to the headmaster, Reverend Al Haig; after I explained our situation, he got right to the point. "Why don't you and your wife and Greg come up here right now?"

"I don't know if we can make it today, Reverend Haig; Brockville's got to be a good four-hour drive from where we are."

"Well, I'll expect you at 11 tomorrow morning, then."

"That's just fine," I said, already encouraged by his enthusiasm.

When we got there, I was immediately impressed with both the school and the headmaster. Al Haig is a good-looking

313

ex-football player who gave up his athletic career for theology school; he has a strong, no-nonsense manner without being overbearing, and he's the kind of man who instantly commands respect.

He interviewed all of us at great length, explained how the school worked, sent Greg to take an exam, and finally spoke to Shirley and me alone. "All right, Mr. and Mrs. Hunter," he said. "We'll take your boy, because there's a light there; it's a dim light at the moment, but it's there."

You know, I could fill an entire book with how I feel about Grenville Christian College. It's one of the most amazing schools I've ever known, with absolutely first-rate teachers, completely dedicated to each and every one of the students. The atmosphere is perfect for kids; in the obvious elements of smaller classes and an excellent curriculum, and even more importantly, in the way the whole school is geared to motivate the students through love and discipline. The whole concept of discipline is taught as a natural attitude that a kid will be able to use all his life, not as a threat held over his head.

You know, I often think that the public school system would benefit enormously by sending a few of their representatives to Grenville and observing the methods this school uses to achieve their fantastic results.

I can never thank the people at Grenville enough for what they did for Greg. He went up to Brockville at Christmas with far from adequate marks, and just one year later, he wrote the highest physics, math and chemistry in his class along with very good marks in all his other subjects.

Of course, all this didn't happen in one day. It took time, and it took some fairly tough methods on the part of the school.

If he was finding the going rough and called us to ask if we could please come, the answer was no, even though that was very difficult to do when he sounded so miserable and we missed him so much. On the other hand, we knew that if we brought him home, we'd be right back to square one again.

When Greg saw there wasn't going to be any soft touch at

314

home, and there certainly wasn't at Grenville, he gradually gave in to the inevitable and decided to accept the situation. Just taking that first step was the hardest part, and the most important; as soon as he saw the results, he tried another step, and another . . . One day he actually called to say how much he was *enjoying* a particular course! From then on, his marks steadily improved, and his attitude became more and more positive.

For the first time in his school life, Greg was actually happy, and to me, it was just like watching a flower bloom right in front of my eyes.

When we saw the positive influence the school was having on Greg, we decided it would be a good idea to send Mark there as well, in order to surround him with all the wide range of options and possibilities that Grenville provides and to help him establish the good working discipline that's so necessary in education and in life. At this stage, Mark is planning to go to college to study design engineering, which would be great for him with his artistic abilities and his interest in mechanics.

With Jeff, it seemed that he had managed all right in the public school system, which by then had done away with open classrooms after a lot of protest from parents, teachers and institutions of higher learning, which were finding that kids weren't learning even basic reading and math before entering college. So we decided that he could finish at his high school, and he did manage to do all right, although I've got to say that it still wasn't an ideal situation for him.

At one time, Jeff had the idea that everything would magically fall into his lap: diplomas, jobs, success. Since then, he's learned that he'll achieve something only by working for it. Shirley and I taught him that, and yes, we say it with a great deal of pride, because Jeff's worth a great deal of pride. All our boys are.

After Greg did so well in his first exams, I talked to Al Haig and then asked Greg if he'd consider switching from the four-year level and taking a five-year course instead.

We explained to Greg that with the five-year program, he

315

could choose either to go to college or university, but with the four-year one, he'd have to make up the extra year if he decided to go to university.

"Yes, I'd like to move up to the five-year course," he said. "By the way, Dad, remember when I was a kid, I always used to talk about flying planes? Well, that's what I want to do for a living; be a professional pilot."

I was absolutely delighted. Two years earlier, Greg had no idea of who he was or what he wanted in life, and now he was very decisively telling me he wanted to be a professional pilot!

"Well, Greg, you keep going the way you are you'll make it, and I'll help you in every way I can," I said. "Tell you what; you concentrate on school, and I'll take care of finding out how you can go about becoming a pilot."

By the end of the year, Greg had worked so hard that he was chosen as a prefect, received an award as the most improved student, and pulled himself right up to the level where he wanted to be in the five-year program. Year after year, he kept improving, and it was a success story beyond my wildest dreams. Here was Greg, graduating with good, solid marks from one of the most demanding private schools in the country!

Ron Peterson, a good friend of mine who also happens to be an Air Canada pilot, suggested to me that Greg should try the Moncton Flying Club in Moncton, New Brunswick. Ron had sent his son, Jim, to the school, and was very happy with the results.

I called Greg on the phone and told him about it, and after he spent a few weeks at home, we went down there together. At that point, all my enthusiasm for the idea started to waver a bit. It just wasn't all that easy to say goodbye. He'd been away at school for four years and now, after only a brief holiday, he was going away to start a new life. Looking at him then, six-foot-two and skinny as a rail, I almost felt as if I was seeing myself at that age, full of big dreams but maybe just a little bit scared.

"You sure you're going to like it here?" I asked.

"Sure, Dad."

"You're going to fly those planes . . . but you know, this isn't the only place to fly planes."

"I know, Dad; quit worrying. I'll be fine."

I'm not ashamed to say that I shed a few tears when I left; at the same time, I was also very proud of Greg's independence and determination. As his courses continued, I hoped and prayed for his success after seeing all the hard work and effort he was putting in. Little by little, the accomplishments kept coming in: his first solo, his private licence, his commercial licence, with always a phone call to share his excitement at passing a test or getting a certificate. Finally, Greg got his Instrument Flight Rating and his multi-engine licence, probably the two most important credentials a young pilot can attain.

Greg's first job was flying a single-engine plane on fire patrol for the New Brunswick forestry department, and after only a few days with them, Eastern Flying Services in Halifax hired him to fly a twin-engine Piper Navajo hauling freight and doing some charter flights. Greg settled in Enfield, Nova Scotia; he fell in love with the place immediately and spent a number of very happy years there.

Unfortunately, the job with Eastern Flying Services didn't last as long; he was laid off when the company started cutting back and Greg just didn't have the seniority. A few days later, I happened to get a call from Doug Robinson, chief of operations for Eastern.

"You know, I never do this," Doug said, "but in Greg's case I felt I should just call to let you know that Greg was one of our best pilots. He's a natural, and I think he'll go far."

(Thanks, Doug; that phone call sure meant a lot to Greg, Shirley and me, and I thank you for taking the time to call.)

Greg was naturally upset about losing the job, and despite all the encouragement he was getting, he began to get discouraged after sending out résumé after résumé without results. "Greg, you've just got to wait and be patient," I said, knowing just how he must be feeling. "I know it's tough, but just remember that you earned your credentials, and nobody can ever take them away from you."

Finally, I got a call one day from a man who introduced himself as Steve Fenton of Soundair Corporation. He asked for Greg's phone number in Halifax. "I hope it's good news," I said.

"Yes, it is," he said. "We've got an opening for Greg."

I'll tell you, nobody has ever been happier than Greg since he got that job; he's logging turbine hours, flying five and six days a week, and absolutely loving his work. Both Shirley and I are tremendously proud of him, and I think that's particularly the case because he's come a long way.

Jeff also had some difficulties to overcome, mostly due to some inappropriate advice he received during high school, when he was advised to take a business administration course for which he had very little liking. He chose to take a real estate course, attained his licence, and spent some time working in the field, which he enjoyed, and did very well. But it was clear to all of us, especially Jeff, that this wasn't destined to be his life's work.

One day, Greg coaxed him into going flying, and when he returned, he was still on Cloud Nine. I've never seen Jeff so enthusiastic about anything in his life, and I had this funny feeling that I was going to give the world yet another pilot.

Jeff quit his real estate job, because he didn't want to take any chances on an unpredictable market; he got another job and worked long, hard hours, sometimes 12 to 15 hours a day, from early spring until the end of August. I just can't tell you how hard he strove toward this goal he wanted to reach, and, by the end of the summer, he took two short days to pack his bags before heading down to the Moncton Flying Club, ready to earn his tuition throughout the entire course, if need be!

In just over six months, he earned all his papers, same as Greg, and we were incredibly proud of what he'd accomplished.

At Christmas, we were heading to Florida, and Jeff was heading back to Moncton. "One of these days, Dad, when you're out there surf-fishing early in the morning, look up and it'll be me."

"Okay," I said.

Well, we got a call in February, at about noon, Moncton time, that Jeff had just passed his commercial test. When Shirley and I went to bed that night, we felt so secure in the knowledge that Mark was doing well, Greg was flying, and Jeff had just received his licence. We felt so proud of their accomplishments.

We usually sleep with the screen door open to get the ocean breezes, and most mornings, I'm already out fishing by 5 or 5:30. But this particular morning, I slept late, and at 6:30 I heard an aircraft go by.

Shirley came out of a sound sleep, nudged me, and said: "That's our boy!"

We grabbed our housecoats and raced out onto the balcony to see a plane peeling off over the ocean, circling in an obvious turn, and heading back toward us. The landing gear came down and the aircraft made a slow pass over the condo, with a dip of its wings. As it passed, I saw the Canadian registration, and I knew who it was.

I looked at Shirley and said: "By God, Jeff did it, just like he said he would!"

CHAPTER 12

"Be the Good Lord Willing"

A friend of mine pointed out to me the other day that I always refer to The Tommy Hunter Show as *our* show. "Why don't you call it *your* show?" he asked. "After all, it's got your name on it."

You know, I've never really been aware of using that expression, but that's probably because I've never thought of the show as rotating around me, so I've always very naturally considered it as our show. All I am, basically, is the end result of a lot of people's hard work, talent and effort, and I never lose sight of the fact that without all these dedicated individuals, we would never be able to achieve the excellence that I believe we attain on our show. That may sound rather boastful, but remember, I'm not talking for myself; I'm speaking in very great appreciation for the people I work with, whom I know to be the very finest in the business.

The people I work with are very much aware of how I feel about them; I've told them time and again how important they are to me, and they know that whenever I've received any kind of award, I've always accepted it on behalf of everyone on our show. I may be tremendously thrilled and flattered, but I want to share the joy with other people, and I always want it to be that way.

There's no low man on the totem pole around our studio;

everybody is important, from the producer to the guy sweeping up after the show. The same applies to everyone on our crew; they are all the very best in their field, and they're all absolutely essential to putting out the kind of show we want to create.

Just being aware of the kind of people I work with, and the dedication and commitment they bring to our show, fills me with such energy and enthusiasm that I can't wait to get in to work in the morning. If my call is at 10 or 11, I'm usually up by 6:30 or 7, practising or looking over my material; and very often I'm still going over my script at 3:30 the next morning. By that time, I've probably learned it backwards and forwards.

That's what I love so much about the way our show is now; I feel I'm in my own world again, working with people who understand and feel what I do about country music.

You know, I'm proud of the fact that I grew up in simple surroundings, and in a family that always pulled together. It's like Hank Williams once said, "You got to have smelt a lot of mule manure before you can sing like a hillbilly." Well, I'll tell you, when I walk out on that stage in a good-looking cowboy suit and fine ostrich boots, there's still a little bit of manure on the soles of those boots; and there's still a lot of the country boy in the television performer.

The same is very much true of the rest of our cast and crew. Just look at Les Pouliot: he's a country boy from rural Saskatchewan who grew up on our music, and he knows what the sadness is, the hardship as well as the joy that makes our music what it is.

Where I once felt like a fish that had been tossed onto dry land, I'm now back in my element again, and absolutely everything around me is geared to the world where I feel most comfortable. It's no longer the out-of-character productions; we now have a team all operating on the same wavelength. The lighting is exactly where it's supposed to be; the makeup and hairdressing people know just what look to achieve; our costume designer probably knows more about Western-style dress than even Nudie, the western tailor to the stars; the sets fit our atmosphere precisely; and as for the scripts, we hardly change a thing.

When I talk about the early mornings and late nights I spend on our show, I have to add that everyone in our whole cast and crew is willing to put in that kind of time and effort. Both Les and I have always felt that placing ourselves and the people we work with under tremendous pressure is the best possible way of doing our show. That way, no one has time to think about anything else; the show is on our minds literally 24 hours a day. We don't go out for lunch and supper breaks; we just have a fast snack and head for the makeup room.

I've seen our crew finish at 11:30 or 12 at night, go in and work till 4 in the morning on editing, grab two hours of sleep, and be back in the studio first thing the next day; matter of fact, I don't suppose any of them sleeps much more than four or five hours a night during tapings.

For us, this kind of schedule is the farthest thing in the world from unpleasant drudgery; all the enthusiasm and excitement we have about what we're doing makes us want to spend so much time on our work, to get it absolutely perfect. At the same time, we also have a schedule set up that enables everyone to use their full range of talent. Every Monday, we have meetings where every detail of the show is worked out to the letter. We know exactly what lighting will be used with a particular guest; all the various camera angles are listed neatly on a sheet of paper; the studio director is aware of each and every sequence in the show; and no valuable studio time is wasted on trying to work out these specifics in the middle of rehearsals or tapings, as was once the case in former days on our show.

At the same time, we're just as demanding on one another as the rest of our cast and crew. *Nobody* gives less than a total effort, myself included.

I'll always remember the time Les came into my dressing room, closed the door, and stood there looking as if he were groping for the right words. "Oh, the hell with it," he finally said. "Tommy, I'll just say it straight out. You are dragging your ass. I know your potential, and that's the difference between a good TV show and a great show. So if we get that extra little edge, that's what will make the difference."

From then on, I gave it everything I had, from the moment I walked in each morning. Rather than saunter out on stage with a cup of coffee, I'd put the coffee down and *run* out on that stage, smiling and performing for all I was worth, as if it were a live show and not just a rehearsal.

Once the rest of the crew saw this, *they* gave it all they had, and everyone else did, too; because anyone who was giving less than 100 per cent would have stood out like a sore thumb. So if we started full tilt at 11 in the morning, you can imagine how much we accomplished even by 2 in the afternoon; we built up momentum just like a freight train rolling through, and we were the engine.

The high-pressure way we work gives us almost the same feeling as if we were doing a live show; we concentrate so much into a day that there just isn't time to do things over. We have to get it right the first time, and that gives us the same kind of edge as the live shows that I was so reluctant to give up when television finally went to taped shows a number of years ago. So while we do tape our show now, I feel we've been able to retain the best elements of live television.

One aspect of television that I can't bring back is the close association there used to be between the shows and the various sponsors. I'm sure many of you will remember sponsors that were completely linked to the programs they represented, like Kraft Foods. The announcer gave that evening's special recipe and then said: "Now, ladies and gentlemen, back to Episode Three of tonight's presentation of Kraft Television Theatre."

There doesn't seem to be that kind of relationship between programs and commercials any more, and I, for one, would very much like to be able to talk about our sponsors on the air, even if it was just to say something simple like: "Thank you, folks, and we'll be right back after this message from Nabisco."

The reason I mentioned Nabisco is that I really enjoyed my

association with them a few years ago. Actually, I did two sets of commercials for Nabisco Shredded Wheat.

The reason I accepted the contract with Nabisco is that I like and trust the product; I remember enjoying Shredded Wheat when I was a kid, and I still eat it most mornings. So once I got involved in the commercial, that was a major commitment for me; I was now part of the Nabisco team, just as with the ads I did for St. Lawrence Corn Oil and Beehive Golden Corn Syrup. Once again, I wanted to go to the sales meetings and say hello to the guys who worked at Nabisco. The company was aware that my enthusiasm for their product meant a whole lot more to me than just the time it took to sign a contract or film those commercials.

On the other hand, I've done very few commercials in all; I feel that in order to lend my name to a particular product, I have to be completely confident that this is something I myself use and believe in totally. Money has absolutely nothing to do with my decision; as a matter of fact, I've turned down some sizable sums from various companies asking for my endorsement. In one case, I was offered more than $100,000 to do a certain commercial, and I had to say no, simply because it was a product I didn't especially like, and I didn't want to give our viewers the idea that it was all right to use this product since I was recommending it. I just have too much respect for our audience to get involved in something like that.

We've done many, many shows that I've been very happy about over the years. One that particularly stands out in my memory was the reunion we had a few years back on our Christmas show, when all the old gang from Country Hoedown returned from near and far to get together once again. We had a wonderful time reliving old memories and sharing newer ones; I can't remember the time ever going faster, because we were all having so much fun. The performer who travelled the greatest distance (he's now living in Los Angeles) was none other than King Ganam; and I'll tell you, it certainly was a tremendous feeling to be performing with him again.

We've also had our share of humor on our show, just as we did in the Country Hoedown days, and one particular incident I'll always remember happened during one of the little visits I used to do with various members of our studio audience, some of whom would ask me questions. On one occasion, I answered a question from a delightful elderly lady who had to be in her late 70s, and when I'd finished talking, she turned to me perfectly seriously and said: "I know you're married and have three children, but I just want you to know that you can put your boots under my bed any time!"

I was utterly speechless at that, so I just laughed and tried not to look too shocked. I remember Shirley saying later that it was the only occasion she could recall when I was at a complete loss for words!

That wasn't *quite* the same experience as I had when I met another elderly lady outside our studio during a break; this was several years ago, when we'd still break for an hour at lunch rather than work straight through. Thinking back on it, I wish we'd instituted our current system a few years earlier!

I never used to want to eat much at lunch, so what I'd do is go visit some really nice guys I'd met in their clothing store over on Yonge Street. They'd have coffee, and we'd sit and chat for awhile. I always used to park my car in the alley as close to the back door of the store as possible, making sure to stay clear of this other door, because I didn't know where it led and I didn't want to block anyone's path.

Well, on this one occasion, I didn't have much time because I was supposed to be dropping a few pictures and a biography off at the *Star Weekly* magazine. So I just stopped in for a moment, leaving the material on the dashboard to remind myself to go over to the office later. The guys and I were just getting to talking when suddenly, there was a knock at the back door.

"Is Tommy Hunter here?" It was a tiny, very sweet-looking elderly lady carrying an umbrella.

"Sure, he's right here," the man said.

She walked straight up to me: "Tommy Hunter?"

"Yes, ma'am," I said, thinking how charming she looked.

"How are you today?"

"Tommy Hunter, you ought to be ashamed of yourself, you ¢%!*!!" she yelled, coming at me with the umbrella upraised. I mean, this lady meant business, and she was cursing worse than a stevedore even though she looked like somebody's dear, sweet grandmother!

Well, she chased me right around the store, through all the stacks of shirts and ties, and right out the back door, waving her umbrella and hollering to beat the band, as all the salesmen howled with laughter to see me fleeing from this tiny woman who couldn't have weighed more than 90 pounds! I just made it to my car in the nick of time, and as I backed up, I could still see her standing there, screeching and shaking that umbrella.

Later on, we pieced together what had happened. That other door next to the store was the fire escape exit of a senior citizen's home, and it seemed the folks who lived there used to leave that way to save themselves the trouble of walking all the way around the corner to Yonge Street.

So when I'd parked my car there, being in a hurry I'd gotten pretty close to the fire door, so when the lady with the umbrella came out, she'd hit the door on my bumper. Annoyed, she'd glanced into the front seat to see all the material about me . . . and the rest is history.

Another unforgettable incident happened to us when a whole group of television performers were flying back from Ottawa after the official ceremonies for introducing the new CBC insignia. There was Fred Davis, Juliette, Wayne and Shuster and many other entertainers and dignitaries, and the entire first-class section of the aircraft had been set aside for us. Somehow, on the way back, the organizers forgot they'd sent us to a special room to wait for our flight, and they had to call the plane back.

Well, we all trooped on board to find this one lone passenger, obviously not an entertainer himself, sitting all alone in the first-class section. He watched us all come onto the plane, one well-known face after another, and he just sat there and stared, utterly dumbfounded.

As soon as we were in the air, Wayne and Shuster moved over to the edge of their seats and started to tell the most hilarious jokes I've ever heard. We all had a terrific time, and Johnny and Frank were obviously having so much fun themselves that they ended up entertaining us all the way back to Toronto.

Sometime during the flight, I went over to speak to the other passenger, who was sitting there as if he just didn't believe his good fortune. After we introduced ourselves, he happened to mention that this was his very first flight.

"Well, how are you enjoying yourself so far?" I asked.

"I'll tell you," he said, "this friend of mine suggested I fly first class because of the in-flight entertainment you're supposed to get, but I had no idea it was going to be anything on this scale!"

There have been so many good memories in my most recent years on television, and I guess the ones that stand out most are some of the wonderful performers who've been guests on our show, ever since Les and I started working together to create the kind of show we wanted for our viewers. If I don't mention absolutely every one of them, I hope they'll understand that after all this time, the list would probably fill an entire book in itself. So let me just tell you about a few of them.

One of the nicest couples as well as two of the finest performers I've ever had the pleasure to meet are Roy Rogers and Dale Evans, whom I was delighted to welcome as guests on our show. We were going to tape their portion of the show Thursday and Friday, and as it happened, both Roy and I had Wednesday free, so I called him at the hotel and we chatted for a little while.

When you first meet Roy Rogers, you can't help but be struck by the legend; but it took me about two seconds to realize that he's one of the most down-to-earth individuals you could imagine: straightforward, humble, just a plain ordinary guy whom everyone would love. Dale is exactly the same way, just the same charming lady you enjoy watching on television.

I didn't know whether they'd have the evening free, but I thought I'd ask Roy and Dale if they might enjoy coming to our home for dinner that night.

"Sure, we'd love to," said Roy, after checking with Dale. "That sounds great!"

I called Shirley to let her know we'd be having guests that evening. "Oh, that's nice, Tom," she said. "Who is it?"

"Roy Rogers and Dale Evans."

"Oh, come on, Tom," she protested. "Who is it, really?"

"Roy Rogers and Dale Evans."

I'll tell you, it was an absolute pleasure spending the evening with Roy and Dale; we sat around chatting until midnight.

Roy said later what a pleasure it was to have a home-cooked meal and spend some time with our family. Both Shirley and I, as well as the boys, found Roy and Dale to be extremely warm, delightful people, and we're both very gratified that they enjoyed spending some time with us, because the feeling was certainly mutual.

I also found Roy and I shared many of the same views, especially the perception of how much we value our private lives. I recall that at one point, we were talking about the Roy Rogers Museum out on the West Coast of the United States, and I asked Roy whether he spent much time there.

"Oh yes," he said, "I'm over there every day."

"I guess there must be many tourists," I said. "Do you sometimes walk around while they're there?"

"Yep," he said. "Every once in a while, I put on my cowboy suit and go and play Roy Rogers."

Roy knows exactly who he is and can always manage to separate Roy Rogers the businessman, father and husband from Roy Rogers the movie star and cowboy.

Another artist I've met a number of times who also has that ability to separate his professional career from his personal life is Eddy Arnold. I've always very much enjoyed working with him on our show, and take great pleasure in some of the wonderful conversations we've had over the years. Eddy and I are alike in a lot of ways; like me, he enjoys working a little and playing a little, pursuing his career but never at the expense of his family life.

At a recent taping, Eddy and I spent some time talking about fishing, boating, and everything under the sun, I guess, except our careers. You see, both of us enjoy our work a great deal, but we take time for other things.

One of the kindest and most hospitable performers I've ever worked with is Mel Tillis, who has been our guest on the show a number of times. I recall that when Shirley, the boys and I were first coming down to Florida, I happened to mention this to Mel one time, and he asked where we were going to stay.

"Well, we'll be just near the Jensen Beach, on the Atlantic coast," I said.

"I know where that is," said Mel, "and it's not far at all from where I live. You'll have to come and spend some time there." With that, he gave me directions to his home along with a key; and before I could say a word, he was on the phone to his brother in Florida, to ask him to get the place all set up for us.

"Hang on a sec, Mel," I said. "This is very kind of you, but you know, we do have a place in Florida."

"Well, I'd still like you to spend a bit of time at my place," he said. "I think you'll like it."

We didn't get over to Mel's place right away, and we didn't end up staying there, but one day, I decided to drive over and explain to Mel's brother why we hadn't shown up.

"Hi there; I've been wondering if you were going to come over," he said. "I've been here just about every day."

"Well, you see, we have a place over on the ocean and the kids are pretty much into the beach scene," I said, "and we haven't had much of a chance to visit anybody."

"Sure, I understand," he said. "It's just that Mel wanted to make sure the place was all clean and ready to go for you if you did decide to come."

You know, even though we didn't stay there, I've always really appreciated all the effort Mel and his brother went to, and every time I see Mel, I keep trying to give him back his key, but he always says the same thing: "Aw, keep it; you might want to drop by for a visit sometime."

Mel also has a real flair for comedy. Now, some country fans who have heard Mel speak may be aware that he stutters; what you might not know is that far from being self-conscious about it, he often uses his stutter to very good advantage. One time on the show, I happened to congratulate him on the movie he was doing at that time.

Well, he started trying to explain the movie to me, and it must have taken him a full 30 seconds to get the first two words out: "W-w-w-w-w-well, T-T-T-T-T-Tommy," before he just stopped, looked at me, and said: "We'll be off the air before I explain wh-wh-wh-what the movie's all about!"

Another unforgettable incident that happened on our show was when Ray Price joined us as a guest artist. We had a beautiful set that went up in tiers from the ground; the top level was about six feet off the floor, and what I was supposed to do was climb up all three of them to join Ray onstage after he'd finished singing.

Well, Ray was just coming to the end of his song, "Danny Boy," and as he hit those last beautiful notes, I started up the risers, listening to the tumultous applause and thinking to myself how superbly he'd sung that song. Suddenly: WHAM!! There I was, back on the ground; I'd missed the stage entirely and fallen down off those risers, landing on my feet with a thud I could feel from one end of my spine to the other.

Meanwhile, the producer was looking around frantically: "Where's Hunter? Where did he go?" and the camera was panning down to find me, standing there with an absolutely panic-stricken look on my face after the shock of that fall. Ray just stood there the whole time, laughing helplessly; and after a moment, I started to chuckle too, even though my back was killing me!

I would have to say that some of my fondest memories were those occasions when we were fortunate enough to have as guests some of the legends of country music.

One such performer who's graced our stage with his presence a number of times is Wilf Carter, whom I'm also very proud to call a good friend of mine. Wilf has stayed at our home on several occasions; he's taken my boys fishing, and we share a lot of the same philosophies about the importance of our families.

Wilf's in his 80th year, you know, and I've never really met another guy like him. His stamina is like that of a 20-year-old; he performs with all that excitement and sincerity, and Wilf's singing is every bit as good today as it ever was!

Most winters now, Wilf lives in Florida, and I remember that before we started going down to Florida ourselves during the winter months, he always seemed to call me *just* when Toronto happened to have a record 25 inches of snow. "It's 82 degrees here," he'd say, very casually, never once letting on he knew anything about our weather conditions up north. "Can't talk now; the fish are biting. So long, now!"

Another very characteristic thing I'll always recall about Wilf is the way he always used to call his car his "little Volkswagen." Well, if you ever went out back to see it, this was the type of automobile that needed two clocks; one in front and one in back, on account of the difference in time zones!

I was also extremely glad that we were able to have Ernest Tubb on our show; I believe that ours was the last network show in which he performed before his untimely death recently, which came as a terrible blow to all of us in country music and to his millions of fans the world over.

I'll always treasure the memory of watching Ernest stride onstage, immaculately attired, lean over the microphone, and sing "I'm Walking the Floor Over You."

Another very precious memory for me was the time Hank Snow appeared on our show. I could recall as if it were yesterday the time Hank was so kind to me after his show in the London Arena. I was surprised and very flattered that both Hank and Ernest remembered meeting me back when I was a boy; I guess that's what makes artists of their calibre special: their fans are so important to them.

You can imagine my enthusiasm when I received a phone call inviting me to appear at Hank's 70th birthday party in Nashville. This was an elegant black-tie affair; many of the people had travelled from all over the United States and Canada to attend this function, and you can imagine how flattered I was when I was asked to be one of the handful of performers to honor Hank.

Among the distinguished guests were Roy Acuff, Chet Atkins, Johnny Cash and June Carter Cash, Johnny Wright and Kitty Wells, Wesley Rose, and representatives of every major music company in America. They were all there to pay tribute to Hank.

I did a tribute to Hank, and one of the songs had me doing a break on the guitar in that unique Hank Snow style of which I am such a fan.

"Note for note, this is how Hank used to play when I was a kid," I said, launching into the break. Well, my finger slipped off the string, and I came to a full stop while the band vamped.

I looked down to see Chet Atkins staring straight into my eyes.

"No, Hank wouldn't have done it *that* way," I said. "That mistake was on Take Four, and the hit record was Take Five. This is it!"

That time, it worked perfectly, and I could see Hank laughing and slapping his knee enthusiastically, as he sat there in the front row!

I have so many wonderful recollections of the great artists who've appeared on our show, and of how much their presence meant to me after all those magical childhood years spent listening to them on the radio or at live shows.

There's a special place in my heart for one particular guest of ours; someone whose very name conjures up the image of a wide-eyed nine-year-old boy sitting in the London Arena and feeling, for the first time, the thrill that is country music.

This great artist, of course, is Roy Acuff.

Just to watch Roy, along with Jimmy Riddle, Charlie Collins, Howdy Forrester, Oney Wheeler, and Oswald (whose real name, incidentally, is Pete Kirby), was a real thrill.

Roy's first song was his most famous: "Wabash Cannonball."

The instant I heard Roy and the boys, it was as if every great memory of the music I loved all my life was all rolled into one. I stood in the wings, trying to wrap my mind around really being here, listening to the same man whose music first put stars in my eyes more than 30 years ago.

I leaned against a post, and just listened . . . The excitement and the memories finally gave way to tears.

I'm proud to say that my feelings for Roy Acuff and his music run that deep.

One time, when I first appeared on Hee-Haw, Gordie Tapp came over to tell me that Roy had been around looking for me three or four times. When he saw me, Roy came right over and welcomed me. "You've seen Opryland, haven't you, Tommy?" he asked.

"No, Roy, I haven't at all."

"Well, we'll remedy that," he said, and turned to Sam Lovullo, the producer. "Do you need Tommy right away? Because if not, we're going on a tour of Opryland."

"Sure, go right ahead," Sam said.

Well, Roy showed me every inch of Opryland; we went all through the theatre and he explained how everything was set up, from the control room and the backstage area to the round piece of the old Ryman Auditorium stage they'd cut out and set right into the new stage. Then we went to the Roy Acuff Museum, where Roy displayed his very extensive collection of stringed instruments from various parts of the Appalachians, including this one old fiddle his grandfather had played.

Finally, we went back to the studio because we both had some taping to do; I thanked Roy for the tour, and he made me promise I'd call him the next time I was in town. Just then, Sam came over and took me aside for a moment.

"You know, you should feel very flattered that Roy showed you around the Opry," he said. "The only other person he's ever done that for was the President of the United States."

That Saturday night, after I appeared on the Grand Ole Opry, Roy came over, put his arm around me and invited me to join him in his dressing room. There were lots of people in

333

there talking and getting autographs, because Roy's door is always open to his fans. When the crowd started to thin out, there was finally just Roy, Charlie Collins and me. Roy stuck his foot out, shoved the door closed and turned the lock, then grabbed his fiddle and began to play, with Charlie and I taking turns on the guitar. We must have sat there and sang harmony for almost two hours, and I'll tell you, I felt tremendously complimented and touched that he'd want to share that time with me.

Folks of all ages and from different walks of life enjoy Roy's shows; you can go as a family and be entertained by a professional who has high ideals and morals, and presents country music as a musical art.

He is proud of his heritage and presents himself with pride, dignity and honesty. A lot of entertainers would do themselves a favor if they dug back and read a few chapters from Acuff's handbook.

Roy has always handled success gracefully and conducted his career and businesses in a highly professional manner.

I've always felt honored to have the opportunity to spend a few private moments together with Roy. In spite of every conceivable reward and recognition a man could ever achieve, Roy is one of the kindest and humblest of individuals. He set a standard for me when I was a kid, and I hope I never let him or country music down.

As I was leaving the Opry, a lady approached me. "You're Tommy Hunter, aren't you?" she asked.

"Yes ma'am, I am."

"How do you do, Tommy," she said. "I'm Dorothy Ritter."

"Dorothy; how are you?" I said. "I've heard so much about you, and it's such a pleasure to meet you."

"Well, Tex was very fond of you," she said. "He often spoke of how much fun he had working on your TV show. You know, he always thought it was the best show on television, and he always spoke very highly of you."

"Thank you so much, Dorothy," I said. "I consider that a tremendous compliment."

Dorothy gave me a little certificate that you receive when

you're a guest on the Opry, and then she handed me a batch of Goo Goo candy bars; they're one of the sponsors of the Opry.

Just as I was going into the hotel, I saw George Lindsay, one of the regulars on Hee-Haw. He took one look at me and started smiling. "Oh, you've just done the Opry and you ran into Dorothy Ritter afterwards," he said, without hesitation.

"How did you know that?"

"It's the Goo Goo candy bars," he said. "Dorothy loves giving those to people, and they're great candies. Just one thing about them, though."

"What's that, George?"

"Don't eat them if you've got caps on your teeth, 'cos you won't have any if you bite into that candy bar!"

The next day, George invited me to lunch along with Grandpa Jones and Archie Campbell. We went over to the Cracker Barrel, across from the studio, and they heaped our plates with ham and country sausage, black-eyed peas, biscuits and gravy, chicken and dumplings, and peach cobbler; it was one of the largest meals I'd ever eaten, and one of the most enjoyable afternoons I can recall, but it did nothing for my diet!

Grandpa told us this one story about how he and Stringbean went fishing one time; on the way back, it began to rain and they couldn't get the windshield wipers to work. So Grandpa hit on the idea of getting some string, tying one end to the wiper blades and putting the other end inside the window so he and Stringbean could operate the wipers by hand.

"Now, here's how you work; back and forth; back and forth," Grandpa said, talking to the wipers with that hilarious tone of voice he gets when he's annoyed.

When I'd recovered from the image of Grandpa hollering at a windshield wiper, I reminded him of another incident that took place when he and Stoney Cooper were both recovering in the same hospital; he'd had a gall bladder operation and Stoney'd had a heart attack.

Well, when Wilma Lee, Stoney's wife, came to visit she'd always drop in to see Grandpa, and one time she happened to ask him if he was getting many letters. "Yes ma'am, I did," he said. "I imagine there's 50 or 60 letters over there."

"Gee, Stoney got close to 300," Wilma Lee said.

"Well," Grandpa said after a short pause, "it just goes to prove that gall bladders don't draw as well as heart attacks."

On our way out of the restaurant, I happened to mention to George how much I enjoyed country ham and sausage. Well, not two hours after I plunked down my suitcase back home in Mississauga, there was a knock at the door and there was a huge carton of country ham and sausage from George Lindsay! That's George; he's always doing thoughtful things like that.

The next time I was in Nashville, Shirley and the boys came along, and I gave Roy Acuff a call. When I reached him, he was just getting ready to leave for Memphis.

"Come on over, Tom," he said. "I'll wait for you."

Roy was right there at the front door to greet us, and I introduced my boys, which was a great thrill for them. "You know," I said, "I'm introducing you to a second generation of Roy Acuff admirers."

"Tommy," he said, "I'm flattered."

A world-famous Canadian artist who's been a good friend of mine for many years now is Gordon Lightfoot. Gordie is one of those very special pals you see only once in awhile, yet the feeling's just as strong as if you saw them every day. Sometimes we play golf together; sometimes we just sit and talk; and we always feel very much at ease together.

I recall one time, when we were both involved in that benefit recording called "Tears Are Not Enough," for the Ethiopian relief fund. The experience itself was tremendously rewarding, and I felt a great deal of admiration for my fellow-performers, who all gave so freely of themselves. To see some of them crying, to feel that compassion and energy, was to feel a real hope for the people we were all trying so hard to help.

After the recording session, I went over to chat with Gordie for a moment; I knew he'd recently given up drinking and I could still remember the feeling of freedom it had given me when I made that decision myself several years earlier.

I told Gordie how proud and pleased I was for him, and we talked about how we'd both felt there was so much more to our lives than drinking. I felt all that much prouder of Gordie, knowing just how much pressure had to be on him constantly as such an immensely talented and creative person: a writer, a performer, someone who's always expected to do great things and who always delivers. I greatly admire Gordie, and I've always been thrilled about his success. When you can look in a person's heart and write what you see, that's a tremendous talent, and that's what Gordie has.

Another interesting writer and performer I got to know was Jud Strunk, whom I first saw on a summer television show broadcast out of Los Angeles. From the first note, I knew I was hearing someone special; he had that unique ability to communicate directly to an audience, which is a rare quality.

When our fall season started, I invited Jud to be our guest; he was absolutely terrific, and we asked him back several times. I also convinced the people at Ontario Place to book him there; I guess they were reluctant because all Jud did was sit on a stool, talk in his New England accent, sing his songs and play his banjo. When they saw how much the audience loved his simple, powerful approach, the folks at Ontario Place joined his list of fans.

As it happened, Jud and I became good friends; he and his wife Marty had three boys about the same age as our boys. We went to visit them one time in Farmington, Maine, and stayed in their ski chalet near Sugarbush Mountain. It was wonderful to see those little Maine communities that so much resembled Jud's songs: simple, descriptive words that paint a thousand pictures. I loved his songs, and I very much enjoyed recording some of them.

Not too long afterward, I was in the studio one day when the phone rang; it was Jud, calling from Los Angeles. "Tom, I've written you this great song," he said.

I was in the middle of a rehearsal, so I asked if I could call him back. "No, I want you to hear it right now," he said, and proceeded to pick up his banjo and sing it all the way through.

"Jud," I said when he'd finished, "that's a fantastic song. Please mail it to me; I'm going into a recording session pretty soon and I'd love to record it."

"You bet," he said. "I'll mail it to you on Thursday."

Well, Thursday came and went, and I never did hear from Jud; but I kept singing the song to myself because I remembered that catchy chorus. Then, one day, I was driving down the road when I heard the radio announcer introduce Jud. Guess what he was singing?

A short time later, I called Jud and jokingly asked what had happened to this song he'd written for me, which was Number One on the Hit Parade by then.

"Tommy," he said, "you may not believe this but it's the truth. I was in the middle of recording it to send to you when the producer walked in and told me what a great song it was, and why wasn't I recording it for him. What could I do?"

"Don't worry about it, Jud," I said, sincerely pleased for him and only upset because he sounded so embarrassed. "It's a fantastic song and I'm really happy it's a hit for you."

A few years later, I was driving home late after rehearsal. I had the radio on, and just as I crossed the Humber River, and I suddenly heard "Daisy a Day." "Wow," I said to myself, "that's still a great song. I've got to give Jud a call."

The announcer came on: "That was Jud Strunk, who was killed today in a plane crash . . ."

It was so hard to imagine that Jud, so full of life and talent, was just not going to be there any more. To this day, I often think very fondly of him and the songs that only he could write.

One time, while we were recording a new album in Nashville, I had an experience I'll never forget. I'd come into Nashville the day before our session to rest up and go over one particular song that was giving me some trouble.

The record producer and a promotion man had come over to the hotel to talk about the upcoming album and to let me know they'd made dinner reservations for 9:30 that evening.

"I'm going to call Charlie McCoy and ask if he can drop by to help me with the song I was having trouble with," I said. "Maybe he can join us later on for dinner."

(Charlie, by the way, was our musical director for the album, had worked on all my recording sessions, and appears each week on Hee-Haw.)

Shortly after Charlie arrived, there was a knock on the door. Andy, our producer, went over to answer the knock, while Charlie and I kept rehearsing.

The next thing we saw was two guys standing there, one with a gun in his hand, telling us to keep cool. One of them hit Andy with his gun; the other punched the promotion man.

Then, the guy holding the gun pointed it straight at my head, and I remember thinking to myself: "Hey, this isn't the way I planned it . . . I didn't mean for it to end this way, in some hotel room . . ." My mind was racing a mile a minute, trying to figure out how I could roll off the bed fast enough if he pulled the trigger, and whether he'd have enough bullets to come back and pump a few into me . . .

He tied my hands behind my back after taking my wallet, jewellery, cash, and credit cards; then, they ransacked the room, emptying every drawer. After yanking the phone out of the wall, they backed out of there and disappeared.

It took me about five minutes to get out of that hotel.

I spent the night at Charlie's place and left for the airport first thing in the morning; I was so eager to get home that I'd have taken the first flight anywhere and then driven the rest of the way. I'd already called Shirley the night before and told her about it, so she wouldn't hear a report on the news and panic, and when I saw her waiting for me at the airport, it was the first time since the incident that I was able to relax.

Once again, it was that cold reality of suddenly knowing your number is up, and there was so much more you wanted to do; and then, by some miracle, a reprieve. Suddenly, life seemed more precious than ever.

You know, Shirley and I have shared many wonderful times together, and one of our most treasured memories is the honor of meeting and talking with Prince Philip. That was an experience I'll remember with pleasure all my life.

How it came about was that my lawyer, Sam Lerner, asked me if I would perform at a special event commemorating the 100th anniversary of the London branch of the Royal Canadian Regiment, London, of which he is the lieutenant-colonel. The guest of honor was to be none other than Prince Philip.

Naturally, I was delighted to accept, and I thought I'd ask Gordie Tapp, who is also from London, if he'd do the show with me. He was just as quick to accept as I was; and Shirley and Helen were absolutely beside themselves with excitement, as were the boys, who were also able to go.

I'd asked Gordie to tell a story concerning the Royal Family, and he told it beautifully; I was watching Prince Philip from the wings and he was nodding and laughing all the way through!

In case you weren't able to be there, why don't I share it with you.

Back in 1939, when the King and Queen were travelling across Canada by train, a number of dignitaries from small communities were brought to one area to be presented to Their Majesties, because there wasn't going to be time for the train to stop at every little station along the way.

Well, the mayor of one small town gave the King a written message explaining that everyone in his community was of British extraction and strongly supported the monarchy; and if the royal train was going to stop anywhere, it should be his town.

The King was apparently quite moved by this message, and even though their schedule showed them arriving in this little town at 4:30 in the morning, he insisted that they stop there briefly. Naturally, this stopover meant all kinds of rescheduling and extra protocol arrangements; but at last, everything was worked out, and the train rolled into the town at 4:30 exactly.

Standing out on the platform, the King and Queen peered into the dense fog and finally saw a lantern light coming closer, as the mayor and his wife approached, along with their family. When they reached the royal couple, they just stood there, staring, as if to assure themselves it really was the King and Queen.

"Your worship, do you not have a chain of office?" asked the King, hoping to break the ice.

"Oh, yes," replied the mayor, "but I only wear it on special occasions!"

I'll tell you, when Gordie finished that story, no one was laughing more heartily than Prince Philip, who'd obviously known all about the incident.

During the show, Gordie and I had introduced our wives sitting in the audience, which seemed natural enough at the time, although we usually don't do that. At the end of the show, Prince Philip walked straight onto the stage and shook our hands; then left the stage, walked over to where Shirley, Helen and Jeff were sitting, and shook hands all around.

As it happened, we had another opportunity to chat with His Highness after the show; he left word with one of his aides to invite all of us to the private reception. I found Prince Philip to be a very friendly, down-to-earth person, extremely charming and gracious, and the kind of person you'd want to talk to for hours. He laughingly confirmed the story Gordie had told about the King and Queen, and also confirmed another well-known story I'd read about a dinner His Highness once attended.

Apparently, toward the end of the dinner, Prince Philip placed his knife and fork side-by-side on the plate in proper formal style.

"Pardon me, Your Highness," said the waiter, reaching down for the plate, "but I think you should keep your fork. There's pie coming!"

I found it a great privilege that Prince Philip shared some of these stories with me in his very delightful way; and ever since then, I've been an even bigger fan of the Royal Family.

I've been very fortunate to have been associated with a great many fine charities over the years, including World Vision, the Cystic Fibrosis Foundation, and many others.

341

One of the earliest of my involvements with a charity was organized by Whipper Billy Watson, the wrestler who has done so much for handicapped children across the country. I recall that we helped to raise money toward the construction of a specially-equipped swimming pool for the youngsters.

Another time, when I was doing a personal appearance in Nova Scotia, I was invited to visit some of the handicapped children at the Cape Breton County Hospital. The plight of these youngsters moved me very deeply, and I decided to contact a magician friend of mine, Evward Myers, with whom I'd worked on many shows, and who was employed at a toy company.

"Maybe we could send just a few little toys to those kids, Evward," I said.

Well, Evward didn't send just a few toys; he shipped a huge crate packed full of all kinds of playthings, and I'd venture to say that there'd never been such a flood of toys to arrive at the Cape Breton County Hospital!

Another charitable involvement I recall very well was a particular message I gave as part of the Cystic Fibrosis Foundation's fund-raising campaign a few years ago.

It was a simple message, and one that came from the heart. I said how fortunate I felt in having three healthy children of my own; I explained that the only way to control Cystic Fibrosis is through the use of dozens of pills and a lot of very costly equipment, which puts a financial strain on so many parents of CF children; and then I concluded by simply asking for the support that is so desperately needed for research that may one day cure this terrible disease.

I can still recall that when the camera crew came to our home to film my message, it took us only one take to make the tape that eventually went out on the air; and I'm sure that was because the message was a sincere and simple expression of something in which I strongly believed.

I was extremely honored and deeply moved to receive the Cystic Fibrosis Foundation's Communication Award for that particular message. That award, to me, represented what I consider a fundamental of my work, and my entire life: communication.

Not too long ago, I received a letter from a couple who talked about a child who had been beaten so severely by his parents that he had to be placed in an institution under very close medical and psychiatric supervision.

Even after a great deal of care, this boy hadn't uttered a single word in a very, very long time; and he had to be watched carefully to make sure there was no violence taking place near him, even the little harmless squabbles that might sometimes erupt among the other children.

The doctor finally decided, wisely, that the best way of handling the situation was to place the boy in a foster home. Great care was exercised in finding just the right environment for the boy. The prospective foster parents had to be absolutely compatible; if they even got annoyed about the family dog getting into the garbage, or the car breaking down, the boy could mistake their frustration for anger and that might suddenly reawaken the memory of that terrible incident which almost shattered his life.

After a great deal of research and many interviews, the authorities settled on the very same couple who were writing me the letter; the little boy was placed in their custody and welcomed into their home.

There were two television shows that the family watched, in the confidence that nothing out of the ordinary would ever happen. One was the Lawrence Welk Show, and the other was our show; two very different styles of music, but both much the same in that you could safely predict what was going to take place on each of them.

The couple wrote that the boy would watch our show every week; never uttering a word or expressing any emotion, just sitting and watching.

Now, there's a particular thing I always do on the show, either after singing the last song or doing the last reading. The guitar is beside me on the stool, and I'll either fold up the book or finish the song; and then, every single week, I'll wind up by saying:

343

"That's our show; we sure hope you folks have enjoyed yourselves. We want to thank you for tuning us in, and thank our guests for dropping by, and all our regulars on the show. Thanks to you folks in the studio audience, and be the good Lord willing, we'll be talking to you next week. Good night, everybody!"

One Friday night, when I was singing the last song, the little boy suddenly ran upstairs where they had an old guitar tucked away in the attic; he grabbed that guitar, ran downstairs, picked up a kitchen chair, and dragged it into the centre of the room. Placing the guitar against the chair, he waited until I'd finished singing and said thanks to our guests and the audience.

Then, for the first time, that child spoke: "Be the good Lord willing, we'll be talking to you next week. Good night, everybody!" he said, word for word, right along with me.

His foster parents just about jumped out of their skins; they raced to the telephone to call the doctor, completely beside themselves with excitement.

From then on, that little boy kept on talking; and very gradually, with the help of therapy, he came out of his shell; began participating in school, and was able to overcome that terrifying memory that had haunted him so long. It seemed, the foster parents wrote in their letter, that it was the constant repetition of that phrase that finally got through to him.

So when I come to the end of our show each week, I recall how I first heard that saying in church; and I think about how much it meant to another little boy so many years later.

If I did nothing else in my life, the fact that I reached one child is award enough for me; I don't need a hunk of wood or a piece of plastic to tell me that I achieved something.

So you see, when somebody else wins an award, I'm always extremely proud of them, but they can never come close to the award I've got.

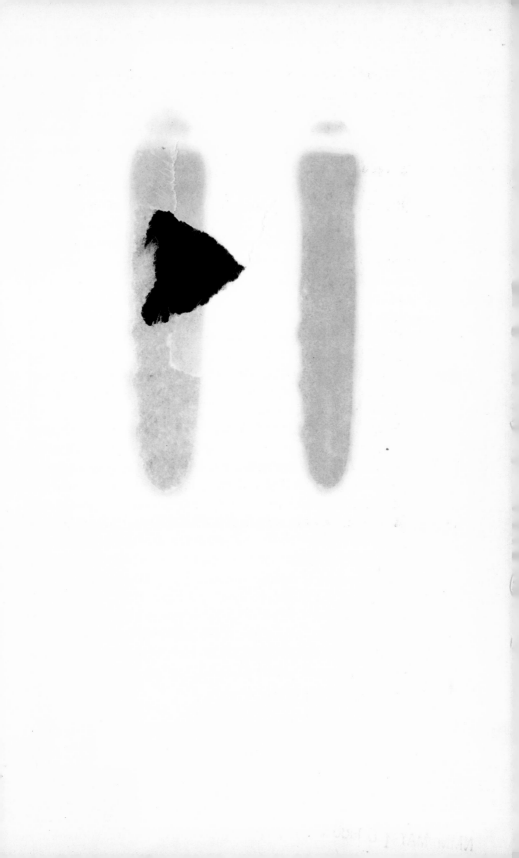